MOTHERLAND, FATHERLAND, WHATEVERLAND

MOTHER LAND FATHER LAND WHATEVER LAND

Searching for Home

ERIK SMALHOUT

Edited by ***Erika Berry***

University Press of Mississippi | Jackson

The University Press of Mississippi is the scholarly publishing agency of the Mississippi Institutions of Higher Learning: Alcorn State University, Delta State University, Jackson State University, Mississippi State University, Mississippi University for Women, Mississippi Valley State University, University of Mississippi, and University of Southern Mississippi.

www.upress.state.ms.us

The University Press of Mississippi is a member of the Association of University Presses.

Photographs courtesy of the author's family unless otherwise noted

Manufactured in the United States of America

First printing 2022
∞

Library of Congress Control Number: 2021948979
Hardback ISBN 978-1-4968-3920-6
Epub single ISBN 978-1-4968-3921-3
Epub institutional ISBN 978-1-4968-3922-0
PDF single ISBN 978-1-4968-3923-7
PDF institutional ISBN 1-4968-3924-4

British Library Cataloging-in-Publication Data available

Contents

Preface

Growing up, Erik Smalhout—my Opa—was my favorite person. As a child, I did not know much about his upbringing other than that he was Dutch, brilliant, cultured, well traveled, and scary strict. I admired him for the many books and *National Geographic*s he displayed in his office, the Dutch magazines that only he could read, his ability to build anything, and his cheeky ways of always making Oma, his wife, feel loved. Sadly, it wasn't until I read his memoir after his passing in 2008 that I realized how fascinating his life story was. From his memoir I not only learned of the exceptional and poignant events that cultivated him into the Opa I loved, but I was also reminded of his humor and eternal curiosity for the world and his fellow man. Fast forward to 2017, when I discussed his memoir with a dear friend who providentially suggested that readers outside of my family may be interested in his story. May God bless friends who want to share our loved ones with the world.

This memoir is organized by "place," with each chapter being a place that shaped Erik. "Home in the Dutch East Indies" details his first home in Batavia, Netherlands East Indies, now known as Jakarta, Indonesia. As a student before the war and as a member of the Royal Netherlands military during the war, "Home in Australia" reflects how multiple cities within Australia became his home away from home. After the war, his time without a home is detailed in "Home in Clandestine" before he found his "Home at Sea." His time at sea afforded him skills that he would eventually use in the home he would call his own: the United States, or more specifically, "Home in the Mississippi Delta." Proving himself as an American and starting a family, he still struggled to fit in, in "Home as a Pariah," as an IRS agent. Finally, "Home Sweet Home" details his life after retirement. This memoir is completely in his words, yet most of the content in his retirement years was withdrawn as it contained mostly reflections from international and—in his later years—domestic travel.

While this manuscript may naturally appeal to World War II buffs, Nederlanders, seafarers, or Mississippians, we hope this appeals to everyone's sense of place: that no matter where you are or what fortunate/unfortunate circumstances placed you there, an eternal curiosity for humanity will always help you find a place in the world.

Special thanks must be given to Mark Wiggs for his guidance throughout the process of publishing this manuscript. It is a true privilege to have Opa's story join the expansive library at Chez Wiggs.

MOTHERLAND, FATHERLAND, WHATEVERLAND

Chapter 1

Home in the Dutch East Indies, 1926–1941

GROWING UP

Although certain memories predate school days, I cannot recall much of anything that occurred prior to age six. All that follows was put down on paper more than half a century later and without the aid of notes at that. My only sister did manage to hurriedly remove some photographs out of a family album as two Japanese soldiers waited outside to escort her to a camp where she was interned for the duration of the war.

My father's first family never followed him to what used to be the Netherlands East Indies and what is now known as Indonesia. He did have a daughter of whom we never even saw a picture; she perished at the Sobibor concentration camp. My mother's first husband worked for the state-owned telephone company and had to travel constantly throughout the archipelago, which was arduous and time consuming; she consequently spent much time alone with her first child, Jan. Human behavior being no different from what it is today, things happened, and divorce ensued, causing her to lose custody of her child.

Mother apparently was an attractive woman; the few pictures I have of her before she came out to the Indies disclose that she had certain physical attributes which made her so. She was also a very independent person, and, on her way back from Holland after visiting her family during World War I, she traveled unescorted via the United States. I remember seeing a picture of her with Jan, my half-brother, both in bathing attire on a beach in Hawaii.

My father was in the import business and prospered after the war. In the late 1920s we moved into a substantial house where we were comfortably attended by a number of servants, and one of the first things I recall is having a swimming pool in the backyard. It was an early version of a rubberized, above-the-ground affair holding about five feet of water, and it even had a diving board. Father was also a car buff and was one of the first to own an automobile, which he tried to drive himself, only to discover that he couldn't stop it; he drove all over town until the gas ran out. After that, he left the driving to a chauffeur. Always resourceful, he frequently managed to call attention to his exploits. As was the case with the car, he was also one of the first to have a radio, which stood as big as a refrigerator and which could pick up the one radio station in Jakarta or, for that matter, in the whole world. Because he owned the radio, I made the cover of the leading magazine as a little boy wearing a pair of earphones.

As is the case in most countries, children were required to attend school once they reached the age of six. This turned out to be a traumatic experience for me, and when the big day arrived, I hid under my parents' bed. They couldn't find me at first, but the servants eventually ratted me out; they must have been impressed by the gravity of the event and I was dragged from under the bed like a dog by the collar, shoved in the car, and taken down to the schoolhouse. However, my mother was unable to get me out of the car, which had lots of convenient things to hang on to. Finally, the principal came out to help and he certainly was big enough to do the job—that is, until he threw me over his shoulder and I got hold of his curly hair. He probably never made that mistake again. Once in school, I must have done well enough, and the only clear recollection I have is that of a brutish female fourth grade teacher who habitually corrected her students by thumping them on the head with a ring which had an oversized stone. This always left a knot on one's head, but it apparently earned no sympathy from parents or else the practice would more than likely have been stopped.

While economic problems loomed on the horizon, life at home continued to be pleasant a little longer. My father was a political activist with socialist leanings, and there were frequent meetings at the house. These meetings plainly irritated my mother, who held opposite views. One night, when a particularly important gathering took place, she spiked the refreshments with a laxative, and soon there was a steady stream of visitors heading for the bathroom. I'm not sure how Father found out about the cause, but a spectacular row followed and my sister and I feared the worst. It so happened that this occurred just before my parents' twelfth—or brass—wedding anniversary. Consequently it was too late to split up, so they decided to have the planned celebration, which also was a spectacular event.

I always loved to be invited to Father's office where he had the most interesting things for sale. He dealt in printing materials, medical equipment, and firefighting equipment, just to name a few. One item which was really splendid was an air-conditioned bed which he sold to hospitals and which was used to let patients recover in comfort following surgery. The thing was shaped like a coffin without a top while the sides were made of curtain material. It was cooled by a fan which blew over blocks of ice stowed on a shelf underneath. Before too many of these contraptions were sold, it was discovered that they caused patients to develop pneumonia. Fortunately, product liability must have been unheard of in those days or, if it existed, it wasn't taken seriously.

The business had an early Model T Ford pickup truck, which chugged around town making deliveries. My sister attended private high school in the downtown area, and on rainy days she was taken there and picked up by car. Occasionally the car wasn't available, and the pickup was called on to do the honors which always provoked a most enjoyable scene. As for me? Why, I rode my bike to school regardless of the weather and did so later when I attended public high school a lot further away than her school ever was. This meant running the gauntlet of hostile Indonesian fellow students who took offense at one's behavior, and I frequently came home with a cut lip or bloody nose. But fights were fair and without weapons of any sort; they just wanted to beat the hell out of you.

The social life of a family of mixed faiths was less than ideal. Marriage between a Christian and Jew had the added dimension of being interracial insofar as Dutch concepts were concerned. After all, the Germans managed to wipe out virtually the entire Jewish community in Holland and could never have done so without an indifferent population. While having a handful of mutually intimate friends, my parents generally went their separate ways and, since I was young, I associated mostly with Mother's friends and acquaintances. Father's Jewish friends were noticeably standoffish when she was around and, rightly or wrongly, I perceived this to be a prevailing attitude toward me in later life.

Most Dutchmen were young when they first arrived in the colonies. Those who came of their own accord without any job prospects never qualified for periodic home leave once they found employment. As a rule, home leave was granted every five or six years to employees hired in Holland and sent out to the Indies at government or company expense. This included the entire family if there was one. Those who didn't qualify for this privilege couldn't even afford to let their girlfriends in Holland come out and join them, let alone take sabbatical and go on leave on their own account. As a result, many Dutchmen wound up marrying Indonesian girls, full-blooded ones during the early period of Dutch rule, and those of mixed blood when they became abundant in later periods. In case of subordinate military personnel, intermarriage was actually encouraged in view of the rigorous conditions existing in the remote areas of the archipelago. As time went by, a sizable segment of the population was of mixed origin and these people, as is unfortunately often the case, wound up in an inferior status.

Not long after I started school, the worldwide economic depression caught up with my father's activities and he lost his shirt in short order. Fortunately, he was promptly hired by one of the large Dutch trading firms and, judging from the location and size and of his office in the headquarters building, he must not have done too badly. Nonetheless, the family's standard of living took a decided beating, and we moved into a modest house. This must have broken my mother's heart because most of her collection of antique furniture had to be auctioned off in the process, but we somehow easily survived all of this.

Among the mutual friends my parents had were a newspaper publisher and his wife with whom we visited often. I wasn't particularly happy doing so because they had three German shepherd dogs—a mother and two grown pups—of whom I was terrified. Good friends of a family were called "aunt" and "uncle" by the children, but the aunt in this case was a finicky old woman who had chosen to remain childless. As a matter of fact, she didn't like children at all, although she tolerated them so long they weren't in her home, where they could possibly damage some of her priceless possessions. She always managed to maneuver me into an overstuffed chair and then lined up the three dogs in front of me like tigers in a circus act. If I made the slightest move, all three would growl menacingly and would more than likely have torn me to shreds had I gotten out of my chair. Today, such behavior would amount to child abuse, but in those days it must have been considered very clever because my parents never protested. I did get revenge of sorts in due course, and that was after the second World War began in earnest. My "uncle" published a Sunday paper called the *Green Morning Post*, which he used mainly to espouse the German cause. The color of the newsprint was actually green, and over the years the publication gained great notoriety. The moment Germany invaded Holland on May 5, 1940, all German nationals together with their Dutch Nazi sympathizers were rounded up to be interned on a small island named Onrust in the Bay of Jakarta. As a Boy Scout, I participated in this roundup, and we went around in a truck to pick up the few personal effects these people were allowed to have in camp. And so we came to my "aunt's" house but only got to see the servants by whom I sent her my warmest personal regards. Being grossly overweight, Uncle later died during internment, but by that time the Japanese were responsible for his well-being.

I didn't dislike these people all that much; it was just those dreadful dogs. The families went out together on elaborate picnics when we all dressed up, with Uncle wearing his plus fours to lend that extra touch of refinement. He was a car fancier and always had at least two of the latest models on hand in which I loved to ride. For a time, they had an Auburn which had a fascinating device with which to shift gears. It was probably the forerunner of the automatic transmission and consisted of a miniature stick shift mounted on the steering column and which was operated with one finger.

There was another couple who were even closer friends of my parents. They were also German sympathizers but had returned to Holland before war broke out. During a family crisis they were always the ones we turned to; indeed, after the war I had to ask this uncle for help nobody else could have provided. It so happened that, when I was born, Father erroneously registered me as being a daughter rather than as a son. This was discovered years later upon receipt of a copy of my birth certificate preparatory to requesting an immigration visa to the United States. To get matters corrected nearly halfway around the world seemed impossible, but someone remembered that Uncle Ben had been a justice department official in the Indies before the war. We found him listed in the telephone directory for The Hague and when I went to see him, I found a feeble old man who hardly remembered me. He was amused by my predicament and recalled accompanying my very excited father to register my birth. He took the matter in hand, and I received an amended birth certificate in short order, no questions asked.

Despite the hard times, my father somehow provided traditional pleasures for the family, such as sending us to a mountain resort each year during the school recess, which coincided with summer vacations in Europe. We would usually go for the entire month of July, and he would come and join us during the weekends. The vacation would begin with a two-hour train ride to Sukabumi, where we would take a taxi the rest of the way into the mountains. There were two hotels, a stone's throw apart, and we would alternate from one to the other each year. Mountain air in the tropics is cool enough to warrant sleeping under blankets at night and was deemed to be restorative for one's health. The hotels were on the American plan, which meant that all meals were furnished. Practically all guests consisted of a mother with one or more children accompanied by at least one servant, usually a maid. There was much tennis playing, swimming, hiking, card playing by adults and, of course, the inevitable sorting out by social groups. The one thing I loved most was horseback riding.

Most of the resorts were situated at higher elevations where tea was grown. Tea plantations covered large areas and were crisscrossed by paths often wide enough to accommodate small vehicles such as a horse-drawn cart or even a small truck. They were also excellent for hiking by adults while children rode small ponies controlled by native guides under the watchful eyes of parents. The vistas were splendid, the air was cool, and plantations were lightly shaded. Tea leaves were picked by women and young girls who went about with large sacks to gather the young growth at the top of the bushes, and the leaves were dried in a factory on the premises. Special arrangements obviously existed between the hotel and the plantation under which guests were permitted to walk through the gardens at will.

The mountains on Java—the heaviest populated island in Indonesia—were a relatively short distance from the coastal cities. All throughout the 1930s people began building weekend retreats a little more than an hour's drive from their primary residence and, occasionally, we were guests in these places, some of which were elaborate. One, built in the style of a chalet, belonged to a German family and had a swimming pool. A member of this household was a nanny for the youngest child and happened to be one of those rare beauties the Aryan race can produce. She loved to romp in the swimming pool with the two boys about my age and they in turn liked to pull the string of her halter which always brought a coy reaction on her part and a scolding from the parents who were sitting on the terrace. This was my first exposure to such delectable behavior, and the memory has stuck with me ever since, not that I dared to participate in any way. The man of the house was, like my Nazi uncle, promptly interned when war broke out, and his wife came by our house late in the night accompanied by her sister to seek my father's advice on what to do next. He decided to buy out her husband's business, enabling her to take her family back to Germany.

Buying out the business brought immediate problems, one of which was how to get into the safe for which nobody had the combination. Someone recommended a previously convicted safecracker, and we all watched with great interest as he went to work on the monstrous thing with assorted tools of his trade. The police had been invited to attend the event, presumably to safeguard the national security. After an interminable period of hocus pocus, we heard a loud click and the door swung open. There was nothing inside but old ledgers and a few days' accumulation of cash, which would have been deposited had the previous owner returned.

In the meantime, tragedy had visited the family in 1937, when Mother came down with cancer of the stomach and, despite the heroic efforts by surgeons, died early in 1938. I was at the precocious age of eleven and, while aware of the seriousness of the situation, do not recall being emotionally traumatized. However, I do remember the last few weeks of her suffering. She had undergone three operations in six months and was at home withering away, fed through a tube inserted in the abdomen below the chest cavity. On New Year's Eve she briefly came out to observe the festivities and when the clock struck twelve, she and my father went out on the back patio carrying their champagne glasses. They stood there for a few minutes as if they were looking at the stars, and then Father assisted her to bed from which she never arose again.

Bringing in the New Year was always a big celebration, but I despised the tradition at home of having a roasted pig with an apple in its mouth grace the dinner table. Although his religion prohibited him from eating pork, Father relished it and did an expert job of carving the creature which seemed to gaze at us reprovingly. The fireworks, on the other hand, were something else. The Chinese grocer, where a household got most of its provisions, would furnish a huge basket filled with all sorts of rockets and explosive devices which would be set off all during the evening by a servant, usually the gardener. During the afternoon he would have hoisted a string of firecrackers, reaching from the top of the flagpole to the ground, and this would be ignited at midnight to provide a deafening racket for about five or ten minutes. I was never allowed to as much as touch a firecracker. I always looked on in amazement and some envy at how today's children play with them with abandon. On New Year's Day, it was the custom for people to sit on their veranda in front of their homes so they could be serenaded by roving bands of native musicians who would play a piece of barely recognizable music for which they expected a tip before moving on to the next house. At one point, the servants would appear, one at a time, to wish us happy New Year and also to collect a tip. We realized that Mother heard all this and would have loved nothing better than to watch this one more time, but she simply didn't have the strength. The ambulance came not long afterwards to carry her away, and she died less than a month later.

Shortly after Mother was buried, Father quit his job to start a new business of his own. This time he kept his office at home for which the front bedroom was remodeled. As usual, he was one of the first to have air-conditioning installed, an American-made window unit which was nothing less than a marvel at the time. His wares were largely the same with a few novel additions, one of which was a fire extinguisher. It was the soda and water type (of which thousands were still in use here in America not so long ago). The patent must have expired by the time he became interested in the product because he had his version produced in Japan under his own trademark. On one occasion he put on a demonstration in cooperation with the fire department, which caused quite a bit of excitement. He first had a small building erected on the city's main square, which was also the site of the annual fair, announced a date it was to be set on fire, and managed to attract a large crowd, including the press. The fire blazed spectacularly and was put out in no time at all by three firemen, each using one of his extinguishers.

Fire was the main scourge of native habitats everywhere in Indonesia. Their dwellings were constructed of highly flammable materials such as bamboo, and they all had thatch roofs. In the big cities there were dense areas of native housing, which were generally out of sight until a fire broke out, when a huge column of smoke rose into the sky, announcing yet another tragedy. Although excellent fire departments were maintained, they were virtually powerless to do more than contain a conflagration. Even though the fire extinguishers Father tried to introduce were dirt-cheap, they were out of reach to the average native, but he did sell great numbers of them to stores and other businesses.

It wasn't long before war broke out in Europe and his next specialty was an air raid shelter of British design. The base was made of angle iron between which sheets of corrugated metal were bent to form a cover. It looked like a miniature Quonset hut, and the whole thing was buried in the ground. An entrance was constructed out of concrete and, presto, there was the shelter. We had one installed in the backyard, and it turned out to be a wonderful plaything and hideaway. It was actually used during the Japanese invasion, but I was no longer at home to enjoy the event.

As in most places, sports were an essential part of human existence, and in the Indies, it was mainly in the form of soccer. While high schools required students to participate in gym classes where, as part of the overall activity an occasional game of soccer was played, there was no organized competition. The latter was entirely the province of sport clubs, and in Jakarta there were about seven or eight of these which formed a league. Holland has always been a powerhouse where soccer is concerned and, as small as it is, has managed to walk away with many World Cups, Gold Cups and other assorted honors. While the Netherlands Indies did not compete internationally, excellent soccer was nevertheless played there, and I remember the touring national team from Austria getting a trouncing at the hands of the club I belonged to as a boy. The club was part of my life from the time I was big enough to kick a ball around. It was a short distance from where we lived in both the old and the new houses, and the only thing that stood in my way was the daily half hour of piano practice under the watchful eye of my mother. Once she was gone, it was goodbye to the piano, much to my regret in later life. Cost of a junior membership was a nominal twenty-five cents a month, and we got to play at least some every day of the week if no more than just before or after the grown-ups practiced. Two days were set aside for a form of basketball I have not seen played anywhere else since. It was a much tamer version of today's basketball and was played by mixed teams of men and women on a grass court at either end of which was a wicker basket on a pole.

Nobody paid any attention to us young fellows, and there was no equivalent of a little league; we learned to play by watching our big brothers, picked up the balls for them behind the goal during practice and did odd jobs like changing the numbers on the scoreboard during a game. If we ever got out of hand, a few sharp words from a senior would be enough to make us cringe. We hoped that sooner or later they would pick us up as a player in the fifth level team to play against other such teams, and thus our march to the top would begin; only a handful made it that far.

In deference to the Indonesian members, a *slametan* would be held once a year. This was sort of rededication of the club's facilities at which time a goat was sacrificed and its head buried at precisely midfield to ensure that the spirits would help us in future contests. The rest of the animal was eaten in the form of *saté*, which were bits of meat on skewers, barbecued over a charcoal fire. The affair usually turned into a drunken brawl, and we were sent home before we got into trouble.

While I did well on the football field, my schoolwork steadily deteriorated. I did manage to finish the seventh grade in elementary school, taught by the same curly-haired principal who carried me into the first grade when I was six years old, but high school was a complete disaster practically from the start. All the teachers in the public school system were Dutch and were extremely well paid. As far as I know, the standards were as rigid as those existing in the mother country and, until a student reached university level, there was no need to go to Holland to further his or her education. To be sure, adequate facilities were available only in the larger cities, and families living in outlying areas had to make housing arrangements in order for their children to attend these schools.

My father was spending two weeks of every month on the road and, initially, my older sister managed to take the place of my mother, more or less. However, she married three months after I entered high school, and the system in which I had such a shaky start completely overwhelmed me.

If there is one irresistible temptation in Indonesia, it is the food. One hundred years of Dutch rule may not have had much of an impact on the Indonesians, but their food is one of the most sought-after culinary experiences in Holland. Surely, many Americans have partaken of *rijsttafel*, perhaps aboard a Dutch passenger liner, in a restaurant in New York or Toronto, or even in prewar Indonesia, and will remember the dozens of tantalizing dishes served by a seemingly unending line of waiters? Well, the truly initiated consider that pure show—good show, to be sure—but nothing like what is sold by street vendors under a lean-to in a *kampong*. While this is the finest of eating, it often turns out to be hazardous to the European digestive system because of the lack of sanitation.

It was a tradition among Dutch families to prepare *rijsttafel* (literally, rice table) at home on Sundays when everyone was there to enjoy it. The rest of the week they ate Dutch food. On the other hand, many people preferred Indonesian food not only because of the taste but also because it was cheaper. Consequently, they ate it every day and had a Dutch table on Sunday, or just the opposite. But such was not the case in our house. Some people even went so far as dressing up like the natives while they were at home, which meant that the man of the house would walk around in pajamas while his wife wore a sarong. The smaller children may have run around naked, although I don't remember ever seeing such. This style of living was mainly adopted by lower ranking civil service personnel and was probably due to their peculiar working hours from 7:00 a.m. until 2:00 p.m. Needless to say, these hours infuriated all businessmen like my father, but there was not a thing they could do about it.

Since I was now living alone whenever Father was traveling, the cook was getting her instructions from me, by then a fourteen-year-old whose tastes tended to be somewhat exotic. Sometimes my preference would dictate scrambled eggs on cocktail-sized bits of toast three times a day and would then change to some Indonesian dish until I got burned out on it too. All of this didn't seem to bother my father, probably because he didn't know what was going on, but my lifestyle generally was becoming a matter of concern among neighbors who looked on with dismay at this budding delinquent in their midst. Shortly, arrangements were made against my wishes for me to eat dinner with my sister and her husband, after which I had to ride my bike to the house of an old family friend to spend the night.

ADOLESCENCE

When I had just about reached the decision to run away from home, pressures abated somewhat, and my father apparently began to accept the inevitable that he had a son who needed his tutelage or else! Just about every time he was about to conclude a business trip, he would call me on the telephone to tell me to proceed to the airport, fly up to meet him, and we would then drive back together. This period lasted about a year, and we grew closer to one another, not to mention the fact that I learned a great deal about regional geography. None of this resembled the traditional upbringing of a boy, and I began to fall further and further behind in my schoolwork. The school administration appeared to be entirely unwilling to consider unusual circumstances, and to put it simply, education was their forte and to hell with individual misfits! One teacher—a math instructor—was openly hostile and even physically abusive. In time, they resorted to expulsion from school for longer and longer periods until I finally quit going altogether. Perhaps all of this was providential since less than two years later, the Japanese Imperial Forces had captured all of southeast Asia while I was safely attending school in Australia. Long before I finally dropped out of school, my father had—unbeknownst to me—begun making inquiries relative to alternative schooling in Australia. In the meantime, I was kept busy on some interesting projects, was sent to "vacation" with a family in the mountain city of Bandung, and became involved in Boy Scouting.

The Scout troop I became associated with was one of four which operated under the leadership of a dedicated scoutmaster, who became the first adult for whom I ever had much respect. We met on Saturday afternoons in a log cabin, situated on a spacious site on the outskirts of town. Each troop had its own facilities, and the individual meetings began with a flag ceremony and ended with one at dusk. The variety as well as the number of projects carried on were a source of amazement, and I recall participating in building a bamboo bridge over a river the very first time I attended a meeting. The bridge was used for quite a long time and opened a whole new area for our activities. We were impressed with the fact that scouting was serious business. We were given the chance to put what we learned to practice in the nearby rice paddies and adjacent jungle. The natives we encountered weren't particularly friendly; in fact, they considered us to be intruders but couldn't quite figure out the difference between a scout, a soldier, or a policeman. As far as they were concerned, anyone wearing a uniform was to be avoided. Badges were not easily come by, and I don't recall ever seeing anyone anointed with the rank of Eagle Scout. Discipline was strict and we worked hard for the few ribbons which were handed out occasionally.

Negotiating the narrow paths on top of the dikes enclosing the rice paddies earned us a good mud bath occasionally, and once a Scout was bitten by a snake, which was identified as being non-poisonous. We would sneak up on one another as if we were having war, and man-to-man combat was carried out with staffs, which were aimed at each other's feet. Once your feet were touched, you had lost.

We had our detractors, too, and these consisted of a troop of fascist youths who marched up and down the streets dressed in white shirts, black shorts, and white knee socks. They carried all kinds of flags and were accompanied by a drum and bugle corps. From time to time they would march out to the entrance of our campground, break formation, and then stand around to jeer for a while. Suddenly, they would fall in and march away with bugles blaring. After the Germans invaded Holland, we never saw them again.

I never quite figured out why I was placed in the house of an army officer during the greater part of one summer vacation. Father certainly was no admirer of the military, and how he ever became acquainted with the major was a mystery. Nonetheless, the episode was enjoyable; perhaps I was in need of some discipline, and I was made to toe the line in that household of an otherwise childless couple. On the other hand, they allowed me to roam the lovely mountain city of Bandung on my bicycle and showed a great deal of interest in accounts of my daily adventures. One of their friends was superintendent of the water works; he would occasionally permit me to accompany him on his daily rounds into remote areas in the mountains. As a result, the sight of large diameter water pipes on the side of a mountain, whether there to supply water for drinking or for driving turbines, has fascinated me to this day.

The island of Java was divided into three provinces: West, Middle, and East. The western province, where we lived, was ethnically different from its neighbors to the east. It was populated by the Sudanese, who, to us at least, seemed a cut above the Javanese. They had their own dialect, had different customs, and didn't seem too fond of the Javanese, who were politically dominant. There was some concern after the war about the future of these people, but their large number must have ensured their well-being, and there have been no reports of any maltreatment. The center of resistance to the reestablishment of Dutch rule after the war was Jogjakarta, seat of an ancient sultanate and temporary capital of the republic after the Japanese occupation. On one occasion I accompanied my father on a trip to central Java and visited the Borobudur temple just a short distance north of Jogja (as we called it) where we were guests of a real uncle on Mother's side of the family who, as a widower, lived alone in a two-story house. He was a finance inspector—the equivalent of an Internal Revenue agent. The house had a splendid bathroom, which was as long as an oversized bedroom. It had a smooth tiled floor with tiles running three quarters of the way up to the ceiling. My favorite pastime at home was to soap the bathroom floor and slide from one side of the room to the other on my bare bottom, but this bathroom where we visited was something else. Try as I would, I could not make it from one end to the other, and I wound up with a badly chafed rear end.

Aside from being inherently dangerous, bathroom games earned me some of the severest beatings while growing up. For instance, I had long tried to make a swimming pool of the bathroom at home, not because I never got to swim anywhere (we were members of a swim club) but just for the sheer challenge of it. The problem was to get a tight seal on the door but one day I ran across a piece of rubber tubing which did the job. It took a long time to let three faucets plus the shower pump about two feet of water into the room and I was getting tired of the whole thing when my father—who had been alerted by the servants that something unusual was taking place—burst into the room with disastrous results. Although the floors throughout the house were tiled, the oriental rugs took a beating, as did Father's expensive new shoes.

A popular pastime in Indonesia was flying kites. At certain times of the year, the wind would blow with a certain required consistency during the late afternoon, and the sky would be filled with colorful creations of all sizes, some of which would reach great altitude. The more serious fliers would engage in a sport which was actually a form of aerial combat; their kites would be of a common shape, without a tail, but with special markings which identified them as fighters. Their purpose was to down another's kite by crossing and cutting its line. The chosen opponent would skillfully evade the attack, and the battle was on. Unofficial champions had staked out their territories and would invariably rise to the occasion when challenged by an intruder. An aerial battle could go on for quite some time before a kite would be seen floating off into the distance, obviously the loser. There would occasionally be a draw when the combatants got tangled up and went down together.

The kite builder in our household was an old house boy—a very old man, really—who had been with the family since I was born. He had mastered the art and, much to my father's chagrin, spent a great deal of time and energy on what he considered looking after my interests. He crushed glass and mixed it with his own glue recipe—just like an apothecary mixed medicine—and would then apply it as uniformly as possible to a light cotton thread which he wound around the trunk of two trees standing some distance apart in the backyard. Drying time was a couple of days, unless it rained and he had to start all over again. The finished product could cut a finger to the bone if a metal guard wasn't worn, and sometimes, I imagine I can still feel the scars earned in a moment of carelessness. When the going got rough, the expert would take over, and the two of us were recognized as masters of a territory, all on account of him, of course.

One day my father decided that a kite could be used for advertising purposes, and he ordered one out of some magazine. It turned out to be an enormous box kite and the only way it could be flown was on the end of a flag line held by four or five strong men. To get it up in the air it had to be towed by a car which almost ran over the crew, and, once in the air, it was discovered that they had forgotten to tie the advertising banner to it. We watched it lumber around for a while, and it attracted lots of attention but to no useful purpose. It was the only time it ever went up.

While I was still struggling in school, my half-brother suddenly appeared on the scene. He had been looking forward to a reunion with Mother, although he did not come to the Indies for this purpose. Like so many before him, he hoped to make a career there and was sent out by an oil company in which his father apparently had some important connections. He claimed to be a geologist, but we later discovered that he was only a geologist's assistant.

Jan was an outgoing person of considerable charm, and, in retrospect, I must have come under his spell from the moment we met each other. Without the slightest hesitation, he addressed my father as if he were his own, and the fact that my father never reciprocated in like manner made no difference to him. He was concerned about the problems I was having in school and made a genuine effort at tutoring me in algebra and geometry, but to no avail. My eighteen-year-old sister adored him, which must have been a source of considerable concern to Father. As a matter of fact, many years later she confided to me that he had actually proposed to her, notwithstanding the fact that she was engaged to be married.

While Jan was in Jakarta, he joined a flying club and earned his pilot's license. Having previously flown gliders in Holland, the transition was an easy one. The flying clubs enabled the air force to back up its scarce manpower and to keep its planes in the air when the Japanese invaded the Indies. After an interval of service at his employer's headquarters, he was posted to the southern part of Sumatra, where the company was prospecting for oil and where it had a refinery. An American enterprise had similar interests in the area and operated across the river.

Before the Germans marched into Holland, the parties to the conflict had their local supporters. My father had started a society called Friends of England on which he spent a great deal of time and which he financed largely out of his own pocket. Its activities consisted of distributing information about the war by means of steel billboards, which had three glass-covered boxes on both sides, each measuring about two by three feet, inside which photographs of the Allied war effort were mounted. Some of these billboards were illuminated so that they could be viewed at night, and they were very popular with the people, most of whom couldn't afford a newspaper even if they could read. We—my sister and I as well as several volunteers—would cut the material out of magazines while two full-time Indonesian employees did the translating and typed the captions. The finished products looked very professional and, it might be said, constituted good propaganda. The big problem was changing the billboards once a week in twenty different locations all over town.

One of the Indonesian employees was well educated, but he was a revolutionary type. Always prepared to take the other side of an argument, Father would bait him and this he would take out on me whenever he caught me alone. One night someone provoked him while he was talking on the telephone, whereupon he stuck the instrument in a carafe filled with water and stomped out the door. This really impressed me, and I have been tempted many times during my life to repeat the feat, particularly since it didn't seem to hurt the phone.

The decision that I was to attend school in Australia was matter-of-factly communicated to me one evening in a "by the way" fashion. That it didn't rattle me was quite a surprise to my father and sister, who never suspected that I had been eavesdropping on some of their intense deliberations about my future. An even greater surprise to them was that I happily took note of the "news" and was prepared to go the next day even though I didn't speak a word of English. To this end, Father had engaged the services of a retired merchant seaman living in a public housing development in a seedy section of Jakarta. The choice was typical, and nobody understood how he ever came to know a man living in such dire poverty, but I found him to be rather interesting and he claimed to have been in many places, including Australia. I doubt if he was very literate because he never once used a book; he would conduct his lessons while sitting on a tiny veranda, dressed in his pajamas, and fanning himself to ward off the heat and flies. What he claimed to be English conversation might well have been Mongolian as far as I was concerned, and when I looked puzzled, he would clarify the matter in Dutch which he spoke with a peculiar lilt even though he was a real Dutchman.

We carried on in this fashion for a couple of months until one day, while I was out with Father, he ran into one of his English acquaintances to whom he proudly explained that I would soon be leaving to attend school in Australia. Being of a shy nature, I was too terrified to utter as much as a how-do-you-do and merely smiled. This infuriated Father, and I was afraid the entire venture was going to be abandoned; at any rate, my English lessons ceased immediately.

There was one other activity which held my interest briefly at the time, and that was radios. Someone had taught me how to put together a simple crystal receiver and, while contemplating my masterpiece at some length, the thought apparently occurred to Father that this might hold some promise. Probably grasping at last straws, he introduced me to a Portuguese gentleman who operated a radio repair shop in the hope that such could work into some sort of apprenticeship. The man was sympathetic and invited me to come in and try my hand at several simple tasks but both of us soon realized that I lacked zero aptitude. I continued to put crystal receivers together for a while longer and became a regular customer at a Japanese electronics store where I bought all kinds of gadgets for which I had little or no use. That venture, too, was soon forgotten and the day was finally fast approaching when I was leaving to attend school abroad. It had been decided that I was to attend school in East Guildford, a suburb of Perth in Western Australia. This meant that I could spend the summer vacations at home, but nobody ever expected that we were not to see one another for four years. When we finally did, home would no longer be what the term implied.

Chapter 2

Home in Australia, 1941–1945

LEAVING HOME

During the early morning hours of August 20, 1941, I said my goodbyes to all that was dear to me—servants, pets, worldly possessions and familiar surroundings—after which my father and sister took me to the harbor to embark on the MV *Charon* of the Blue Funnel Line. Although ready to sail, the ship did not observe its scheduled departure time because of the possibility of being intercepted by an Axis raider which had been lurking about the northern parts of the Indian Ocean. We would be blacked out at night while at sea and were only allowed to burn dim lights in our cabins. Fortunately, my father and sister decided to take their leave so as not to prolong the agony of a final farewell, and I was free to explore my new surroundings.

There were two other passengers besides myself who came on board in Jakarta, a boy my age who was headed for the same school and with whom I shared a cabin, and a girl who was about three years older. The *Charon* was known as a "dormitory ship" because it regularly transported students between Australia and East Asia, principally to Singapore and places on the Indian subcontinent. Whereas the British had traditionally been sending their children back to England for an education, they had increasingly opted for Australian schools after war became a distinct possibility during the late 1930s. A vacation traffic jam occurred twice a year, once late in January at the beginning of the school year in Australia and again in December at the end of the school year.

Before anyone realized it, the ship slipped its moorings shortly after 3:00 p.m. and began rapidly picking its way through harbor traffic while heading for open sea. At the harbor entrance I spotted the family car with Father standing on the running board frantically waving goodbye. Poor man. Luckily he had no idea of the horrible times he was to endure shortly.

It was the first time I had been at sea or, for that matter, really away from home at all, and we quickly settled down to shipboard routine with a lifeboat drill as the first thing on the agenda. After a brief stop at *Banjuwangi* on the eastern tip of Java early the next day, we passed through the Strait of Bali before entering the Indian Ocean, where we ran into rough water and I promptly became seasick.

The first port of call in Australia a couple of days later was Derby—no more than a cattle station in those days—where we picked up cattle. What a strange place it seemed after never having seen anything but the lush vegetation of the Indies. So, too, were the other stops at Onslow and Carnarvon farther south before we reached Fremantle ten days after leaving Jakarta. We were met by Canon R. E. Freeth, headmaster of the school we were to attend who, after assisting us in clearing immigration and customs, drove us to Guildford about ten miles east of Perth. It was midwinter and the day was drab and rainy, but we were all eyes and excited. Attempts at conversation were awkward due to language difficulties, but as usual in such cases, we somehow managed to communicate with one another.

The Guildford Grammar School is what is referred to as a public school and operated by the Church of England and, while I was there, had two hundred boarders and about fifty day students. It was one of five such establishments in the Perth area, the others being Hale School, Scots College, Aquinas College (Catholic), and Wesley College. Except for the last, the institutions competed with one another in sports, which were as important an element in the educational process as academics were. Paramount was the development of each student into a gentleman after the English mold so admired—if not envied—by much of the world. While they did their utmost, I merely wound up among the admirers, possibly because I was a hopeless case to start with but more than likely because the habit requires unceasing reinforcement by one's peers. Then, too, most of the students had been entrusted to the separate preparatory school at the tender age of six.

In the A division, students were prepared for future intellectual pursuit—i.e., Latin and Greek—whereas the B division was meant for average students. At the conclusion of the Upper IV form, one was required to sit for an examination administered by the State University. A pass meant that one received the Junior Certificate, and one qualified for the Leaving Certificate after having

<table>
<tr><th>FORM</th><th>FORM</th></tr>
<tr><td>III A</td><td>III B</td></tr>
<tr><td>Lower IV A</td><td>Lower IV B</td></tr>
<tr><td>Upper IV A</td><td>Upper IV B</td></tr>
<tr><td colspan="2">The Junior Certificate</td></tr>
<tr><td colspan="2">Fifth Form</td></tr>
<tr><td colspan="2">Sixth Form</td></tr>
<tr><td colspan="2">The Leaving Certificate</td></tr>
</table>

Organization of grammar school classes

successfully completed the fifth and sixth forms. The only examination I ever sat for was at the junior level, and it was anything but easy. To pass a foreign language, one had to demonstrate a proficiency in both its written and oral forms. The last was administered some time in advance of the former and consisted of one half-hour of conversation with two examiners, and I never spoke French or German as well since that time. English was the most comprehensive test of all, and the school miraculously prepared me in a little over two years to pass the subject with distinction. (When I had arrived in Australia I knew only how to say "yes," "no," and "good morning.")

An important requisite of a boy's upbringing apparently required that he be periodically exposed to primitive conditions in a camp so that he could learn to cope with them with equanimity. The school had gone into a two-week, end-of-term recess just before our arrival, and the two of us had to join the other overseas students at a camp outside Pinjarra, a town located some fifty miles south of Perth. During the one night we spent in school before leaving, we were under the supervision of the housekeeper—a Miss Morgan—who treated us kindly (although we later learned that she was known as "the battleship" on account of her size and temperament). Except for staff, quarters buildings were devoid of heat, and all showers and wash basins had only one handle, and that was for cold water. Being unaccustomed to the climate—it was the middle of winter—we failed to take a shower, but that was the only time—ever!

We took the early train to Perth the next morning, where we caught the Bunbury express, which stopped in Pinjarra. While most people used the train in those days, rail travel was primitive and slow, one reason being that it had evolved in a rather peculiar manner. Each Australian state had engaged a different engineer to build its railway system. As a result they all wound up with different track widths. Western Australia and Queensland both had narrow-gauge beds, while New South Wales and South Australia both had standard widths. Victoria chose extra wide rails, as in the Soviet Union. In traveling from Perth on the west coast to Brisbane on the upper east coast once required changing trains six times.

In Pinjarra, we were met at the station by the mail carrier, who also happened to own the camp where we were headed. If they intended for us to rough it, they could not have picked a more appropriate place, and I was ready to wire home, begging to be repatriated. The boys were housed in four dilapidated cottages, some six or seven to a unit. They did their own cooking, bathed in the river, used outdoor privies, generally lived like savages, and seemed to love it. We, the two newcomers, were each given a large jute bag and told to go and fill it up with straw at the horse barn. This was our mattress, commonly called a *palliasse*. Two rough, olive-green blankets served as sheets, and I later found out that this was the way it was in the Australian army and that we really fared better because we at least slept on cots, while soldiers slept on the barracks floor. My cot was beside the front door and my first assignment was K.P.—what else? Then they forgot me, that dumb Dutchman, for two whole days as I struggled with all the unpleasant tasks, all the while trying to figure out how to complain without the help of a dictionary. Finally, the one master in charge came to the rescue and invited me to have dinner with him, which wasn't exactly first class but was at least edible.

The two weeks were soon over, and we returned to school to start the last term, and this opened up a whole new world. For a start, they placed me in Form Lower IV B, but it became readily apparent that this was too difficult for someone without sufficient knowledge of English, and they dropped me back to III B, where I got along reasonably well. School was very formal; the boys wore charcoal gray suits, white shirts with detachable collars, and navy-blue ties. The masters wore caps and gowns, and those who had special degrees were adorned with various colored vestments. When they entered the classroom, everyone would rise until invited to be seated. Classes lasted forty-five minutes from 9:00 a.m. until noon, followed by an hour's break for lunch. They resumed from 1:00 p.m. until 4:00 p.m. There was no school on Wednesday afternoon; instead, we had school on Saturday morning. We rose early, took a mandatory cold shower, dressed next to our beds, then rolled up the bedding and placed it on our night stand. Maids made up the beds and we would not be allowed in the dorm again until after study period at night.

The school was organized into four houses, namely, St. George's House, School House, and Henn's House for the boarding students, and Sterling House for the day students. We fell into formation by houses to enter the dining room, to march to chapel or, for that matter, to attend any function. Breakfast was at 7:00 a.m., to be followed by chapel every day at 8:15. One rarely saw masters have anything to do with boys outside the classroom and day-to-day operations were carried on under the direction of prefects, of whom there were eight. Four of these were captains of the individual houses, each of whom had a number of prefects of a lower order. They had broad jurisdictional powers and enforced general discipline by handing out demerits called "fatigues" for any infraction of the rules—including not holding one's eating utensils just the right way. The captain of a house could, at least theoretically, administer corporal punishment, but I don't recall that ever taking place. Corporal punishment by the masters was an everyday event, involving a three-foot-long cane applied to the rear end. Six strokes were the maximum permitted on any occasion, and most of the time it was just one or two hard whacks, which would leave welts for a few days. For misbehavior in class, one was summoned to the masters' common room, where punishment was administered in a small anteroom. A housemaster would deal out whippings in his personal quarters, located at the head of the stairs between two dormitories. On occasion, the whole house would listen in while lining the stairs, but this was risky business because they would sometimes be caught doing so and receive an equal number of strokes with the cane. During midmorning break, the entire student body participated in doing calisthenics called "PT." We stripped to the waist and fell into formation on the parade ground in summer and winter. When it rained, we stayed in the locker rooms, which was rather uncomfortable because of the lack of space. The sports fields were adjacent to the preparatory school about a mile down the highway. Cricket was played during the warm months and Australian Rules football during cold weather. Both were practiced after the last period, when we had precisely thirty minutes to get dressed and run the mile down to the fields. After practice, we got forty-five minutes to run back, shower, and prepare to fall into formation to enter the dining room for supper. At this point, there was a little relaxation time when everyone had a chance to spend some pocket money at the Tuck Shop, where they kept a supply of all sorts of candy, jam, and other goodies to supplement an otherwise bland diet. If one bought a jar of marmalade, it would rest at the center of the table with one's name on it. We ate at long tables, ten on each side, while sitting on a bench with a comfortable back. A prefect would sit at the head of the table while a housemaster would take a seat at the other end during lunch, which was the main meal of the day. Masters would generally take their meals while seated at a long table on a dais at the end of the dining room. All meals were served by uniformed maids; one of these happened to be very pretty and therefore popular with all the boys. But she knew how to handle improprieties and spilled a plate of hot soup on a fellow sitting next to me who had been uttering lewd remarks meant for her. He got a good caning to boot afterwards.

Try as I would, I could not manage to serve the ball at cricket, which was the most important sport from a social standpoint. Games against other schools—referred to as meets—were elaborate affairs during which all players turned out in crisp white uniforms and the only distinguishing team garment was the school cap. The game could go on for days and it was advisable to show up from time to time in order to display proper respect for this great and very British cultural event. Fortunately, there was a substitute sport for those not adept at playing the game, and that was rowing.

The Swan River flowed serenely several hundred yards behind the school and became an estuary in the middle of Perth ten miles to the west. It looked very much like the Thames River just before it reaches London. Our boathouse contained a practice eight and a racing eight, as well as two practice- and one racing four—five boats in all. They were stored in racks upside down and had to be carried only a short distance to a large jetty. A boat is carried on the shoulders of an equal number of crew on each side and, once near the water, is turned over and placed on the thighs of the crew on one side and held there while the crew members on the other side scramble underneath to assume their share of the weight in the same fashion. It is then lifted by the struts and gently lowered in the water.

No matter how much—or how long—one has rowed, the first time a boat is taken out at the beginning of the season, crew members look like a bunch of novices. To get in the boat requires that one foot is placed on the keel while a hand is quickly placed on top of each of the sides; to miss stepping on the keel could result in damage to the thin shell. Once seated, the oars must be placed and secured in the oarlocks, and then the wobbling really begins. If the novices survive this without turning the boat upside down, they are ready to proceed on command of the coxswain, who is the tiniest member of the crew and who faces forward to steer the boat. The first time out, they usually go no further than a couple of hundred feet and then turn around to come back. The amazing thing is how sore one gets from that initial outing. After a few times, however, the awkwardness passes and the sport becomes a delight beyond compare.

Once a year, in the fall, the four public schools would meet in Perth for the head-of-the-river race, which measured a mile. In the spring, the four houses competed intramurally on the Swan River behind the school, two at a time because the river wasn't wide enough at that point. The spring rowing season would be topped off with a regatta at Aquinas College to which we were always invited. To compete in the events in downtown Perth and at Aquinas College required that the boats be rowed from ten to fifteen miles downstream and back again afterwards. The river enters the Swan estuary on the edge of downtown Perth, and on one occasion there was a stiff breeze blowing across the open water, which caused us to swamp. Rowing in the bow position, I had to endure most of the water breaking over the front until we abandoned ship. We were some distance from shore, and our predicament was beginning to attract attention. They had taught us to stay with the boat, no matter what, and to turn it over, if possible, but the water was deep and we never gained our footing until we got close to shore. Somehow, we managed to hold all the gear together and push the boat into the safety of the Perth Yacht Club, where it was stored for the night. We received much praise for this feat but were nevertheless issued a citation by a bobby (a policeman on a bicycle), who was quite unimpressed by it all. The charge? We never found out, but it probably was "disorderly conduct."

THE WORLD AT WAR

The first term at school was about to come to an end when we woke up one morning to learn about the Japanese attack on Pearl Harbor. The event quickly embroiled more nations, this time including the Netherlands East Indies, but it took a long time before I heard anything from home. Meanwhile, we lived off rumors. Arrangements had been made for me to spend the summer on a farm owned by one of the school's former students. This turned out to be an education in itself, and I can remember virtually every detail of my surroundings as well as most of the events which occurred from day to day.

The Australians were making an important contribution to the Allied war effort, and the effects were obvious at home. Available manpower was rapidly dwindling, and the government had decreed that all able-bodied males over a certain age—it seems that this was either fourteen or sixteen—be required to work whenever they were idle. There was plenty of work available, and those who couldn't find a job to suit themselves were put to work picking grapes—a job which had somehow earned a dreadful reputation. For that reason, I opted for farm work but not entirely without the urging of my father, who had grown up on a farm in the eastern part of Holland. I took the train to a place called Broomehill, where I was met by a Mr. Stuart who drove me out to his three-thousand-acre wheat and sheep farm. Having never seen wheat before, I was impressed by the endless fields standing ready to be harvested. Even more impressive was the family home situated on top of a hill about half a mile from the main road where I was introduced to Mr. Stuart's mother and sister. Old Mr. Stuart was deceased, and the son and daughter were in their late twenties. There was also a farm hand on the premises who lived in a shack behind the house. He was able to impart the entire vocabulary of Australian foul language in record time, much to the dismay of the lady of the house, who one day caught me proudly practicing the art while harnessing a balking horse.

The home had all the conveniences of a city dwelling except for a telephone. Furnishings were elegant, and came from one of Australia's largest department stores in which the lady of the house reputedly had a family interest. Water came from two sources: wells and rainfall, the latter of which is adequate in southwestern Australia. Virtually all buildings in the outback had corrugated galvanized roofs, and rainwater was collected in round metal tanks. Well water was pumped by multibladed windmills, which all seemed to be made by a company named Southern Cross. A separate windmill drove a small generator, producing electricity, which was stored in a room full of automobile batteries wired in series so as to produce thirty-two volts of power, enough to run a refrigerator, small appliances, and all lights.

Every working day began at 5:00 a.m., and I was assigned small chores such as milking two cows, operating a hand-cranked centrifuge which separated the cream from the milk, and grooming the horses. Occasionally I would accompany the boss on his motorcycle to pick up rabbit carcasses. Australia was infested with the offspring of thirteen rabbits which were introduced in 1859 for hunting purposes and had since become serious pests. They lived in burrows, sometimes single ones, but more often in communities, covering as much ground as a large house which had scores of entrances. Farmers waged a relentless war against these creatures by using traps, poison, or gas, or by just shooting them. In the evening, I made the rounds with a horse-drawn buggy, which made a shallow trench in which poisoned pellets were dropped. We went out the next morning to collect dead rabbits, which I would drape over my lap while sitting on the back of a motorcycle driven by the boss. The Australian government paid a bounty for every skin, and we would sit around and skin rabbits for an hour or so.

It was harvesting time, and they had hired me principally to drive a huge tractor which pulled a combine. After a breakfast of Wheaties and strawberries covered with fresh whipped cream, followed by bacon and eggs, plus toast and all the butter one would ever want, we would head out to a distant part of the three-thousand-acre farm and fire up the Massey-Harris tractor, which was fueled by charcoal. Gasoline was rationed and was available in sufficient quantities only in the remote northern territories. A bag of charcoal the size of a hundred-pound bag of horse feed was emptied into a steel tank about three feet in diameter and about five feet tall. This was set on fire the same way a barbecue grill is lit. After the fire had caught up, the tank lid was closed, and the fuel system of the tractor was primed by means of a crank which drew the gas into the carburetor. If all went well—sometimes the system would be troublesome—the engine was cranked, and the only noticeable difference between burning petrol and charcoal was a slight hesitation upon revving the engine. Every so often another bag of charcoal was emptied into the tank, and the machine kept going all day long.

A couple of drawbacks existed insofar as the tractor was concerned. Any fire source constituted a hazard in a wheat field, and we had to exercise extra caution when opening the fire box. The charcoal tank was furthermore mounted beside the hood immediately behind the clutch, and this caused extreme discomfort to the driver. I sat practically on top of a furnace from about 8:00 in the morning until 5:30 in the afternoon every day of the week except Sunday but never seemed to suffer any ill effects. I did roll up my sleeves three inches higher than usual and wound up with a nasty sunburn which caused a blister of equal size on both upper arms and left a mark for the rest of my life.

Trucks and automobiles were also fueled with charcoal, the only difference being in the way a tank was mounted. Cars carried tanks in the trunk, which required removal of the trunk's lid. Some people objected to this and placed the system on a two-wheeled trailer, which was hitched to the bumper. My boss made his own charcoal by setting logs on fire in a shallow depression about twelve feet square and then covering them with a light layer of dirt. Letting the logs smolder for a certain time turned them into charcoal.

All of the combine's inner workings were activated by a drive wheel equipped with cleats so that the tractor did not just pull it along but rather operated the whole affair by setting it in motion, a heavy load indeed. While I drove the tractor, the farm hand operated the various controls on the combine. The wheat bin was emptied into jute bags after one or two rounds in the field, after which the bags were taken to a local silo by the boss in his truck. Nowadays, combines are self-propelled and empty the wheat into a wagon, which is pulled to the silo where the load is dumped.

In the middle of the morning and again in the afternoon, we would stop to boil a billy of tea. We built a small fire, poured water into a can and when it came to a boil, threw a handful of tea in it. No self-respecting Australian would drink tea made any other way while working in the open. Everyone carried a canvas bag holding about a half-gallon of water, which was hung outside a car, truck, or any other moving vehicle. Just enough moisture seeped through the canvas so that air moving over the bag caused evaporation, keeping the water inside cool. The day's lunch was driven out to the field by one of the ladies and was always a feast, which made going back to work no easy task.

Quitting time was 5:30, and the drive back to the barn took about a half-hour, sometimes longer. We would shower and dress for dinner which was served around 7:00. Dress was casual but by no means sloppy, and afterwards we sat on the front porch to await the "Albany doctor," which arrived at a certain time each evening. Albany is a port city on Western Australia's south coast, about one hundred miles from where we were. The "doctor" was a cool breeze, which quickly lowered the temperature to comfortable levels. There being no land mass of any kind between Australia and Antarctica, cool air currents flowed unobstructed to replace hot air over land. Dusk at that latitude would, furthermore, not come until about 10:00 which allowed plenty of time for talk and relaxation. The favorite refreshment at such a time was homemade root beer.

The weather was predictable from day to day—dry and hot. We did have a cyclone one day. It came upon us out of the north and consisted of a towering black wall stretching as far as the eye could see from west to east. The wind was hurricane strength and did considerable damage to the windmills and the tin roofs covering the buildings; however, repairs were quickly made and the event soon forgotten. The boss did tell me that a sheet of corrugated roofing came within inches of decapitating me as it sailed over my head during the height of the storm.

Other than riding a small pony as a child, I had never been on a horse before, but one cannot round up sheep very well while on foot. The hard work is done by sheep dogs—wily animals without equal—but to keep up with the whole flock one needs a horse. Fortunately, the farmer had a gentle old nag which was afflicted with arthritis, just the right specimen for learning to ride. We were meant for each other, and as we roamed all over the place, it seemed as if the animal was actually trying to show me certain things of interest.

Toward the end of my stay, I was allowed to ride the boss's own horse, a spirited stallion and, wonder above wonder, I lived to tell about it. While riding it one day, I decided to provoke the resident bull by charging him. Other than snorting a couple of times, he showed no interest. I got a much better response from a herd of semiwild horses roaming a neighbor's farm. They had cautioned me to keep my distance, but I wrongly surmised that that only meant while being on foot; since I was on a horse, I decided to join them. As soon as about a dozen mean-looking critters had surrounded us, one wheeled around and let fly with his rear legs missing my head by inches, and I beat a hasty retreat but not before my horse decided to retaliate, connecting solidly several times. I hastily dismounted and, while I was fumbling with the gate, my mount decided he had better not hang around. As a result, I had to walk a considerable distance back to the barn. When I arrived, I found him in his stall munching hay. Miraculously, nobody found out about the episode, but it sure taught me a lesson.

I was on excellent terms with a huge Clydesdale which was used to pull things around and had been given strict instructions never to let him go faster than a trot. But he loved to gallop, and whenever I thought we were out of sight I let him have his way. It wasn't long before they caught me, and it seemed as if my whole adventure was about to come to an end. I never had any intention of doing him any harm, but it was explained to me that a draft horse could easily overheat or, because of its sheer size, could injure itself should it ever stumble. Fortunately, I was able to make amends shortly after that when it was time to dip sheep to rid them of maggots, and this was done by immersing them in a foul-smelling solution. Among the herd was a particularly troublesome ram of respectable proportions which, at a critical moment, decided to turn and run the wrong way—towards me! Without the slightest idea what I was doing—ignorance is bliss—I stood firm between him and freedom, grabbed him by the horns and we both went tumbling. I managed to hang on long enough until help came, and this so impressed the boss that he managed to brag about it for days.

At least once during my stay, we all went into the town of Katanning to go shopping. Outback towns were drab-looking affairs, but to farmers, the Saturday outing was something to look forward to. Not many roads were paved in those days, and going anywhere was a dusty adventure. I don't remember anything we did, exactly; frankly I was bored. The best description I can think of is that, aside from the architecture peculiar to Australia, the town looked like someplace remote in Texas or Oklahoma during the Depression, as is depicted in old Wild-West movies. Come to think of it, it was about that time in the world's history.

The family never went to church on Sunday. Again, come to think of it, churches seemed to be nonexistent, although we always had a special service in the Church of England cathedral in Perth at the conclusion of the school year. This is not to say that religion did not play an important part in life, but its practice in Australia was more like that in Europe, where it is far less pervasive than in the USA.

On another occasion, we attended a community picnic, and there was much excited talk beforehand about all the lovely young ladies I was about to meet. Well, amazing as it may seem, the only girl I ever remembered having anything to do with thus far in life had been the one sitting in front of me in high school before coming to Australia, and she didn't like me because I kept dipping her pigtails in my inkwell. Girls simply had not been a part of my life and were not to be for quite some time. My behavior must have been terribly awkward during what turned out to be a splendid get-together, and my hosts seemed genuinely disappointed.

Christmas passed virtually unnoticed, or so it seemed to me. People did decorate their houses for the occasion, but not to the extent they do in the northern hemisphere. Perhaps local commercial interests have learned to exploit the event since I was there, although it is hard to imagine that anyone could be inspired to dream of a white Christmas when the temperature hovers around the hundred-degree mark. And so the time came for me to return to school after eight weeks of toil, for which I was paid ten shillings a week, for a total of four pounds Australian currency. Free room and board was in addition thereto and was invaluable. There is but one item I can resort to for comparison and that was the cost of first-class transportation from Jakarta to Fremantle only a few months earlier, which came to thirteen pounds. All things considered, I suppose my compensation was fair enough.

EVACUATION

The new school year started the first week in February, and we quickly settled into a common routine. My greatest concern was what was happening in the Indies, and the paucity of news from home wasn't helping matters. In one letter I learned that Father had been hospitalized because of high blood pressure, and an entry in my diary on March 6, 1942, mentions that by then all of Malaya, half of Borneo and Sumatra, plus all of Celebes (Sulawesi) had been overrun by the Japanese but that Java had not been invaded yet.

A week earlier I was called out of the classroom because I had a visitor who turned out to be none other than my half-brother Jan, resplendent in his uniform, which looked foreign even to me after only such a short time. He was accompanied by a fellow officer, and they had just arrived in Fremantle that morning on one of the last ships out of Tjilatjap on the south coast of Java. They told me that the Dutch had lost virtually all their planes and that they were part of a contingent with orders to carry on the war from elsewhere. They were on their way to Melbourne, which had become the gathering place for the various Allied commands which were driven out by the Japanese. They were in a hurry to get back to the ship, and my brother promised me that he would keep me informed as to his future whereabouts. A few months later, I received a letter from him in Jackson, Mississippi, where the Dutch had established an air force training base.

War even reached us in Perth, although only in the form of false alarms. We dug a series of trenches behind our dormitories, and at 9:00 one night, a practice session was held. We evacuated all buildings to see if we could find our way to safety in the dark.

The few letters I received from home were becoming less and less optimistic before they ceased coming altogether. On March 7, 1942, the newspapers reported that Jakarta had been occupied by the Japanese, and a couple of days later the Dutch capitulated. I could only imagine what was taking place and did not find out until many years later what actually happened because people were so reluctant to talk about their wartime experiences. Anyone who was a government official was immediately locked up in central prison where they remained until the end of the war. My sister's father-in-law was thus treated; he survived but came out with a bad case of tuberculosis. All military personnel were treated as prisoners of war, and most of them wound up on the infamous Burma Road, where many succumbed to tropical diseases such as bacillary dysentery. My brother-in-law, Piet, was fulfilling his military obligation as a truck driver when evidence mounted that all was lost. He drove his truck to the vicinity where he lived, abandoned it, and walked home where he burned his uniform. He was interned shortly afterwards in a camp for civilians where my father also spent the war.

The Japanese selected two areas in town, well separated from each other, and erected a barbed wire fence around them. Dutch males twelve years or older, as well as males of any other nation at war with Japan, were locked up in one camp, while females and children under twelve were placed in the other. Living conditions, bad from the start, steadily deteriorated during the war. People were hungry and there was no medicine to treat the sick. My sister later told of her experiences as an assistant to the surgeon who had operated on my mother. He was a professor of medicine, who crafted his instruments from eating utensils and was able to save many lives.

Internees were required to work within the confines of the camp and were often brutally beaten; those who were tall were particularly despised by the guards. The old were excused from work, but my father worked anyway and got a hernia from lifting heavy objects. It became strangulated, and a Japanese doctor successfully operated on him just before the end of the war.

About a month and a half into the first term, the entire student body was to be evacuated to Pinjarra, the place where I spent the first two weeks after arriving in Australia. The Church of England owned a farm there called Fairbridge, which had been used as an orphanage. Orphans were no longer arriving from England because of the war, and only a small group remained. They were to vacate the premises so that we could move in. Our school plant had been leased to the United States for use as a military hospital. We spent the next three days packing, and on a Saturday morning, an Australian military convoy assembled on the parade ground to load and transport us and our belongings to our new abode. The whole job was accomplished in a day—really a marvelous exercise in efficiency. The ones who entertained us the most during the trip were the military police on motorcycles, who maintained order among the convoy and kept it moving at a steady pace. If the lead truck needed to be headed off, one of the cyclists jumped the ditch and raced full speed through the bush, a sight which would have delighted today's trail blazers.

Contrary to expectations, our new home turned out to be acceptable. We were housed in cottages, about a dozen boys to each, under the supervision of a faculty member. The lower floors of those which had two stories were used as classrooms, crowded but not bad. We had washrooms equipped with showers and washstands—cold water only, of course—and had to use outhouses for latrines. That was tough, particularly on days you had to empty the slop-pot used in the dorm during the night. It is amazing how much liquid a dozen bodies will void in one night—almost five gallons! It required two boys to negotiate the rather steep and narrow stairway with almost a full pot which had once been a paint bucket. The lead boy had to shoulder the stick on which the bucket was hung, while the one at the other end had to crouch to keep it level. The first time my turn came for this delectable job, I lost the toss of a coin and was the lead boy—to my utter horror! Halfway down the stairs, something happened and I didn't wait to see what it was; I just jumped the rest of the way and out the front door before the pot slid off the stick. It earned me three licks with the cane, not because of the mess, but because of resorting to language unbecoming to a gentleman. The fact that I had only recently been tutored in the common man's language by a real Aussie didn't impress anyone.

Other than being isolated, the farm was really a nice place. It had a central kitchen and dining room, a handsome chapel, and several football fields; it even had a golf course. A fast-flowing creek with the purest, ice-cold water provided us with a swimming hole where we spent many hours cavorting on hot days and where we even managed to train for swim meets in Perth. We did well at the meets because they were held in brackish water, which provided additional buoyancy and therefore required less physical effort.

Apart from large quantities of fresh bread, the food was positively awful. We were allowed to supplement our diet by buying even more bread and would line up at the back of the kitchen late in the afternoon as the bread came out of the oven. They stopped furnishing butter, ostensibly because it was rationed, and substituted a substance called "dripping," furnished at the table. The stuff was actually leftover grease, and our efforts to make it palatable with tomato catsup were to no avail; I just refused to eat the muck.

Each cottage had a fireplace, and we were allowed to light a fire on weekends. We learned to gather mushrooms which we sauteed in butter—our private supply—and eat them on toast, quite a delicacy. Sleeping quarters were open to the weather on one side, a substitute for the balconies at our regular school which were reserved for seniors. Once you become accustomed to sleeping in fresh air, it is hard to do without, even in the coldest weather.

It was soon wintertime, and I was introduced to Australian Rules football. The game is played on an oval field twice the size of a soccer field, and each team has eighteen men. They play with an egg-shaped ball which is never thrown but is continually kicked for long distances, if possible. Players take up position all over the field, rather than in an advancing or retreating formation as is done in soccer or in American football. The game is started with the referee bouncing the ball midfield, after which two players from opposite sides try to gain control by tipping it to a teammate. The one who gains possession of the ball will kick it to one of his teammates standing closest to the opposing team's goal. The receiver is guarded, and several players will jump to catch the ball. Whoever succeeds in doing so gets a free kick, and so the ball continues down the field or goes back towards the other goal, depending on who gets control. Finally, when the ball is in possession of a player close to the goal, he will attempt to kick it between two tall posts which are flanked by two shorter posts on each side. If the ball goes between the tall posts, he makes six points for his team; if it goes between a tall post and a short one, it will count only as one point and if it misses altogether, it goes out of bounds. Kicking is a fine art, much more so than in soccer because of the shape of the ball. A drop-kick is the most accurate, has a low trajectory and is easier to catch. A good punt (a ball kicked without it first hitting the ground) generally goes further but is not as accurate. Once a ball hits the ground, a scramble ensues and whoever recovers it can kick it, run with it—in which case he must bounce it every third step—or pass it to another player by punching it with one hand out of the other. There is never any throwing, unless the ball goes out of bounds; then the player from the nonoffending team faces away from the players and throws it over his head back on the field. It is an extremely fast game and an exhausting one because of it. Never much at sports, I failed to make the school's first team, but I drove them crazy in practice sessions by knocking the ball out of an intended catcher's hands by sneaking up behind him at the last moment causing it to go wild. Some threatened to knock my teeth out if I didn't quit, but it was legal. I never mastered the drop-kick on a consistent basis; hence, I always punted, which they dubbed the "Dutch special."

Before I knew it, it was time to make arrangements to stay somewhere during the two-week break between first and second terms. Given a choice, I selected a vineyard where they packed currants and raisins for shipment abroad. The operation belonged to a gentleman who had inherited it and who lived alone in the parental home, which was situated on a hill overlooking a beautiful valley. The farm wasn't too far from where the school was located at the time.

Grapes had been sun-dried and were being packed when I arrived on the scene. As usual, there was one farm hand helping the owner, and they had fallen behind filling orders, mostly destined for shipment to the United Kingdom. Products were packed in neat wooden boxes about six inches deep, which were lined with waxed paper. A mechanical press compressed the contents, and the power source was an ancient internal combustion engine which fired noisily every third or fourth cycle, keeping a flywheel in motion. It drove a shaft from which various devices took power by means of leather belts. Two people worked at this task while a third operated a machine which put two steel straps around the boxes after they had been nailed shut.

I had a comfortable room in the house and the food was outstanding. Although it seemed to be a traditional item on the menu of every farmhouse in Australia, I specifically remember the fresh cream for breakfast every morning. There must have been a cook, but for some reason I can't recall thanking or saying good-bye to one upon leaving. Even though there were only two of us for dinner at night, we both wore coat and tie. As on the previous occasion, my employer/host had attended the school where I was going and paid me well.

Soon after returning to school for the second term, I was called in by the headmaster to hear the dreaded news I had been expecting for some time: my funds were running low and I should consider the possibility of leaving school. I was sixteen years old by that time and, while the news increased my apprehension, I was able to cope with the situation.

The quality of education never suffered while we were in exile; if anything, it was enhanced by our isolation. All sorts of shortages began to manifest themselves, and that of shoe polish stands out in my memory. Footwear took a beating walking dirt roads, but the school authorities never let up on the requirement that shoes be properly polished. Protests of not having shoe polish brought the retort, "You see that laboratory out there? Well, go and make some!" And sure enough, one of the brainier seniors made a huge pot full of the stuff, which he divided among the cottages so that we could resume polishing our shoes. It turned out to be superior to anything which could be bought in stores, assuming one could have found some.

One afternoon while we were playing golf, we were startled by a loud explosion coming from the laboratory located nearby, and people came running from all directions to find a couple of dazed boys staggering around outside. Although several windows were blown out, we never found out what happened but, after that incident, any experimentation in the lab could be carried on only when a senior student was present.

Apart from the splendid beaches, the Australian landscape is generally not inspiring, but where we were, things were different. On Sundays they would pack all the boys a lunch so that we could explore the countryside after chapel. Just a short distance up the creek, we had to negotiate a narrow gorge to reach open space where we could hike long distances and hardly ever come across each other, let alone strangers. As long as I lived in Australia, I never once saw a kangaroo in the wild, although, when riding in the train, one would occasionally get a glimpse of a wallaroo, a much smaller cousin of the kangaroo, scooting out of the way. Stories of the big "roos" were plentiful, however, and they warned everyone never to fool around with one because of their ability to rip a person apart with their powerful hind legs if cornered. Australians hunted the animals with dogs and, while they can outrun anything, they can be worn down. Their favorite defense is to enter a pond and wait for the dogs to come after them, when they will simply sit up and drown them.

Our school maintained a cadet corps under the auspices of the Australian army, and enrollment therein was mandatory upon reaching a certain age. Tuesday afternoons after school were devoted to "Cadets," and once a year we had to attend camp for a week during which we received general military training. The school had an armory, which had an adequate supply of rifles until we had to pack them up for shipment to England where they were running short of small arms. They were ancient .303 caliber rifles used in the Boer War at the start of the century, and we were puzzled as to how they could ever expect to defend British shores against a German invasion with that kind of a weapon. In the meantime, we had to drill with wooden rifles supplied by the army, and these were replaced about a year later by the standard Lee-Enfield rifle used by the British armed forces.

The first camp I attended was held during a break between terms and, since we were already in the country, we attended it on school grounds. The thing I remember best is the day we were ordered to lay out and dig a series of trenches. Our training manuals were of World War I vintage and provided detailed plans for trench warfare as well as drawings of tactical movements on battle grounds divided by impenetrable hedgerows or strong walls, neither of which were part of the local landscape. Digging those trenches proved to be a backbreaking task, and they failed to tell us that they were to serve a useful purpose shortly—very shortly, as a matter of fact. It all started with a faint rumble in the distance which we were unable to identify but which grew steadily louder. Suddenly, we heard yelling, instructing us to get into those trenches and keep our heads down. Most of us took our time until we spotted a tracked vehicle coming straight at us, and we wasted no time doing what we were told to do. It turned out that arrangements had been made for a couple of Bren Gun Carriers (essentially light armored personnel carriers) to participate in our field exercise. After a couple of feints, presumably to be sure that we were out of harm's way, they drove right over us, scaring us out of our wits.

Within a week after school resumed, I was called out of class to go and see the headmaster. Fearing the worst, I found two gentlemen in the office who represented the Dutch government in exile and who wanted to talk with me. During the course of long questioning, they asked if I was satisfied where I was, adding that if I was not, arrangements could be made for a transfer to another school.

"Any school?" I asked.

"Yes, indeed; any school in Australia," was the answer.

Her Majesty the Queen, then living in London, had instructed her government in exile to find her subjects anywhere they might be in the world and to see to it that they were properly cared for. I asked if I could think about it, and they agreed. In parting, they instructed me to contact the Dutch consul in Perth if I needed anything. No request for repayment of fees was ever made after the war.

I could only greet the end of the school year in December 1942 with misgivings since I had been unable to land a job and had nowhere to go except back to a boarding house run by an old lady in Darlington—a village in the hills east of Perth—which served as a sort of halfway house for people caught in unusual circumstances. It was where commuter trains from Perth turned around and headed back to the big city. On the way in, the train stopped behind our school, which had red crosses painted on all the roofs and where the Stars and Stripes fluttered on the front lawn.

Fortunately, two interesting boarders had moved in since my stay three months earlier; they were a middle-aged army officer and his wife whose home was in Sydney. The husband was a colonel recovering from war injuries, and they were as glad to see me as I was to find them there. Why they didn't send them home to the east coast was a mystery which was never explained.

As the officials who came to visit me at school had suggested, I contacted the Netherlands consul in Perth to see if he could find me a job, and he invited me to come in and see him. He turned out to be an honorary consul, a very kind, elderly Australian gentleman who recalled talking to my father over the phone about recommending a school where he could send me. While he could not help me find a job right away, he did say that he probably could locate a more suitable place for me to spend my vacation. Pursuant to his efforts, I was invited shortly after Christmas to move in with a Dutch lady who lived within walking distance of a popular beach and who had a small room for rent. She had come to Australia with her three-year-old son while her husband remained in Indonesia to take care of some last-minute business before the Dutch surrendered, but he never showed up. All she needed was a bonnet, a long black frock, and a pair of wooden clogs to have made a perfect advertisement for a fishing village on the Zuiderzee so popular with tourists after the war. She even had a gold tooth which glittered when she smiled. She was a godsend if ever there was one.

RETURN TO CIVILIZATION

The Australian continent has a varied and interesting coastline, and I regret not having seen more of it, especially the northeastern segment, including the barrier reef. If anything constitutes the Australian Way of Life, it has to be life on the beach. In accordance with British custom, every beach seems to have been dedicated to the public use with a paved road separating it from private property.

Australian lifeguards are unique. On heavily used beaches, teams of half a dozen men are stationed a hundred feet or so apart, each equipped with a reel of rope to which a harness is attached. When a bather gets in trouble, a member of the nearest team dons a harness and goes to the rescue while his teammates let out the rope, then reel it in on his signal once he has gotten hold of the victim. These rescue operations are practically an everyday affair and are executed with precision in even the roughest surf. To be a member of a team requires that one be a strong swimmer and training is rigorous.

Another team mans a rowboat which is launched from the beach whenever a shark is spotted and drives it off. The operation of such a boat in heavy surf requires a great deal of brawn and skill, particularly upon returning, when the crew must time its strokes to make maximum use of an incoming wave. If it gets caught short, turbulence can cause it to be broadsided by the next wave, which is an unpleasant experience.

The main pier and pavilion in Cottesloe—then the most popular beach in Western Australia—was the central attraction where, among other things, daredevils entertained the crowd by bodysurfing as close to the jetty as possible without getting killed. Occasionally, someone would misjudge the direction of a wave and get wrapped around a piling, but when the surf got too bad, they would be warned by the lifeguards to cease and desist.

A few blocks from the pavilion, there existed a popular open-air movie theater which was cozily nestled between several buildings. Seating was similar to desk chairs but were actually long pieces of canvas held up by two horizontal poles. A piece of canvas gave way one night and an entire row of spectators went down hard on their bottoms. The obese and elderly had a difficult time getting up because the lower part of their legs were hanging over the front by the crook of their knees and most of them had to be helped up. Everyone took it good-naturedly, even though some looked like they might have gotten a nasty jolt.

The brownout over the southern part of Australia had been suspended several months earlier, but one morning we were startled by gunfire coming from the direction of the beach. Without warning, the army had set up an antiaircraft battery during the night and was having target practice using a drone, which was flying out over the ocean a few miles out. People thought the coast was being fired on by enemy warships.

Service personnel from Allied nations were much in evidence everywhere, mostly American, but also British and Dutch. During a party celebrating the birth of the latest Dutch princess, I met an officer from a Netherlands destroyer who invited me to tour his ship in Fremantle. He showed me the latest device with which the enemy could be detected at long range in the dark. It looked like a round table with a slightly convex and opaque glass lens about three feet in diameter. It was an early model radar about which he offered no further details.

When school resumed in February, we found that several new masters had joined the faculty. One was the former British high commissioner to Malaya, a courtly old gentleman who taught history. A second was a British army captain who had received a medical discharge after a bad case of smallpox had affected his eyesight; he taught English. The third was a German prisoner of war who had been an officer in Field Marshal Erwin Rommel's *Afrika Korps*. He had a Ph.D. in physics and was on leave from a prison camp; he was fat as well as jolly and quickly endeared himself to the students. We all suspected that he had deliberately run in the direction of the British lines during a battle. His lessons in applied physics were fascinating. He also consented to teach me German in his spare time.

A month or so into the first term, I finally received a letter from my brother, Jan, who was in Jackson, Mississippi, where they had set up a Dutch base to retrain a bomber, a fighter, and a transport squadron. I learned something interesting many years later during a reunion of the various squadron members held in Jackson. Among memorabilia displayed on a long table in the convention hall was the Legion of Merit awarded to a gentleman sitting next to my wife, Ruth, at the dinner table. He, like so many present, had become a United States citizen and was, understandably, quite proud of the award. He explained that it would have been signed by President Roosevelt, had he lived; instead, it bore President Truman's signature. The man in question had been a senior member of a prewar commission working out of the Netherlands embassy in Washington. The commission's task was to acquire new military aircraft to replace the outdated Glen-Martin bombers and Brewster-Buffalo fighter planes in the Dutch East Indies. Insofar as the bomber was concerned, a company in Los Angeles had agreed to develop and build a plane according to the commission's specifications, and it turned out to be the famous B-25 bomber. The Dutch government had paid cash for a considerable number of the aircraft—some sources reported as many as 160, but the attack on Pearl Harbor came before any deliveries were ever made. The United States placed an immediate embargo on war materiel when hostilities broke out but then released five of the initial eighteen being shipped to Australia for use by the Dutch air force, too late to stem the Japanese tide. The Dutch government was subsequently refunded the money it had paid. A group of B-25s, also known as the Mitchell bomber, was led by General Doolittle in the first air raid on Japan in April of 1942.

My hostess for the summer vacation kept me supplied with all kinds of goodies during the school year, and I had a standing invitation to come back whenever I could. I was surprised to discover when I returned for a brief stay between first and second terms that most of the beach had disappeared. They explained that ocean currents always carried it away during the spring.

Toward the end of the school year, in November, we moved back to Guildford the same way as when we were evacuated—by military convoy. We had been in the country roughly a year and a half and were pleasantly surprised that all buildings had been completely renovated and that, except for the plumbing, there wasn't a sign that there ever had been a hospital. The new plumbing put in by the Americans had been modified so that only cold water was available, except in the bathtubs. We did get two hot baths every week, fifteen minutes each, and had to take turns because there were only two tubs in the bathroom. Baths started during the evening study period which lasted from 7:30 until 9:30 and everyone knew precisely when it was his turn to quietly leave, dash upstairs to undress and then run to the bathroom to jump in the water which his predecessor was expected to have drawn. One had to be careful, however, and test the temperature lest one be scalded.

We had not returned in time to take all of our examinations for the junior and leaving certificates, hence some segments had been administered while we were still in the country. We found out that our masters had been a lot tougher than the proctors at the University of Western Australia. In one instance a boy had asked to be excused to go to the bathroom. The answer was a firm "NO," unless he was ready to turn in his papers. He solved his problem by doing what he had to do in his handkerchief, then holding it out the window to squeeze it out. The master in charge calmly observed what he was doing and made no comment.

Once back in our regular quarters, we began to realize how much we had missed by being forced to evacuate and wondered why we had been the chosen ones, particularly since our school was the furthest away from the metropolitan area. The services which were once provided were never reinstated, and the food continued to be inferior. They blamed it all on the war.

I was fortunate to be able to line up another job for the summer of 1943, this time with the State. I had just one day to take my belongings to Cottesloe, where my more-or-less permanent hostess lived, before leaving for Narembeen, which was located about two hundred miles inland from Perth. The train left on a Friday morning at 8:30 and arrived at 6:00 p.m. Unbeknownst to me, two other fellows aboard had been hired by the same agency, and as we stood forlornly on the platform watching the train go out of sight, we instinctively approached each other to introduce ourselves. Not knowing anybody, we decided to check into the one hotel for the weekend.

While having breakfast on Saturday morning, a robust, no-nonsense type bushman strutted into the dining room and headed straight for our table. He introduced himself, although he need not have because we realized that he was our boss the minute we saw him. He had come to get us to sweep out a grain storage facility, which we found not to be too unpleasant a task. We later had fun in a dancehall, where we found everyone to be quite friendly. A lovely young schoolteacher took us under her wing and showed us around on Sunday, even treating us to a picnic. At breakfast on Monday, they hardly gave us any time to finish and told us to load our belongings on a heavily laden, beat-up Model T Ford truck and then climb on top of that. The first stop was a country store to buy provisions. Provisions? We had never considered such an outlandish thing and had presumed that the matter of food would—as always—somehow be taken care of. How wrong we were! Having to find bedding during the weekend should have warned us. I picked up a few cans of "bully beef" (corned beef) and a couple of loaves of bread without really knowing what else to get. We pulled out of Narembeen at 9:30 a.m., amidst a roar from the engine—which lacked a muffler—and chugged along a dirt road beside the railway for some twenty miles before reaching our destination at 12:30.

Production of wheat had either been increased as part of the war effort or there existed a shortage of shipping space; in either case, they had run out of storage facilities and were piling the stuff up at railroad sidings. It was our job to pave an area half the size of a football field, let them dump a huge pile of wheat on it, and return to build a roof over it. This required pounding long poles into the wheat, wiring cross pieces to them, and nailing sheet metal on top as a roof.

At that first work site, we found one completed storage facility full of wheat and another recently paved area, which we had to sweep during the afternoon. We unloaded our belongings into a tiny shed, which served as the station house, and that is where I slept fitfully that night, worrying that the conductor of a passing train would throw me out. The old hands, who loved nothing better than to pull our legs, didn't tell me that there were no trains during the night.

The third day out we began by paving a new storage area further along the line and wound up being covered with tar. Our uniform comprised a pair of shorts, hobnailed boots, and one of those floppy hats Australians love to wear. We bathed out of a bucket of water, which we filled up anywhere we could find water, and we looked awful! Fortunately, we worked in an arid climate and the heat, while uncomfortable, was not as debilitating as it is where the humidity is high. Later during the week, we visited a wooded area to find suitable trees for poles. Chainsaws were unheard-of in those days and trees had to be chopped down. Nobody ever wore gloves, and the hands of workers looked like they had been mangled. Even people who worked behind a desk took little trouble to keep their hands presentable.

Friday was payday, and I felt rich for the first time in my life because the pay was good. We were only five miles away from Narembeen, and after a mere hour of work on Saturday they decided to call it a day. On the way back to town, the truck broke down and we had to wait a long time before they patched up whatever was wrong. No sooner were we back at the hotel and ready to jump under the shower when they began rounding up people to help put out a fire in a distant wheat field. This time we rode on an empty, late-model truck, and at one point I managed to glance through the rear window of the cab to see the speedometer register seventy-five miles an hour—on a gravel road! When we arrived at the fire, they had almost succeeded in putting it out, but we nevertheless joined the group and started beating the remnants with empty jute bags. That night we were back at the dancehall, and I had to be rescued from what, at close quarters, looked to be a mob. Coffee had been served during the intermission, and they had placed a pitcher of milk and a bowl of sugar in the middle of the dance floor. I failed to see them while walking across the hall and kicked the sugar bowl, causing its contents to spill all over the beautifully polished floor. There was an instant reaction of hostility on the part of some local yokels and, luckily for me, others restrained them. We decided that dancing was a dangerous exercise after that, but we had been introduced to several hopeful families who had young lasses in the house, and they invited us home any time we were in town.

To spend the night under the stars on a half-empty stomach was an experience which took some getting used to. We usually quit around 6:00 in the evening, and everyone would retire to the living quarters he had staked out in the bush. Some were elaborate affairs such as a bed sheet stretched between some scrubby trees, but my abode was no more than a palliasse without even a groundsheet. While somewhat better stocked than the first week out, my cupboard—an old box which also served as a seat—was a pitiful affair. For dinner I usually opened up a fresh can of bully beef, sopped up what little juice came out with a piece of stale bread, and downed the lot with a cup of tea brewed over a small fire. The old hands cooked some good-smelling stuff, but nobody ever invited anyone else to share what he had. The three of us kept our distance like a bunch of dogs chewing on a bone. Right or wrong, I figured that five days and nights of this wouldn't do anybody much harm so long he could make up for it during the weekends. The proprietress of the hotel was somehow aware of our trials and tribulations and took very good care of us. Keeping reasonably clean was another matter and one evening, when we could no longer stand ourselves, we took a dip in a beautiful pool of sparkling blue water, ignoring the NO SWIMMING sign put up by the local community water department.

The morning the official state examination results were published in the newspaper turned out to be a sad day for my coworkers, both of whom learned that they had failed. I was relieved to find that I had passed, and it made me look forward to the next school year.

Christmas fell on a Saturday in 1943, and we got an extra-long weekend as a result. Someone invited us to ride an empty tractor-trailer truck to Perth and back. We left at 6:00 in the evening, stopped in Northam for four hours of sleep, and arrived in front of our school in Guildford at 6:00 in the morning, where we caught the train the rest of the way. Three-fourths of the way had been on gravel roads with many stretches over washboard surfaces. We had to hang on for dear life because we were riding on a flatbed trailer, and the constant cloud of dust was but a minor problem. The two days of swimming in the ocean and being treated to good food by my faithful hostess made up for it all. I was sorely tempted not to go back, but the good pay was too much of an attraction; besides, three more weeks wouldn't hurt anyone, or so I reasoned. The trip back was terrible, but we arrived in Narembeen at the reasonable hour of 11:00 at night, which gave us a chance for a good night's sleep before getting on the road with the roofing gang again.

New Year's Eve a week later brought people into town from miles around to celebrate. Before it turned into a brawl, I decided to withdraw to my room upstairs, and the singing of *auld lang syne* in the pub barely registered as I struggled to fall asleep.

LAST CHANCE

Without realizing it, 1944 was to be the final year during which I was to receive any kind of formal education. I had experienced much difficulty in adjusting and, in the process, was becoming more and more of a disciplinary problem. My relationship with my fellow students had reached a point where I was constantly getting into fights. Open hostilities were not tolerated, and if two adversaries insisted on physical combat, they had to wait until a Saturday night to don a pair of gloves and settle their differences in a boxing ring set up in the gym for the occasion. They would fight three rounds, refereed by a master who declared one to be the winner, after which the contestants shook hands and, at least theoretically, ended their hostilities. Perhaps my father had made a mistake when, while I was still at home, he made me enroll in a boxing class at a local gym. A classmate—a scion of a wealthy family—was usually my sparring partner, but he was big and immensely strong, and he good-naturedly let me try my best on him without the least result. After I arrived in Australia, Father insisted that I maintain proficiency in the sport because he felt it to be important that one could defend oneself against bullies, who are always around.

Where I grew up, the casual use of guns was unheard of, and people simply had no access to them. Violence did exist, of course, and people were stabbed, clubbed, and even shot to death, but not with today's degree of callousness. At any rate, there came a low point in my relationship with other students when I accidentally knocked a sparring partner out cold during practice one afternoon.

The instructor, who was a professional boxer but not a member of the faculty, became enraged about such unsportsmanlike conduct and called on three of his strongest boxers, one after the other, to mete out similar punishment, which they never succeeded in doing. Needless to say, I considered this to be most unfair, and it set a whole series of events in motion which culminated in me getting the ultimate punishment of six strokes with the cane, administered by none other than the headmaster who had a final warning of, "Behave, or you're finished!" This was a turning point in my life. Aside from the humiliation, it was the first time a caning had actually drawn blood, and I was in pain for a number of days. Clearly, this was a case of abuse, or was it? It gave me a chance to reflect that conformity to the norm could, after all, have its advantages and perhaps I should start doing something about it. A very pleasant discovery followed soon afterwards, which was to make me a lasting admirer of the system. As soon as I showed signs of coming to my senses, I was met with encouragement from all sides, and rewards were not far behind. There were never any recriminations, and all that had previously occurred was treated as if nothing ever happened. Acceptance by the group was quite sincere.

At about the time I went through this metamorphosis, there occurred an incident in Western Australia which gave substance to the justification for corporal punishment. A habitual rapist by the name of Sutton had once again managed to escape from prison and promptly repeated the criminal offense which had already earned him a life sentence. The exasperated judge who had put him behind bars before, decided to subject him to a flogging with the cat-o'-nine-tails, one of the most feared punishments of earlier times. They had difficulty locating an executioner but finally found one in the eastern part of Australia. There was never any outcry against the administration of such cruel punishment, and Mr. Sutton must have decided that enough was enough and stopped escaping from jail.

There were eight students in the fifth form that year and about that many in the sixth and final form. Instruction in these senior classes was practically personalized, and I remember history as the most rewarding course. It was taught by one of the housemasters, a big man with a great sense of humor who had the habit of sitting on his desk to "discuss" history with us. Having graduated from either Oxford or Cambridge, he imparted knowledge of the subject purely from a British standpoint and often resorted to anecdotes. One of these was the innocently charming one of the visits by Paul Kruger, president of the Republic of South Africa, to England. While he was the dinner guest of

Queen Victoria, "Oom Paul," as he was called, picked up some food with his hands whereupon the queen did likewise so as not to embarrass him. Well, that was just too much like what was in Dutch history books, where it was reported that President Kruger allegedly drank water out of his finger bowl, whereupon Queen Wilhelmina diplomatically did the same thing. After I brought this detail to the attention of the class, they never failed to enquire sarcastically whether British history squared with Dutch history on a particular point.

Shortly after my eighteenth birthday, I received official "greetings" to report for a physical examination preparatory to being drafted by the Australian armed forces. This had been anticipated, and the Netherlands consul-general in Sydney had earlier given me instructions on what to do. As a Dutch citizen, I was obligated to serve in the Netherlands forces, and I was given a draft deferment until I had completed my studies. It was soon time for another cadet camp which, this time, was held at an army base in Northam. We were transported by troop train, consisting of box cars of a type suitable for men, animals, or both.

There was no doubt that the tide at the front had turned, and an air of confidence prevailed among the military. Supplies were abundant and we were issued new boots instead of those salvaged from dead soldiers at the front. Other than the rigorous training, our stay was actually pleasant, except for the indignities inflicted upon us by the drill sergeants. Entertainment was provided at night, and the Salvation Army furnished free refreshments after first locking us up in a chapel for a short interdenominational service. At the firing range, one fellow caused a commotion when, upon ordering arms in close formation, his rifle went off and a .303 slug whizzed past his head within inches. Another did a poor job hurling a live grenade over an embankment, causing several members of a squad to experience a mild concussion but, other than that, few mishaps of any consequence occurred.

Back at school, matters steadily improved and they even informed me that I was being considered for an appointment as prefect the next year. In the cadet corps, I was advanced to the rank of lance corporal, which was to prove my one and only promotion in a uniformed environment. This might not have been much, but it probably helped to stay out of the brig later in military service because gold stars and stripes, as well as other military insignia, have the same effect on me as a red cape does for a bull.

For the summer vacation at the end of 1944, I had signed up with the State Forestry Department and was sent to a place below Nannup some thirty miles north of Flinders Bay on the south coast of Australia. It is the region where Jarrah trees grow; their dimensions approach those of the California Redwoods. There were about fifty of us, and our job was to create a pattern of fire lanes by burning the undergrowth. We walked around with a water tank strapped on our back and a squirt gun which could send water a distance of at least twenty feet. Whenever a fire broke out in unexpected places, it was our job to extinguish it quickly. While so engaged, lumberjacks continued felling trees with huge saws operated by two men standing on a platform about ten feet high, and occasionally we would hear the shout "Timberrr . . ." and look up in time to see a giant tree begin to lean ever so slightly, gaining momentum and crashing among other giants without touching them, its crown having been previously removed. To reach our camp from Perth, a distance of about 225 miles, took most of a day and part of a night by train and by truck. As usual, our foreman was a foul-mouthed bushman, and we were soon talking just like him. He displayed great organizing ability from the start and, upon reaching the camp, he dared us to move and escorted us to our cabin, two at a time. Just before midnight, we were ordered to assemble in the dining hall where a feast of lamb chops and fried eggs awaited us, a meal worth remembering. The cook was an Italian prisoner-of-war who managed to endear himself to everybody.

Taking a bath at the end of a day's work required two helpers, one standing on top of a platform to fill a five-gallon container with a shower head attached to the bottom, and one to carry water from a nearby creek to the person standing on the platform. The one taking a shower could control the water flow with a short rope, but it was by no means a comfortable experience because the water was ice-cold, particularly when there was a breeze.

As usual, Christmas and New Year's Eve passed without leaving any indelible memories and, since we were needed only a short time at our summer job, I was soon back in Perth to enjoy the remainder of my vacation, or so I thought. A few days after returning I received a letter from the consulate in Sydney, advising me that my draft deferment had been canceled. In time, I was to learn that there had been some disagreement between the authorities as to who had jurisdiction, the Australians or the Dutch. The latter decided to exercise theirs and closed the matter. I was ordered to report at an Australian recruitment center at once for a physical, where they classified me "1A," and that was the end of my formal education.

Although it was no longer a vacation, I enjoyed my stay at the beach. My former hostess had departed for the east coast, but I managed to find pleasant quarters with an Australian lady who had a large home in Cottesloe and whose children were grown, married, and lived elsewhere. It was a sad time, however, when school resumed and I had to stay behind and wait for instructions on what to do next. Fortunately, I didn't have to wait long and was directed to proceed by train to a place named Casino in New South Wales, about thirty-five miles south of the Queensland border and thirty miles from the coast. It took a week to secure a priority permit from the Railway Department to travel across the continent, which gave me time to take care of personal matters such as packing a trunk full of mementos which I intended to send for at some future date. Unfortunately, I never saw that trunk again, and repeated pleas to the lady I left it with remained unanswered. She was in her sixties and not quite well, so she may have died, but it would have been so easy for her daughter to honor my request. The trunk contained numerous photographs of my school years, magazines my father sent me after I left home, and clothing such as my school uniform.

Chapter 3

Home in Clandestine, 1945–1946

LIFE IN THE ARMY

The Westland Express left Perth at 8:00 p.m. for Kalgoorly, 375 miles to the east. I had seen it pass the school countless times and looked wistfully out the window to catch a glimpse of familiar buildings as we sped by, somehow sensing it would be the last time I would ever see them again. Even though it was a night train, it lacked sleeping accommodations, and all compartments were occupied. We reached Kalgoorly after lunch the next day, two hours late. I had wanted to look around the famous mining town but didn't get to see much of it. The landscape was barren, and there was a pub on every corner, wherever one looked. It was said that only ten years earlier, before a pipeline from Perth was installed, water cost five shillings a gallon.

We had to change to the Transcontinental Express, which ran from Kalgoorly to Port Pirie in South Australia, a distance in excess of a thousand miles. We were on that train for two nights and had a most enjoyable journey. There were four of us in a compartment, all strangers and got along just great. Seat backs were hinged at the top and would make into beds at night. There were showers and toilets at both ends of each carriage, one for women and one for men, and an attendant would summon each passenger when his or her turn came to bathe. The dining car served three meals a day at a reasonable price but, if one preferred, sandwiches were also available for consumption in one's compartment.

We traversed the Nullarbor Plain, a seemingly endless expanse of desert-like land with scrubby trees and made two or three stops on the way. Because of the locomotive's oversized wheels, we needed an assist from a yard locomotive to push the train from a standstill; once moving, its water supply was replenished by being scooped up from troughs between the rails. We couldn't see any of this, but the train did slow down from time to time for no apparent reason. At each stop there were usually a number of aborigines selling souvenirs. I had seen them before at ports along the coast on our way from Jakarta to Fremantle but never in Perth. Anyhow, one is never quite prepared for the rather shocking sight of the filthy and half-starved looking creatures. At one place there was a chap sitting on his haunches who looked different and who seemed at ease among white people. He told us that he was a member of a squad of police trackers whose job it was to pursue criminals as well as to keep aborigines away from populated areas. A growing number of passengers kept crowding around while he was talking, which made it hard to follow what he was saying. We regretted hearing the all-aboard whistle so soon.

We reached Port Pirie early on a Saturday morning and had to change trains for Adelaide, about 175 miles further south; the trip took about four hours, and we pulled in at about 2:00 in the afternoon. My traveling companions on the Transcontinental talked me into taking an hour's tour of the city by taxi, which, at that stage in my life, was of little interest to me and I was glad to get back on the train later that afternoon for Melbourne, some 425 miles to the southeast. The night's ride was wearisome since there were no sleeping accommodations available and, indeed, would not be for the remainder of my journey.

We arrived at nine, the next morning a Sunday, and the city looked like a ghost town. The first thing we had to contend with was to try and secure a seat on a train to Sydney, and everybody was waving their priority tickets about. After standing in line for two hours, it turned out there was plenty of room. The only problem now was to get through the day somehow.

For some time, I had carried on correspondence with a pen pal who lived with his parents in Melbourne and who attended school as a day student. We had alternated writing in English and Dutch in order to keep up our skills in our own language. Since my train did not leave until the evening, I decided to go and meet him and took a cab which had a rather long distance to travel before reaching his address. Arriving on a Sunday morning unannounced was a perfectly stupid thing to do, and it caused quite a commotion in the household, but things soon calmed down and we had a pleasant lunch hour. It was a Jewish family who had an overly protected son, very studious, and they seemed pleased to see someone take time with him. I excused myself early in the afternoon in order to look around some before continuing my journey. Melbourne is a lovely town, probably the nicest in Australia. It was where the Dutch army maintained its headquarters throughout the war—and quite some time afterwards—a comfortable distance from hostilities.

The next segment of the journey included an interlude which I had been looking forward to. Between Melbourne and Albury, which is situated on the border between Victoria and New South Wales, they had recently introduced a new train called the *Spirit of Progress* which traveled at the unheard-of speed of seventy-five miles per hour. Its most remarkable feature was the absolute lack of noise coming from the roadbed and, even at top speed, only the creaking of the coach work was barely audible, due to the normal stresses of movement. Everyone on board obviously enjoyed the experience and reluctantly changed to a regular train for the rest of the way to Sydney, where we arrived the following day (Monday) at 9:00.

Sydney was where it all happened in those days; it was considered the fun city. It was crowded with Americans in uniform, and getting a taxi for someone dressed in civvies was well-nigh impossible. I finally managed to snag one which took me to the consulate, where I needed to beg for some more money, which was readily provided. Like all long-distance trains, the Brisbane Express departed toward the evening, and I had about eight hours to kill. The famous bridge across the harbor looked inviting and I decided to walk across it but never even made it halfway, fooled by the distance. Late in the afternoon, as people were leaving to go home from work, the crowds seemed overwhelming. Unless one lives and works in a large city, this is always a somewhat unsettling experience, leaving the observer to wonder if something unusual is happening.

The last leg of the trip—some 350 miles—was truly a grind, and the train pulled into Casino shortly before noon the next day. The entire journey over a distance of roughly 2,900 miles had taken about 132 hours—not bad, considering wartime conditions. According to a recent Australian travel guide, it now takes eighty-two hours. The only sleeping accommodations were available for two nights, on the segment between Kalgoorly and Port Pirie, and the other four nights were spent sitting up.

As soon as I got off the train, I spotted a couple of Indonesian soldiers walking down the platform toward the exit. Once outside, I asked them if they happened to know where the Dutch camp was—a rather stupid question—and they answered in the affirmative. In fact, they were looking for a cab to go there, and I was invited to join them.

Victory D Camp, as it was called, was the temporary home of the First Infantry Battalion of the Royal Netherlands Indies Army. Ninety percent of its personnel was Indonesian, and ten percent of the commissioned officers were Dutch. Nobody was expecting any new draftees, and I was beginning to feel like a persona non grata when someone motioned for me to follow him. Walking through the camp in civilian clothes behind a soldier must have looked like I was under arrest, although only a few persons seemed to take any notice of the strange sight. We finally entered an office where a captain brusquely asked me in English if he could help me. Stupidly, I asked him if he spoke Dutch, which seemed to irritate him, and when I explained what I was doing there, all he could utter was, "Well, I'll be damned, you poor bastard!" He picked up the phone to seek advice on the matter from higher up and after a short discussion, it was apparently decided that I should be inducted at once before I had a chance to run away. He swore me in on the spot as a member of his own company, the fourth in the battalion.

The first and most important thing one learned in the Dutch armed forces was how to petition his Excellency, the Commander in Chief, for a discharge. Anyone who had access to a typewriter had a distinct advantage in that he could keep up a barrage of petitions, the trick being to resubmit one immediately after one was rejected. I was out in a little over a year after a sympathetic senior officer acted on the umpteenth request, but by then the war was over except for the police action to restore Dutch rule in Indonesia, which was ultimately abandoned anyhow.

There were two other newcomers besides me. One had been a sergeant in an oil battalion (whatever that was) and had given up his stripes in the hope of being allowed to attend officer candidate school. The other man was really an Australian but was for some reason considered to be a Dutch citizen. He didn't speak a word of Dutch while our instructor spoke hardly a word of English, which was fortunate indeed for him, else he might have wound up before a firing squad.

It wasn't long before the battalion was reorganized and we wound up with a new company commander, a fussy young captain by the name of Santman. He ran into problems almost immediately because, within days, our complement was increased by five newcomers who had escaped from German-occupied territory in Europe by walking across the Pyrenees mountains into Spain. These fellows had been through hell and were not inclined to take any nonsense, whatever the source. We were housed in large tents and training got underway. They soon concluded that our Australian friend was a hopeless case, and they sent him home. He was replaced by a highly decorated Eurasian who didn't seem to need any training. He wound up in our tent and spent most of his free time rubbing his face against his shoulder, pretending that he was necking with a girl. He claimed to have been dropped off on several occasions by a submarine in various parts of the Indonesian archipelago for intelligence gathering purposes. He would swim ashore in the middle of the night to be met by a local agent who furnished him with clothes, usually consisting of a sarong and perhaps a ragged shirt, and who would then take him into a village to live among the natives until it was time to rendezvous the submarine which let him off. To do so, he would swim out in blind faith—always on a moonlight night so he could see the sub's silhouette to be picked up without ever a hitch. During his stay ashore he was at considerable risk because many Indonesians were sympathetic toward the Japanese cause. People would be told that he was a survivor of a fishing vessel which had sunk. We took all these stories with a grain of salt, but an authoritative source published after the war told of the Dutch submarine K-19 which operated during the entire conflict under the command of a captain Van Boetzelaar, who did drop off and pick up agents, just as our friend had related. His decoration furthermore tended to support his claims and, finally, he seemed crazy enough to undertake anything.

Our select group might have been destined to become officers, but the infantry was not where my interests lay, and I requested a transfer to what was then the army air force in the hope of becoming a pilot. Meanwhile, I tried to muster as much enthusiasm as was necessary to keep all options open. We were in the Netherlands Indies Army, which meant that they fed us a diet of rice, fish, and spices, as we would have received had we been in Indonesia. This suited me fine, but it was tough on the fellows who had recently arrived from Europe. We wound up eating a lot of steak and eggs in Casino's greasy spoon joints for at least as long as our miserly monthly pay lasted. For entertainment, we found that Lismore, some fifteen miles to the east, had the most to offer, and it was there that I first learned to dance with girls. We did have dance lessons at school, but we had to practice with other boys. They used to get together with St. Kilda's, our sister school, but our evacuation had prevented this. My obvious hesitancy to mix with the opposite sex was of grave concern to my new friends from Holland, and they conspired with several girls to get me on the dance floor. It didn't take a whole lot, and, once I got the taste of it, my shyness evaporated.

Most of our training was meant for raw recruits, which I found hard to endure. The poor captain who instructed us seemed to be little more than a recruit himself, and he became defensive when corrected with regard to some of the light weaponry involved. I never could figure out where he came from or how he achieved the rank of captain. Fortunately, less than two months after arriving in Casino, I was transferred to the air force and was ordered to report to headquarters in Melbourne for a physical examination.

In Melbourne the Dutch not only maintained a well-staffed military headquarters but kept up a fancy club in a hotel. The latter was where much of headquarters personnel was housed, and the club was the hub of the Dutch community's social life. There was an excellent dining room, which served both Dutch and Indonesian food, and the idea of war hardly ever entered the consciousness of those present. The whole affair became so entrenched that, after the war, it remained there for a long time before all those high-ranking officers were sent back to the East Indies, where they belonged.

It seems that I stayed in Melbourne an inordinate length of time without recalling precisely what for, other than undergoing a physical examination administered by an Australian medical officer. Everything was fine except for the fact that I was myopic, particularly in the right eye, to which the doctor came back repeatedly. He finally instructed me to come back in a couple of days, suggesting that I have a good rest the night before. Upon returning, he greeted me with, "Well, let's see if we can squeeze you by today," and back he went to his instruments, peering into my eyes and having me call out letters and numbers from I don't know how many different charts. Finally, he straightened up and said, "Sorry old chap, but I just cannot pass you." That was a blow, to be sure, and I didn't look forward to returning to army boot camp. However, it soon appeared that they had something else in mind for me, and I was kept around long enough to become acquainted with a young lady, who showed me much of Melbourne. She was my much-admired companion at the Dutch club, but, as usual, good things came to an end and I found myself on the train heading for an air base in Canberra, Australia's capital city.

THE ARMY AIR FORCE

Like everything else in Canberra, the air base looked new, clean and prosperous. There were three large hangars: one used by the R.A.A.F., one housing the governor general's plane, a large four-engine aircraft, and one in use by the Netherlands Army Air Force, where it maintained its personnel and equipment pool, or P.E.P. for short.

The remnants of the Netherlands Indies Air Force, which had managed to escape from Java, ultimately wound up in the United States where it regrouped in Jackson, Mississippi, to undergo training in the process of which some thirty or more fliers were killed, either while trying to fly under a bridge spanning the Mississippi River or carrying out other unauthorized maneuvers. The group returned to Australia to become the 18th Bomber Squadron (B-25s), the 19th Transport Squad (C-47s), and the 120th Fighter Squadron (P-40s and P-51s).

One of the oldest airlines in the world is KLM (Royal Dutch Air Lines) which has traditionally maintained a worldwide network of routes. In the Netherlands Indies, a subsidiary named KNILM maintained air service in the Far East. Every time new hostilities broke out, Dutch planes and their crews would be caught abroad like chickens without a roost, and equipment was promptly commandeered by Allied forces. Crews were likewise absorbed, a good many of which came to serve in the Far East. The bomber and fighter squadrons were under Australian command and were carrying out sorties from bases in the northernmost part of the continent. The transport squadron was kind of an odd bird and was based at the airport in Brisbane.

People were constantly rotated in and out of the Personnel and Equipment Pool, which served as both a refreshment and training center. It was there that I reported for duty before its commanding officer, Lt. Colonel Asjes, a kindly gentleman of some renown in aviation circles prior to the war. He greeted me with, "Well, where do you come from young man?" Again, nobody had let anyone know that a nineteen-year-old private second class warrior was coming in, but at least the reception was cordial and the interrogator seemed bemused. In Melbourne, someone did mention that they might be needing gunners, but the colonel said that they had plenty and that none were being trained. "All right, just speak to the adjutant, and in the meantime, we'll think of something" was what he dismissed me with, and sure enough, before the day was over, they did find suitable work for me. The squadron maintained an extensive library where pilots and bombardiers could access all manner of intelligence relative to enemy targets. It had so far been run by a lady volunteer from the embassy in Canberra, and her work had increased to the point where she needed help, but it was preferred that someone take over the task entirely. She wore a uniform but had no rank, and they had been looking for someone with a good command of English to take over her job.

The library received large quantities of secret information every day without any security precautions being taken. Photographs of enemy installations had to be viewed with a stereoscope to obtain a three-dimensional effect, and the most spectacular were those of techniques like skip bombing where bombs would be visible up to the moment of impact, as would the facial expressions of a ship's crew looking for cover. Standard size of the photos was that of a sheet of typing paper. All of the material had to be catalogued and placed in three-ring binders stored on bookshelves at one end of the room. Long tables and swivel chairs occupied the rest of the room, and models of every conceivable model airplane, enemy as well as friendly, were suspended from the ceiling. The room was upstairs in one of two building pods, which supported the arch covering the hangar space. There was an unimpeded view of the airfield on one side, and on the other side one could see across a glassed-in corridor directly into the hangar.

Flight crews were billeted at a hotel in Queenbeyan, a town adjacent to the capital territory and about five miles from the base. The rest of us occupied two buildings at the end of the barracks row where accommodations were Spartan: hence, bunk beds with a mattress and two coarse wool blankets. (Here my memory fades, for we may have had khaki sheets because the air force was considered to be a cut above the infantry.) For heat, we had a pot-bellied coal stove in the middle of the barracks which could be approached only with some effort because it was the precise spot where interminable games of *songo* were played. The latter was an efficient means to part troops from their money, and at the end of the month the games would go on uninterrupted all night long or at least until everybody was broke. The professional game sharks played all month long, and that was just about all they did in their spare time. Fortunately, I had a top bunk at the end of the barracks located furthest from the street. Bathrooms were about a thousand feet away, and running to and fro on cold mornings when dressed in shorts and a pair of wooden bath clogs wasn't very comfortable. One was treated, however, to an abundance of hot water spewed out by rows and rows of showers on arrival.

There was a mix of personnel ranging from Dutch to Indonesian to people of African descent who came all the way from Surinam and who had joined up while training was going on in the United States. One of the latter, a fellow by the name of Lobato, was a superb soccer player, and a few of us soon gathered on a corner of the playing fields to kick a ball around. It wasn't long before we had organized a team and were playing against British naval personnel from as far away as Sydney. We were good, too, and achieved quite a reputation. One day, after a game of soccer, I casually joined the Aussies in kicking a ball around and was promptly invited to play Rules football with them. Although the number one sport in Australia, it appeared to be played by relatively few people, much as appears to be the case with American football; both are more a spectator sport than anything else, probably because they are too difficult to master, especially in America where one has to be exceptionally big and strong.

A couple of nights a week we would dance the hours away in a club in Kingston, a suburb of Canberra. British dance halls are the same the world over; boys and girls sitting on opposite sides in rows of straight-back chairs, sizing each other up, with a small combo consisting of saxophone, clarinet, piano, and drummer beating out the latest tunes. When the music starts, boys walk over to ask the girls to dance (one is rarely refused), and then the dancing couples circle the hall like a roundabout. It is crude, entertaining, and, above all, an effective way of mixing. Occasionally we had amateur night during which the same would-be artists invariably repeated previous renditions of a song. There was one middle-aged tenor who always sang "Amapola," or something like that, which he would practice for hours in the barracks until it became too much for the gamblers, who threatened to wring his neck if he didn't quit.

One night we missed the last bus back to the base, and we had to take another one which merely passed the airfield going elsewhere. It was late, and night flying had long since ceased so we asked to be let off to take a shortcut home. We had just passed midfield, when guard dogs chained to the planes came alive and this brought out the MPs, who took all of us to the guardhouse where we had to wait for the officers of the day. The poor Aussies were locked up, but the Dutch officer didn't see it that way; we simply didn't take matters of discipline that seriously.

It wasn't until after the war that pilots and bombardiers automatically became officers. Many of the ablest flyers were NCOs (non-commissioned officers), while one fighter pilot in the squadron was a private first class. He had been a relatively young airline pilot who had decided that he might as well have some fun during the war and fly fighter planes. He was quite a disciplinary problem and, as soon as he climbed up to the rank of sergeant, would do something outrageous and get busted back to private.

In time I became a familiar fixture in the library and often helped people find material they needed to read. Air crews were notoriously clannish, but I came to know several flyers quite well, at least well enough to solicit an invitation to go flying. "Well," one of them said one day, "ask the colonel; he probably won't mind." It took a while before I mustered up courage to ask for permission, but one morning I walked into the adjutant's office on impulse to ask him. He shook his head and grinned, got up out of his chair, and disappeared into the commander's office.

"OK," I suddenly heard him say, standing behind me, "but don't take this to be a blanket permission, is that clear?"

"Yes, sir," I replied.

"Are you caught up with your work?"

Again, "yes sir!"

"Hmmm, all right," and that was all there was to it.

That same afternoon, I met my favorite pair of pilots—a sergeant-major and a sergeant—and climbed aboard a B-25. The first thing I noticed were the close quarters crews had to cope with, enough to give one afflicted with claustrophobia some second thoughts as to whether such an adventure was really worth it, but I soon became accustomed to them. Most of the time I would stand in a stairwell behind the pilots and look over their shoulders. I was actually standing on top of the disappearing stairs by means of which one entered the forward portion of the aircraft. To the left of where I was standing and underneath the cockpit, there was a crawl space which gave access to the nose cone, where two machine guns were mounted. This was also the place where a bombardier would lie on his stomach and operate the bomb-sight.

One has never really flown until having had the privilege of looking out of a cockpit window; it is positively addictive, and I was soon going two or three times a week, fortunately without more than a cheerful nod from the adjutant, who didn't seem to get any complaints about my work. Over the weeks and months, I observed all sorts of situations, from blind flying to flying on one engine as well as a number of capers the pilots had to account for afterwards. It seemed that most of the complaints would come following skip-bombing practice over a remote area. Without meaning to, the pilot would pull up over a farmhouse he had not seen in time and scare the daylights out of every living thing on the ground. The plane could fly on one engine while the propeller on the other was feathered, but seeing them have trouble restarting an engine was no fun, particularly after having been told that a B-25 would drop like a brick without power.

Occasionally, I had to make room for an inspector, who would board at the last moment, and I had to sit in the back of the plane behind the bomb bay. The B-25 was reportedly the noisiest plane ever built and after flying in the back for even a short while one would be practically deaf until the next day. I learned to grab a pair of earphones before relocating but sometimes forgot to do so.

The most exhilarating experience was when they practiced flying at low level and skimmed over treetops at 230 miles per hour. I should have asked for permission before crawling into the nose cone during the first such flight but didn't dare to distract the pilots. They must have found out anyway because the captain came by not long afterwards and asked me to come with him. As we walked toward a row of planes, I noticed that one had something sticking out of its nose and at closer range saw that it was a tree limb. He just wanted to show me what could happen if someone flew too close to the ground. That particular plane survived, even though the limb almost reached the instrument panel. Planes did come to grief on occasion, most of them while either landing or on takeoff, and the junk pile at a corner of the airfield bore testimony to that fact. Fighter planes were the most accident prone, although I don't recall any fatal crashes while I was there.

One day we heard a terrible racket followed by much running and shouting. Planes were always parked facing the hangar, and an armorer had accidentally discharged the forward firing .50 caliber machine guns of one of them, sending a burst through the hangar doors. A couple of mechanics servicing a B-25 were knocked off a scaffold, and one was killed instantly while the other was badly injured. The Australians were more shaken by the event than we were; they were concerned about damage to the governor-general's plane in the next hangar since they found more bullet holes in the doors on the entry side than there were on the exit side. Some slugs even went through the doors of the next hangar. They were able to save the life of the wounded mechanic at the Australian base hospital. All the Dutch had was a crotchety old army doctor, who walked with a slight limp and always carried a cane. Everyone suspected that he didn't need the cane but used it solely to lend emphasis to his warnings about the dangers of venereal disease. Whenever he diagnosed another case, his standard remark would be: "Dammit, you people put that thing where I wouldn't even dare put the tip of this walking stick."

The fact that we had a constant flow of personnel in and out of the squadron ensured that we were never short of real characters. One was the parachute officer, so called because he was in charge of that section which issued and maintained parachutes. Lieutenant Baker (not his real name) had copiloted a plane which had been ditched due to engine trouble. All aboard were able to get into a dinghy and were rescued by a friendly warship. For reasons not entirely clear—some said it was because his name was Anglicized—the Australians awarded him the Distinguished Flying Cross, and during his well-earned rest and recreation in our squadron, he had begun sporting a mustache befitting any R.A.A.F hero. However, he achieved the greatest fame through his manner in which he answered the telephone which he would do with "'Leftenant' Baker DFC speaking." People would call him up just to hear him say that.

There was one flight crew which was decorated for undertaking an extraordinary mission which was prepared under our very noses in Canberra without us knowing what for. They stripped a B-25 bomber of all its armaments except its tail guns; installed auxiliary fuel tanks in the bomb bay as well as further to the rear of the plane; removed all paint and exterior markings; and then painted huge Dutch flags on the underside of the wings and on both sides of the fuselage. All this was done—as we later learned—to enable the craft to make a nonstop trip from Darwin to Jakarta, zigzag across the island of Java to fly over prison camps at low level, and then return to Darwin. Coming in low over the south coast of Java, they headed for Jakarta, where they were seen by thousands of prisoners who later confirmed that the flyover had the desired effect of boosting morale. It took the Japanese completely by surprise, and they were through before the reaction came, just as anticipated. The plane then flew a few feet above the surface of the Indian Ocean with Japanese Zeros in hot pursuit, but the tail gunner was able to ward them all off. By flying just above sea level—a dangerous maneuver—the angles of attack by enemy planes were severely limited. It was deemed to have been an exceptional performance, and the hero of the venture turned out to be the tail gunner who had volunteered for the job.

The greatest excitement on base occurred when a corporal (nonflying) got into a frenzy when he heard that his American wife had left San Francisco on the S.S. Mariposa for Sydney. He became more and more depressed as the time of her arrival drew nearer, and one day he disappeared from the scene. We never found out how his Australian wife reacted when she found out about the competition. Bigamy must have been a problem for the authorities because it occurred among both officers and enlisted men. An even bigger problem was interracial marriage, solely because of the economic aspects involved. Australian brides were promised great riches upon their spouses' triumphant return to Indonesia, even though most of these people came from dismal native habitats. In this connection, I never could help but wonder what happened to my friend Lobato from Surinam who taught me much about soccer and who was slated to marry a tram conductress from Melbourne.

Winter arrived, the Germans had surrendered in Europe, and the Japanese were treated to the atomic bomb. Just after the last event, they notified us that the squadron was moving to a base 175 miles north of Brisbane. Anything that couldn't fly, or couldn't be put on an airplane, was loaded on railroad flat cars and covered with tarpaulins. I was instructed to pack everything in the library in ammunition boxes, number them, and prepare detailed inventory of the contents. It was to be the last time I saw any of the precious material (it simply vanished) which must have been by design because nobody in command ever exhibited the slightest concern about the matter.

Perhaps it was meant to be an appropriate farewell, but a somewhat distressing incident occurred during a victory celebration at the cenotaph in Canberra, for which our unit contributed a small detail. As luck would have it, we wound up next to a unit from Duntroon Military College—Australia's West Point—and not ten paces from where I was standing, I noticed a former schoolmate who pointedly refused to acknowledge my presence. Now, I must admit that we probably looked pretty ragged in comparison to the country's finest, but the two of us were more than just allies; we had gone to school together—we were Old Boys!

AFTER THE WAR WAS OVER

The fact that the war was over took a long time to sink in. Bundaberg looked depressing after Canberra. The base had recently been vacated by the Australians and was in a deplorable condition. Within a short time, a new base commander appeared on the scene, a colonel who had just come out of a Japanese prison camp. He didn't seem to be impressed with us nor were we with him. The first thing he did was ground all the planes to save them for use in the Indies. Next, he ordered all personnel to report to the parade ground after work every day, dressed in shorts, T-shirts and tennis shoes to participate in calisthenics. He had a platform built on which he stood to lead the exercises personally. One couldn't help but be amused by the way the poor fellows moaned and groaned. They lacked all insignia of rank, and occasionally everything would be stopped while a particular person received a scolding for not putting forth enough effort.

My intelligence section had ceased to exist, and the boxes which I had so carefully packed never showed up. Eventually I came to realize that the material must have gone into some archive for historical purposes and wished I could have saved at least a couple of those magnificent photographs for my personal future library. The train arrived and we were kept busy for a while getting the base in order, but not without some unusual incidents.

While stationed in Canberra, I had learned to drive a motor vehicle. Nobody had ever taught me how, and the order to go to the motor pool and pick up a jeep came unexpectedly one day. Fortunately, I did not have to leave the base to deliver the material that was given me, hence, if an accident had occurred, at least the civil authorities would not have been involved. The sergeant in charge of the motor pool never bothered to ask if I was able to drive; he just pointed to a jeep in the back of the garage and said, "Help yourself." I did as directed and with a throbbing heart cranked the engine, put the gear shift in reverse and ever so slowly backed out of the parking place. Perhaps things were going a bit too slowly because, when I looked up,

I saw the sergeant watching me. Finding first gear didn't go swiftly, and I let the clutch out too fast, causing the engine to stall. When I checked again to see what the sergeant's reaction was, he was nowhere in sight. My first drive along the base boulevard was without incident. Years of watching how it was done, as well as driving all sorts of vehicles in my youthful imagination, had paid off. Within a week, I was the proud possessor of a military driver's license issued by the adjutant and was racing about the base with abandon. And so I came to volunteer to drive a truck from the railroad station to the base after the train arrived in Bundaberg.

They had loaded everything on trucks first, which in turn were driven aboard railroad flat cars. The trucks were called six-by-sixes, had twelve forward speeds, and the one I got to drive was loaded with a spare aircraft engine. I had not learned how to double-clutch and only managed to shift into the third or fourth gear without too much damage and, since I was going fast enough, I decided to leave it at that. The road to the base was paved but was very narrow, and about halfway, I met an old truck loaded with sugar cane, which was sticking out about three feet on both sides. Neither of us made much of an attempt to move over, and I didn't have to hold my breath too long before feeling the inevitable jolt. My truck had a left-hand drive, and the rearview mirror was knocked awry. I had to drive on a bit before being able to see, in the mirror on the right side, that a pile of sugar cane was lying in the middle of the road. Not knowing what to do next, I just kept going and upon reaching the base parked the truck, and went back to my desk. The next few days were traumatic, but I never even heard the incident being mentioned by anyone.

Once things quieted down, they put me to work in the movement office, where all travel orders originated. This provided me with an excuse to fly down to Archer Field in Brisbane occasionally, where the Nineteenth Transport Squadron was located. A couple of times I even managed to make a coveted trip back to Canberra, where they were deliberately slow in winding up affairs. On the way back during one of those trips, we ran into violent weather at night between Sydney and Brisbane. Our pilot, a naval officer, had remained undaunted by the reports of adverse weather conditions, and we experienced some anxious moments. About four of us were isolated in the rear of the B-25—where speech was impossible—and at one point we noticed one of our comrades from Surinam busily counting his rosary beads.

On another occasion I happened to catch a flight during which the new base commander was being checked out for the first time by a major who was an old airline pilot. I anxiously looked on as they went through a long procedural check before cranking the engines and again as the plane was poised for takeoff at the end of the runway. The colonel took off without a hitch and made a butter-smooth landing in Brisbane—quite remarkable after such a lengthy stay in prison.

There wasn't much in Bundaberg by way of entertainment. Although the Great Barrier Reef wasn't too far away, there were no sightseeing facilities in operation in those days. Even if there had been, few of us could have afforded to take advantage of them anyhow; our soldier's pay was a mere pittance. We did try out the beach a couple of times, which was about a twenty-five mile ride each way, but it looked more like a mangrove swamp than the fabulous beaches further south. For the occasion, I was able to check out a truck which provided standing room only for those not lucky enough to sit up front in the cab.

At about this time, several instances of outright rebellion occurred among the Indonesians who were demanding instant repatriation to their homeland, now that the war was over. One morning, we were hastily instructed to fall into formation in front of the hangar where a plane was parked. An armed detail with bayonets mounted and wearing steel helmets was standing guard over half a dozen Indonesians dressed in fatigues without wearing headgear.

"Good God," I thought. "We're fixing to witness an execution!"

Directly, the base commander strode into view accompanied by an officer who had his saber drawn and who was also helmeted. A short speech was made, and the prisoners were ordered into the plane. When they refused, the colonel walked over, grabbed a man by the collar with one hand and by the seat of his pants with the other and crammed him into the hatch under the plane's belly at the rear. Being a big fellow, he had no trouble picking up every one of them and putting them aboard in the same manner. That done, the stairs retracted, engines were cranked, and we bit the dust as the plane wheeled around and headed for the runway. The armed detail marched off, and we were dismissed without being provided any explanation. We did notice that some Australian personnel had gathered nearby and later realized that the purpose of our presence had been to deter any interference on their part. Upon the plane's return several hours later, the crew related that the prisoners had been flown to a detention camp and that their reluctance to enter the plane had been due to the fact that they feared being thrown out during the flight.

We did not have a military police force as such; instead, the provost marshal would select one or more individuals to assist him on a regular basis. My turn came while stationed in Bundaberg, and I was issued a pair of canvas leggings, an armband emblazoned with the letters MP, and a rubber truncheon which must have been fortified with lead. The only instruction I received was that the stick was to be used to slap the side of my breeches while walking, and under no circumstances was it to be used to hit someone over the head. The provost marshal's preferred steed was a Harley Davidson, which he handled as if it were a physical extension of himself. Every day, for a whole week, the two of us diligently searched the Australian bush for deserters, and during the evening we would make the nightclub circuit looking for drunks. Aside from being boring, I found the latter to be embarrassing because as soon as we entered a dance hall, we became the center of attraction. Bravely slapping my leg with a truncheon only earned me a nasty bruise on the side of my knee.

The last night I was on duty I talked the boss into checking out a club frequented exclusively by officers. He showed considerable reluctance and argued that such had never been done before. Jokingly, I suggested that all ranks were entitled to our protection, and that seemed to impress him. The instant we made our appearance, a senior officer came charging through the crowd, drink in hand, obviously not to welcome us but to tell us to get lost. While he engaged the provost in an unfriendly discussion, I slowly strutted around the perimeter of the dance floor and ducked out the first available door to wait for my leader outside. When he finally emerged, he didn't look happy at all.

It was Saturday night, and the troops could be expected to drink too much. For this reason, we were driving one of those British lorries with huge wheels where one really had to do some climbing to get aboard. Outside one of the rowdier places, there were four or five drunks sitting on the edge of the sidewalk as if they were waiting for transportation back to the base. The sergeant went inside to recruit some volunteers who tossed all of them into the back of the truck and I was instructed to take them home and have them locked up in the guardhouse. From town to the air base was about a twenty-minute ride during which the prisoners in the back didn't utter a sound.

"What you got there?" the sentry on duty wanted to know when I didn't drive on after he motioned me to do so.

"A few drunks sarge wants locked up," I answered. He casually walked around to the back of the truck, and I felt him climb up and then jump down again.

"There's nothing back there," he said. It took a moment for that to sink in; I got out, climbed up the back and, sure enough, no prisoners! Not far from where we had them put aboard, I remembered having to wait for one of the few red lights in town; as we sat there, they must have all climbed out. So much for my turn at playing policeman.

With planes grounded, there was less than nothing going on at the base and the troops were becoming restless. Apparently, they were awaiting orders to move to Jakarta, which, by common agreement among the Allies, was occupied by British troops. The Americans had long since bypassed the Netherlands Indies bound for the Philippines and Japan.

The Dutch maintained a warehouse in Brisbane from which they supplied the eighteenth and 120th squadrons, which had been moved to Hollandia on the north coast of New Guinea, as well as the Isle of Biak not far from there. The former had been a US naval base and the latter a Japanese air base. Less than two months after arriving in Bundaberg, I was suddenly transferred to Brisbane to work in the warehouse.

LAST CAMPAIGN

Only a handful of people were working at the warehouse, and we had to make our own housing arrangements for which the army provided an allowance. I wound up living in Sandgate, not quite the beach the name implied, but it was near the water and affordable. It was still winter, and I was the sole guest in an old clapboard boarding house run by a tough old lady with a gold heart who came from way in the real Australian outback. The only disadvantage was the daily one hour commute each way by train.

At work they introduced me to the thrill of operating a forklift truck which soon lost its appeal. My immediate supervisor was a Eurasian sergeant, and we took a dislike to one another. It drove me to submitting petitions for a discharge with increased urgency, and in the meantime, I tried to stay away from the monster. He was a spiteful character and one day ordered me to wash the lieutenant's car, inside and out! That was a grave mistake. The vehicle in question was a new station wagon which had only recently been issued, and as instructed, I washed it inside and out; it took at least a week for it to dry out. Asked by the commander what in the world induced me to do such a stupid thing, I answered that I was carrying out orders, a fact which at least two people were willing to corroborate. The lieutenant appeared to be amused, and I saw the sergeant go into his office shortly after I was dismissed. He stayed inside for quite some time (presumably for counseling), and his attitude improved remarkably after this incident.

The warehouse also employed an old Dutchman with the honorary rank of sergeant who had lived in Australia a long time. Big, fat and loud, he personified a typical wheeler-dealer, and he was responsible for acquiring the daily quantities of fresh meat, dairy products, and vegetables for shipment to the distantly located squadrons in New Guinea. He bought these in a big public market in Brisbane and took them to Archer Field, where they were loaded aboard a C-47 to be transported over the hump in New Guinea to Hollandia and Biak. The "hump" was a mountain range running the length of New Guinea with a height of more than 12,000 feet. He had been looking for someone just like me (he said) to make the daily run from market to the airfield and back to the warehouse. I took the job, which turned out to be a lark.

The market opened long before most people were awake in the morning, and by the time I arrived to visit the half dozen or so suppliers, it was so congested that I often got stuck an hour and a half at a time just pushing my way through traffic. It took all morning and part of the afternoon to fill up the truck, which had to be at the plane's side no later than 3:00 p.m. It would depart before dark, make one refueling stop during the night, and arrive at its destination at daybreak the next morning. Once my truck was unloaded, I would stop by the movement office to pick up cargo for the warehouse and quite often wound up with human cargo which needed a ride downtown. It was when making one of these stops that I spotted my long-lost half-brother talking to a group of officers. Not quite sure whether it was him or not, I shyly walked up to ask if he was Jan Theunissen. Indeed it was, and my hesitation became a source of laughter forever after. He had married during his stay in America, and it so happened that his wife had just arrived in Australia. They were living in an apartment downtown, and that evening, during dinner, I caught up on news about my family. Jan had been the first among the group to return to the Indies and had already been back and forth several times. On the first trip he had gone to the women's prison compound in Jakarta where he somehow found my sister among the thousands of prisoners. Together they had gone out and found her husband in the men's compound and had then gone looking for my father. They had to search all the hospitals before they found him in the biggest one, all skin and bones and unable to get out of bed.

The city was in a state of chaos. Coming from Australia, the initial flight approached its ultimate destination by way of Biak and then the east coast of Borneo, where they were delayed while the group's commander flew on to Singapore in an effort to secure permission from the British to proceed to Jakarta. It was first denied outright but then reluctantly given because the group's safety couldn't be guaranteed. What safety? They were prepared to take care of themselves, and when they landed at the airport, the B-25s menacingly rotated their gun turrets in all directions to show that they meant business. When nobody challenged them, they stopped the engines and got out.

Instead of surrendering their weapons, the Japanese had abandoned them in place, thereby providing the Indonesians with an arsenal which, fortunately, they didn't know how to use until much later. The center of resistance was mainly in the middle of Java, although from the start, countless atrocities were committed in Jakarta against defenseless women and children by roving bands of rebels. Decapitated bodies floating in canals were a familiar sight for quite some time to come.

A provisional government randomly assigned houses to former prisoners, although many proceeded to occupy them without benefit of a license. Their own homes had been plundered by the Japanese, and what was left was later looted by members of the Indian army, which temporarily occupied the city. About the only decent houses left had been occupied by Japanese officers, and my sister and her husband ended up in one of these.

On his most recent trip, Jan had tried to talk my father into coming to Australia with him. The plane carried two flight nurses, and he would have easily qualified as an emergency case, but he refused and preferred to wait for evacuation to Holland instead. A few days after our reunion, Jan called me one evening to tell me that he had arranged to sign me on as a crew member and would I please be ready to depart in forty-eight hours. When I protested that I would never be able to get permission he said that everything had been cleared and not to worry about a thing.

The C-47 was loaded to the limit with all kinds of supplies. Jan was the pilot and, besides the copilot and flight engineer, there were two flight nurses on board. I don't recall what exactly my designation was. The first leg of the journey took us to Cloncurry, 900 miles to the northwest, still in Queensland but in the middle of the desert. The plane barely managed to clear the end of the runway on takeoff, and the flight lasted about seven hours, the top speed of a C-47 being about 130 miles per hour. It became increasingly rough as the day progressed, due to turbulence caused by heat rising from the desert, and we landed in Cloncurry at about 4:00 in the afternoon to spend the night. Air conditioning was an unknown, and the heat was unbearable, making sleep impossible that night in the otherwise comfortable hotel.

The first part of the second leg of the journey was virtually a repeat of the previous day. We departed early in the morning and stopped in Darwin to refuel before heading for Kupang on the island of Timor. Almost four and a half years had passed since I had seen the Indies, and my excitement mounted as Timor loomed on the horizon. As usual, I was looking over the pilots' shoulders while occupying a foldaway seat behind them. A small Dutch army detail was guarding the air strip, and the Japanese were still doing all the work associated with airplanes. We spent the night in barracks just off the airfield and witnessed an unusual flag ceremony just before sundown, when a Japanese detail came down the road on the double, continued around the flagpole three times and then bowed three times before lowering the flag. The officer in charge of the field had thought up the ceremony and had it performed twice every day. The prisoners did everything on the double and managed to look like a ballet troupe while rolling fifty-five-gallon gasoline drums around.

The evening meal was very tasty; it consisted of Indonesian cuisine of rice, spices, and a meat dish, which looked questionable. Someone later swore that he had heard that it was either a dog or a cat they had served us. Anyhow, I have always partaken of meat sparingly and barely tasted it that night; besides, nobody suffered any ill effects.

We rose early the next morning, and our destination was Balikpapan on the east coast of Borneo about 800 miles to the northwest. Ours had been the only plane on the airfield since it landed, and the Japanese had disappeared after the morning flag ceremony. The runway was rather short, and the pilot had to rev the engines before suddenly releasing the brakes in order to achieve maximum takeoff power. We had barely gained momentum when the engines were cut and the brakes applied to bring the plane to a shuddering halt. For once, I was sitting in the back with the flight nurses and, on looking out the window, we noticed that the starboard engine had stopped running and that the plane was slowly turning around to go back to where it had been parked during the night. Directly, Jan came charging out of the cockpit and ordered the flight engineer to check the fuel supply. He told us that he suspected that the gasoline was contaminated and, sure enough, they found water in one of the tanks. Now the question arose whether the prisoners had been responsible or whether it was merely a question of condensation which had formed in the gasoline drums. The Japanese officer in charge was summoned and, after being questioned, was ordered to drain all the gas out of the plane. Afterwards, every drum was tested by the flight engineer before the contents were loaded into the tanks. We were later told that we had been lucky because the starboard engine had started to lose power just before we had reached takeoff speed. There were some anxious moments when the plane finally rolled down the runway after having wasted a good part of the morning, but all went well and there was no more trouble that day.

After lunch, I was invited to take the copilot's seat and got a chance to watch the towering cloud formations which were beginning to show up all around. I had always thought that a plane could fly through any cloud with impunity but was shown that such was not the case. Instead of flying around one, we gained altitude barely grazing its top and experienced violent turbulence. I accepted the offer to try my hand at flying and found that what looked so easy really wasn't. I was told to keep my feet off the rudder pedals and could only bank or go up and down. No matter what I did, the altimeter showed that the plane was continually gaining altitude. We cleared the next thunderhead nicely, but before I had a chance to concentrate on maintaining level flight, I had to give up my seat to the copilot. That was some thrill!

Why we had to go by way of Balikpapan was never clear. The place was devastated and had been fought over at the time of the Japanese invasion and again upon recapture by Allied forces. The eastern part of Borneo is an important oil-producing region, and it was said that oil coming from the nearby island of Tarakan was of such high quality that it could be used without being refined. We spent the night in tents set up amidst stripped coconut palms, abandoned tanks, large caliber guns and other assorted war material half buried in the mud: a dismal scene indeed.

Jakarta was reached the next afternoon, and the plane first circled the city a couple of times. I have never understood why it is so difficult to get one's bearings over what one knows to be familiar territory and had it not been for a guided tour, so to speak, I would not have recognized any part of the terrain. Jan told me that he had promised my sister to announce his next arrival by buzzing her house. Perhaps he needed to get his bearings before recognizing his target and, once he did, he began making a gradual descent until he reached what seemed to be a dangerously low altitude before gently pulling up; he explained that one does not make sudden maneuvers with a fully loaded plane. Shortly, we were on the ground at Kamajoran airport, not far from the downtown area of Jakarta.

Well, there we were, home again, but were we really? No, this was no longer home, I thought, and would just as soon have turned around and left again. It was a sultry afternoon and the place looked awful. No sooner had we parked and gotten out than a young British officer briskly approached and ordered the plane moved to another spot on the tarmac—at once! An argument ensued, but Jan must have realized that protesting was futile; after all, the airdrome was still under British command, so he was forced to comply. Something must have been wrong with the plane's batteries, or perhaps it didn't even have any. Neither did there seem to be any auxiliary starting equipment available, and the flight engineer and copilot took turns cranking a flywheel to bring it up to the required speed to start an engine.

Both engines were hot, however, and refused to cooperate. After a lot of sweating and cursing, one finally sputtered to life, and it was decided to move the plane on just the one engine. That turned out to be a tricky job, but it was finally accomplished.

Before leaving the airfield, we were checked for weapons; only side arms were permitted. A six-by-six truck provided service to the famous Hotel des Indes downtown, and only one route was safe to travel. Everyone was cautioned to dive for cover in case of attack by rebels. Dive for cover? Where? Under the truck's benches, was the reply. The driver drove at breakneck speed, sitting on his horn Indonesian style, and we sighed with relief as the truck pulled into the hotel's entrance. Jan disappeared and came back with a jeep he found somewhere; he wished the crew a happy stay and told them that we were to depart the third day after we arrived.

Jakarta was a treacherous place. It was officially occupied by the British who used Indian troops for the job; the most in evidence were Sikhs with their turbans. Indo terrorists were doing their dirty work without hindrance, and people probably would have been happy to crawl back into the prison compounds. The streets were in awful shape and were congested with all sorts of vehicular traffic, making progress agonizingly slow. Having heard the plane when her house was buzzed earlier, my sister was sitting on the front porch waiting. She didn't recognize me at first and thought that Jan had brought along a guest, which was common in those days. Needless to say, it was an emotional reunion.

My brother-in-law worked for a steamship company which, besides maintaining inter-island transportation, had a network of shipping lines in the southern hemisphere as far away as South America. During the flight from Brisbane, I had carefully nursed several items such as butter (still rationed in Australia) and cured hams, only to find the refrigerator crammed full with an array of items which came from visiting ships. Other than living in a perpetual state of fear, people didn't seem to want for the basics, and all city conveniences such as water, lights, and gas were operational. Servants, however, were unavailable because they were threatened with death if they worked for the Dutch.

We learned surprisingly little about camp experiences, and it would take many years before the whole story unfolded. Everyone's health had obviously been affected and many people never fully recovered from the ordeal. They had suffered from hunger. Oddly enough, the thing that sustained them most were food advertisements in old magazines. Women in particular told stories about how they used to spend hours gazing at tantalizing illustrations of food.

The morning after arrival, Jan and I went to visit Father in the hospital. The instant I saw him, I realized that he was a doomed man; he was skin over bones and could hardly stand beside his bed. As mentioned earlier, he had suffered from a strangulated hernia which had only recently been repaired by a Japanese surgeon. Food had been so scarce, however, that he had become emaciated. Just before the end of the year, he was evacuated aboard the hospital ship *Oranje*, but he died the day before arrival in Amsterdam, probably of heart failure. As the years passed, I never ceased speculating as to what the man's inner feelings must have been during those last three weeks on the way back to Holland. He had worked hard all his life, only to fail repeatedly through no fault of his own. In the end, at sixty-one years of age, his only worldly possessions consisted of a pair of threadbare pajamas my sister had found somewhere at a flea market. He was laid to rest in a grave shared by three others in the Jewish cemetery in Amsterdam. My mother's brother-in-law, whom he had never met, made the funeral arrangements and was the only person present besides the undertaker's staff. Word of his death reached me one evening when I came to visit Jan and his wife in Brisbane for dinner, even though it was no news to me. A couple of nights earlier, I dreamed that I was waiting for his arrival at an airport, and as his plane touched down, it went end-over-end to burst into a ball of fire. It happened to be precisely the night in Australia on the day that the ship was approaching Amsterdam on the other side of the world. It was good that we had the opportunity to see each other. Even though he was no more than a shadow of himself mentally, he was obviously relieved that he had done the right thing by sending his son abroad. My sister later told me that he was proud of the result.

I went to see the house where we used to live and heeded the warning given people not to attempt entering one's property if it looked occupied, which it was. At one place I thought I spotted the old family car but then remembered that Father had bought a new one after I left to go to Australia. However, as I looked up, who would be standing there but the old family chauffeur's son, who had also spotted the car and had come over to look. Some coincidence! He was obviously ill at ease to be seen talking to me, but he did tell me that his father had died during the war. That was all he had to say, and he abruptly walked away before I could ask him anything else.

We seriously discussed our individual futures, which looked uncertain at best. It was just a matter of time before my sister and husband would be eligible for evacuation to Holland. Both the latter's parents survived the war but were in bad shape and had to be evacuated at once. Being a ranking government official, the father had spent the entire war in central prison and had contracted tuberculosis. Now that I was more or less a product of one of its institutions, Australia seemed holding the most promise for me, and I had more or less decided to stay there for good. I had received a kind letter from my old headmaster who invited me to come back to school and complete my final year so I would have no trouble qualifying for admission to a university. I would be close to home and at the time we were all laboring under the delusion that Father could somehow salvage his business. Truth of the matter was that we couldn't even find any of the books and never realized one penny of amounts deposited in banks. He was wiped out completely. C'est la vie!

As planned, we departed on the third day after our arrival. The only time we sensed any danger during our stay was when we were awakened in the middle of the night by someone trying to enter the front of my sister's house. Jan and I were sleeping in the living room, and both reached for our revolvers at the same time. We could see two persons through the glass-in-lead double doors and heard them stick something into the lock, probably a key. They would have been easy targets had they succeeded in entering, but in a minute or so, they left. We breathed a sigh of relief and slept little the rest of the night. It was the sort of thing people had to cope with every day.

The plane was loaded with sick people, many of whom were on stretchers, and it looked like the flight nurses had their work cut out for them. I don't even recall where we spent the night, although we must have done so somewhere at least once because we did not fly at night. My guess would be Darwin in the northwestern part of Australia, which was within flying range and where there were hospital facilities in case they needed them. The journey was boring, and horrible conditions developed as we crossed the Australian desert the second day. It was hot, and severe turbulence caused most passengers to become airsick. It took some resolve to traverse the cabin in order to reach the tiny toilet in the rear, only to stand seemingly up to one's ankles in vomit. The flight nurses were magnificent and without doubt saved several people from dying.

I was glad to get back to the routine of gathering the daily supply of foodstuffs and deliver it to the airfield. Christmas was just around the corner, and I had been invited to spend the holidays at a friend's house. I had lined up a seat on one of our planes to Sydney, only to discover on the day of departure that I had been dumped. No amount of pleading could change things, but someone suggested asking the Americans for a ride; they had a separate airfield called Eagle Farm, and one of our trucks happened to go in that direction. Once there, I found a plane being loaded which was supposed to go to Sydney, but regulations prohibited them from taking anyone along. When asked whom I should see for permission, someone tersely replied, "Try the base commander." They seemed irritated to have to give directions as to where I could find him and, as I hurried down the road, someone yelled, "You'd better hurry, 'cause we're leaving in ten minutes," which brought laughter from everyone.

They were nice at headquarters and showed me where to go. When I knocked on the commander's door, he looked up with surprise and asked, "What can I do for you soldier?" He was a bird colonel, and those were still pretty scarce in the days before high ranks were given out like candy. I told him my predicament, and he wished to know where I had seen a plane loading.

"The water tank?"

He had to think for a moment, but then said, "Oh, OK." and picked up the phone to dial a number.

"You have a plane leaving for Sydney?" I heard him ask. Pause. "I have a boy here from that Dutch outfit who needs a ride. Any room?" Pause. "All right, wait, and put him on." "They are waiting for you. Merry Christmas," and he dismissed me by resuming whatever he was doing.

They weren't laughing when I returned, and as soon as I climbed aboard, the engines started, the door pulled shut, and the plane started rolling toward the runway. It was my first ride with the Americans, and I was impressed by the casual efficiency of the crew, their neat appearance, and the cleanliness of the aircraft. I thanked the captain upon arrival, and we wished each other merry Christmas.

From Sydney I had to take the train inland a piece, reaching my friend's hometown around 8:00 in the evening. She was waiting for me at the station, and at home they had kept supper warm for me. It was the first thing I had eaten all day, and I was so nervous that I couldn't hold my soup spoon steady. Hers was a Catholic household and I noticed that a Bible and other religious literature had been placed on my nightstand, an unmistakable sign that matters were getting serious. Her sister—a nun—was home for the holidays and frequently crossed herself whenever I had something to say. We brought her back to a convent some distance away, where I was introduced to several jolly clerics (I have often wondered why Protestant clergy have such a hard time assuming a similar demeanor). It was a beautiful place, which had a genteel air about it. Gasoline was still scarce, and we were invited to pull the car around to the garage for a fill up, and I wished they offered us a set of new tires to replace the bald ones, which restricted us to a speed of thirty-five miles per hour. At the time, I lacked a reference point for the pretty scenery of tree-lined roads and rolling hills we passed; I was reminded of them many years later when we were vacationing in Ireland.

After Christmas and New Year's, we moved to Sydney, where my friend knew lots of people and we began a round of social calls, which I did not enjoy. The redeeming factor was that I received a comprehensive tour of the city and surrounding area in the process. The many peninsulas jutting into the Bay area with the famous bridge as a backdrop were unceasingly spectacular. There were two popular night spots, *Romanoffs* and the *Princess Club* where one could dine and dance to the sounds of a big band in style. The latest song was *Sentimental Journey*—a timely reminder that wartime romances were hopeless affairs. It turned out to be the last time we saw each other, and a "Dear John" letter caught up with me less than a year later in Canada.

Not long after returning to Brisbane, a severe swelling developed on both sides of my jaw which forced me to go on sick call at the US air base. A doctor diagnosed it as a case of the mumps and had me transported straight to an Australian military hospital by field ambulance. After the usual processing, they locked me up in a communicable disease ward with at least twenty-five other mumps patients. Was there an epidemic? Yes and no; it was not uncommon to have that many cases, and I must have picked up the disease in a swimming pool during the holidays.

Patients were able to watch open-air movies from a distance while seated on benches in an area enclosed with chicken wire at one end of the barracks. The food was good, particularly the asparagus sandwiches the night nurse would make just before lights went out. Every day at least one person would suddenly come down with orchitis, when one side of the scrotum would become swollen almost as big as a football. It was treated with complete bed rest and if the afflicted person didn't obey doctor's orders, the sister, who was a lieutenant, would chew him out. Once on the mend, patients were detailed in pairs to fetch food carts from the kitchen, which, for us in the isolation ward, meant a long journey past countless wards three times a day. It was a sobering experience, especially for those who had never seen combat casualties before. Six months after hostilities had ceased, and there were seemingly countless horribly maimed persons with wounds which had not even begun to heal. One can't help but wonder how many of those unfortunate souls became permanent residents of military hospitals and how many more came to join them each time some police action or war of liberation took place.

Within just a couple of weeks after returning to work, word reached me that they had acted favorably on my most recent petition for a discharge.

So, what now? I had no funds and no job prospects; neither were there any programs similar to the G.I. Bill of Rights in America, and even if there had been, a noncitizen would not have qualified.

"Why don't you go back to Jakarta and get your bearings?" my brother asked, and that is what I ended up doing. Even though I no longer was in the army, he again arranged for me to be included as a member of a plane's crew, and I said farewell to Australia before I had a chance to reflect on such a momentous decision.

A BRIEF INTERLUDE

Once back in Jakarta, my sister invited me to stay at her home where there were already two paying guests, both employees of a steamship company. One was married and was waiting for his wife to come out from Holland to join him, while the other was a bachelor. I discovered that the frivolous atmosphere prevalent during my previous visit was not just to celebrate a reunion, but was a nightly affair and, quite often, a drunken one as well. My sister's husband, Piet, vowed that he would never again be deprived of liquor if he could help it, something he was to pay dearly for later in life. The others merrily joined in.

It was three months after my first homecoming, and things had begun to change. The British had departed and had been replaced by Dutch troops from Holland. The first shipload had at first been quarantined outside the harbor of Jakarta until there were indications that the parties were about to come to blows, which would not have been the first time in history. Once differences were resolved and the Dutch took over completely, some semblance of order was quickly established, at least in the coastal areas. The situation was different in the interior where hostilities intensified and finally culminated in a police action. The Dutch wound up with 100,000 troops in Indonesia, an enormous number considering the total population of Holland at that time. The way logistics were handled, not to mention the way the troops had been trained in such a short period since the war, was truly remarkable.

Not long to sit still very long, I found a temporary job with the Department of Finance. The Japanese had debauched the currency, which had to be completely replaced, and new money was brought into circulation through food distribution centers of which there were about a dozen in Jakarta. People could exchange bank notes for new ones at a rate of a hundred to one (or some other such fantastic rate) and could then purchase basic supplies at the food stores. I was part of a crew of three uniformed men who delivered fresh currency to a number of stores and picked up the previous day's collection of worthless money, which was taken downtown to be counted before being destroyed in an incinerator. The supply we took out in the morning was contained in a locked trunk; what came back filled huge canvas bags which left little room for us to sit in the back of an open pick-up truck. We were easy prey for anyone intent on robbing us and authorities had furnished each of us with a .38 caliber revolver. Fortunately, we never needed to use them even though terrorists were busy committing atrocities against civilians.

Whenever time permitted, I tried to run down information concerning my father's business in the hope of salvaging some of it and possibly starting it up again but never discovered even the first lead. The person who had kept the company's books had died, and her whole family had vanished.

Jakarta in 1946 was a city under siege. Its European inhabitants were confined to an existence within the city's borders. Although a large area, things were a lot worse in reality since actual living space was limited by the degree of one's fears. The harbor—located about ten miles away—was called Tanjung Priok, and the road to it was one of the few safe zones. It was kept that way out of necessity because it constituted a lifeline to the outside world. A camp-like atmosphere persisted in most households, and one was inevitably caught up in it. There was never a quiet evening, and alcohol consumption was horrendous. Newcomers were inclined to look on incredulously for a while, but things inevitably got on one's nerves sooner or later. Within a short time, my brother and his American wife joined the household. Then there were three married couples, plus three men, since the owner of the house had recently shown up and had readily accepted the invitation to join us. He didn't stay long, however, and departed for Holland where his wife and children had gone. The house was fairly large but had obviously not been designed to accommodate eight adults. There were three bedrooms, which took care of the couples. One of the bachelors occupied a room meant to be used as servants' quarters, while I slept in a converted garage. My sister had been fortunate to locate a cook who was willing to risk coming to work, and all of us took our meals at the same table, at least until the couple from Holland began to eat apart, to be followed by Jan and his wife, Virginia, who, as was to be expected, had a difficult time adjusting to life in Indonesia. The drunken parties at night continued unabated, however, and I was getting more and more disgusted with the whole setup.

Since three of the men in the house were associated with the shipping business, there were occasional visitors who were members of a ship's crew which happened to be in port. One in particular, a good friend of Mil and Piet, was chief purser of a passenger liner which plied the route between Rotterdam and Jakarta and who was therefore in port for about a week every other month. The purser on a ship is the equivalent of a hotel manager; he is in charge of housing, feeding and entertaining passengers and controls the largest staff aboard a ship. Our friend's demeanor was that of a person in high authority, and he had considerable charm to boot. Visitors like him introduced a certain civility into our lives, and it was always a relief to learn that one was expected for the evening.

My temporary employment was coming to an end and the prospects of finding a new job were not encouraging. I mentioned my predicament in a letter to the headmaster of my old school in Australia and he suggested that I contact a certain party in Singapore who more than likely would be able to put me to work. The problem was how to get there when I was largely penniless.

I became intrigued by suggestions that I should follow the time-honored tradition of Dutch youth going to sea, if not forever, then at least for a while. Soon, a ship of the Rotterdam Lloyd came into port. It happened to need an assistant to the chief steward, and would I be interested to come in and talk about it? Well, why not, and before I realized what I had done, I had signed up as a crew member and was instructed to come aboard that same day since the ship was leaving the next afternoon. I hurried home to collect my few personal belongings and bade my sister good-bye. It turned out to be a lucky break.

Chapter 4

Home at Sea, 1946–1950

THE WANDERING YEARS

1946

The MS (for "motor ship") *Bantam* was a 12,000-ton freighter, 575 feet long, which ordinarily carried twelve passengers. The ship was built in Rotterdam and was placed in service in 1939; its cruising speed of sixteen knots (19 mph) had been a contributing factor in enabling it to survive the war during which many of the company's older and slower ships had been dispatched to the bottom of the ocean by German U-boats. They put me in a cozy little cabin right around the corner from the radio room on boat deck where, in time, I became used to the incessant squeals, crackles and chirps of the speakers whenever the radio officer wasn't using his headset.

The ship was on its way to Calcutta in India and was transporting about thirty American missionaries who had come aboard in Los Angeles. After having been aboard more than a month, they were old hands at finding fault with everything. My presence only added fuel to the fire, as I discovered the next morning when I was assigned to supervise the serving of breakfast by the dozen or so Indonesian stewards for whom I had to take everyone's order. The elaborate menu confused me, and a mix-up in orders resulted in an uproar in the dining room. The chief steward casually came to my rescue, and I noticed that he had a look on his face of a cat which had just eaten a canary. On subsequent reflection, I became convinced that he had used me as an instrument of revenge, but for the moment I was through and decided to quit my job. As I went to my cabin to collect my belongings, I resolved to hate missionaries for the rest of my life. Before I had time to finish packing, I heard a knock on the door and there stood the chief officer, cigarette dangling from his lips and with a broad smile on his face.

"Good morning," he said, "heard you were leaving us."

"Yes, sir, "I answered, "I don't think I'm cut out for that kind of work."

"Well," he said, "the captain wants to see you—come on, let's go."

Captain Reyneke was the archetypal Dutchman, rather short, receding reddish blond hair, piercing blue eyes, a slight gap between his upper front teeth, and speech betraying his humble origins. He was immaculately dressed in a white tunic, and I was awed by the obvious splendor of the world on the bridge. He expressed his regrets at my misfortune in the dining room and assured me that he understood.

"Tell you what," he went on, "I badly need someone to help me with my administrative duties, and I hear that you speak good English. Do you have any knowledge of bookkeeping?"

"Yes, sir," I replied, and I wasn't lying because I did take a course in it at school in Australia.

"Well then, why don't you stay with us? You'll strictly be working with the chief mate and myself, and I'll bet you'll find life agreeable."

And so began my career as a ship's clerk, sometimes referred to as the purser on bigger ships.

Adjoining the chief mate's state room was a narrow office, which was to be my domain. It had a rectangular window overlooking the main deck between midships and the passenger quarters, and also had a porthole on the side. A telephone was mounted on the wall with which one could talk with the captain, the chief engineer and the officer on duty in the engine room, but I was cautioned only to answer a ring and never, ever, initiate a call for any reason.

As the ship was being prepared for departure that afternoon, my thoughts went back to childhood days when, as a family, we often went to say goodbye to friends and relatives returning to Holland on leave or to retire. The departure of a ship was a festive occasion, with lots of flowers and champagne flowing while the ship's orchestra played cheerful waltzes. Excitement would mount when the first long blast on the ship's horn sounded as a sign for well-wishers to take their leave. The second blast would come about fifteen minutes later and, by the time the third one sounded, members of the crew would already be busy dismantling the gangway. As we stood ashore amidst streamers tossed over the sides by the lucky ones, we would suddenly become aware of a widening gap between ship and quay, and then the ship's orchestra would strike up the national anthem. Once far enough out, water would begin to boil behind the stern and the ship would quickly move away. A depressed mood would prevail on our way home and would sometimes persist for days.

That was then, however, and I wasn't at all depressed when later that afternoon I suddenly realized that the ship was moving. On the contrary, a great sense of relief came over me as the harbor receded into the distance. I could foresee nothing but trouble back there and had lost all confidence that things would ever return to normal.

The first thing I was called on to do was to type a letter from the captain to the owners in Rotterdam which was to be mailed in Singapore, the next port of call. Tradition required that the master of a ship submit a detailed narrative of all activities during the past thirty days to keep management informed. Having to type it kept me equally well informed, although I rarely got to see instructions, which came from management to the captain.

The rule requiring the presence of a doctor on board when a ship carried more than twelve passengers had not yet been reinstated after the war, and accommodations were overloaded. The dining room, however, operated on a first-class basis. The only members of the crew who mixed with the passengers were the captain, the chief officer and the chief engineer.

The officers' mess was amidships and was a main gathering place. One did not enter the crew's quarters located in the stern of the ship. It was a world away in human deportment, and the man completely in charge there was the boatswain who had a private cabin. Dress code among the officers was strict: full uniform at all times, although engineers were allowed to come into the mess in overalls during coffee break in the morning, and again for afternoon tea. Lacking a uniform at that time, I was the only one accepted who dressed in civilian clothes. One was expected to wish all present a good morning or good afternoon upon entering the mess; failure to do so earned one a withering look from the second mate, who was in charge there.

There were four mates, also called deck officers, and two apprentices. The chief mate's watch was from 4:00 to 8:00; the second mate's from 12:00 to 4:00, and the third mate's from 8:00 to 12:00, around the clock. The fourth mate assisted the first. Apprentices were more or less nonbeings who served for a year at sea before returning to the merchant marine academy to finish their final year and then began their career as deck officers. They did whatever one of the mates ordered them to do, which could be anything. The story was told about an apprentice who had to go down into the engine room of a passenger liner one Sunday morning to turn on the organ in the chapel. He had on his best whites and carefully negotiated many catwalks before he found the engineer on duty to ask where the switch was located. After he finally found him, he was told to open one of a row of steel doors which, unbeknownst to him, were inspection ports to a crankshaft of one of the diesel engines. Oil splashed all over him, and then he got chewed out to boot for not attending church service. Although apprentices took their meals in the officers' mess, they sat at a separate table. At one time, they did not even have a place to sit and had to eat standing up.

There were six engineers, also known as engineering officers: four regular ones including the chief and two electricians. These people were not just glorified mechanics but were capable of repairing an engine under any circumstances. They were an abrasive bunch, but once you got to know them, they would do anything for you. They constantly reminded me that I was the most useless crew member on board with which I fully agreed, but I was also the one who, among other things, typed up announcements for the bulletin board and purposely used the salutation: "To all officers and engineers," which never failed to bring howling protests.

And then there was the service staff, which I would have been a part of if I had remained assistant chief steward. The chief was a nice man—a clown, to be sure—and I tried to help him out as much as I could. His ship had been torpedoed from under him three times in a row just outside New York and everyone was convinced that it had made him a rich man. It was said that he would claim that all cash in the safe belonged to him but what they didn't know was that very little cash was ever carried on a freighter.

Besides a cook, the ship had a baker who made fresh bread every day and who made the most delicious pastries for the passengers. During stormy weather we usually got to eat these. One could always tell when some special dish was about to be served because the cook would then be loitering near the entrance to the mess wearing crisp clean clothes and hat. As the stewards brought the delicacies out of the pantry, he would stand expansively in the doorway to wish us "bon appétit."

Aside from the vibrations of the giant diesel engines, one could hardly detect any movement of the ship, which is one of the pleasures of sailing in the tropics. There was one navigational hazard, however, which gave the officer on watch a great deal of concern. Fishing boats called *prauws* would drift at sea without lights. Collisions were virtually unavoidable during the night, and while they did not endanger a large ship, they would be devastating to the *prauws*.

Singapore has always been a crossroads of the Far East. In those days, it had relatively little docking space, and most visiting ships rode at anchor in the roads where they loaded from, and loaded into, barges brought alongside. Chinese stevedores boarded the ship in droves to do the work. We were to call at Singapore many times and only came alongside a wharf, also known as a *godown*, once. The rest of the time we were one of as many as fifty freighters riding at anchor in the roads, swinging in unison first in one direction, then back again, according to the currents. Something went wrong on a later occasion when either a neighboring vessel or our ship swung in opposite ways, and the sterns slowly closed in on each other while everyone stood by helplessly waiting for the inevitable collision. It came not so much as a thud but rather as a crunching when the two superstructures mounted on the vessels' sterns came together. Our ship was subsequently repaired in New York at a cost of $30,000.

Travel between ship and shore was by means of a water-taxi which tied up not far from the famous Raffles Hotel. Singapore was a far cry from the place it is today, but even then, so soon after the war, luxury goods were more plentiful there than in any other place which had been occupied by the Japanese.

The MS *Bantam* was in the Java-Pacific Line of the Rotterdam Lloyd and maintained service between Bombay and Vancouver with many places in between. Port Swettenham (now known as Port Klang), the harbor of Kuala Lumpur, and Penang happened to be on the ship's itinerary that trip.

One of my duties was keeping the ship's payroll and making cash advances in local currencies to members of the crew. Anyone needing money had let me know prior to arrival how much he needed so that our agents could be notified to have the required amount of cash on hand, which I would often have to pick up in town. We had a crew of between fifty or sixty people, far larger than ships have today because container ships and tankers are heavily automated and seldom carry passengers.

A steamship company had four operating divisions, i.e., navigation, engineering, service, and administration. The last one concerned itself only with passenger ships where a full purser's staff was on board. On a freighter, the clerk, or "quasi-purser," was under the navigation division. An average freighter would be manned as follows:

Navigation
Captain (1)
Deck Officers (4)
Apprentices (2)
Boatswain (1)

Carpenter (1)
Seamen (12)
Purser (1)
Total: 22

Engineering
Engineers (4)
Electricians (2)
Oilers (9)
Total: 15

Service
Chief Steward (1)
Stewards (12)
Cook (1)
Baker (1)
Laundry men (2)
Total: 17
Grand Total: 75

Except in large harbors, a ship needs its own tackle to load and unload cargo. Prior to arrival, seamen rigged up all booms and tackle, and removed the tarpaulins off the hatches. During a short trip in the tropics, such didn't need doing because everything had been left in place since the last port-of-call. While in port, the seamen performed maintenance work, usually consisting of chipping away rust and then repainting the surface. It would be the only time they could do anything to the hull because, once at sea, nobody was allowed to even lean over the side.

The hardest working people on board were the mates. At sea they had their watches—four hours on and eight hours off—whereas in port they looked after a particular cargo hold for which they were responsible. They had to know precisely where everything was stowed so that nothing was left on board. In my office there were two six-foot-long drawings of the ship's cargo holds, one providing a view from the top and one from the side. On these, each mate would enter minute descriptions of cargo and its destination. The drawings served several purposes, the most important of which was to enable the chief to determine the ship's center of gravity before it got under way. It had to be within a certain range and could be adjusted by shifting water or diesel fuel from one tank to another. A wrong computation could cause a ship to capsize, the ultimate disaster.

The most relaxing way to travel is bound to be as a passenger aboard a freighter, provided it has acceptable amenities and good food. In spite of being crowded, our missionaries appeared to be comfortable and were interested in everything going on. Among them was a teenage girl of average looks, who, while being safely beyond reach of the crew, was nevertheless a center of attraction. There were several real characters among the crew, the most notable being the second engineer, who was truly an inspiration in his own way. Bald-headed and scrawny, and approaching the mandatory retirement age of fifty-five, he would spend most of his off-duty hours standing on deck wearing pajamas and wooden shower clogs while watching every move our shipboard beauty made. He was our dirty old man. Any young female on board invariably created dissension among crew members, and the chief steward became the principal target of envy because of his association with the passengers. To make matters worse, he would often go out of his way to provoke envy. The longer a female remained on board, the worse the situation became, sometimes approaching violence. The moment she disembarked, all was quickly forgotten until the next load of passengers was about to come on board, and speculation grew hot as to whether another pretty girl would be among them. As always, beauty lay in the eyes of the beholder, and tastes would become less and less discriminating the longer the subject remained on board.

Our missionaries went as far with us as Calcutta in India. On arrival at the mouth of the Hooghly River, we were treated to the grand spectacle of a pilot boarding the ship to guide it the rest of the way to our destination, a distance of about fifteen miles. He was an Englishman, dressed in a splendid uniform and accompanied by an Indian servant who carried all of his paraphernalia. They didn't have to climb the Jacob's ladder since the gangway had been respectfully lowered. The Hooghly is the westernmost part of the Ganges Delta and serves as the navigational channel to Calcutta. It is a treacherous stretch of water for a ship to negotiate and its pilots were reportedly the highest paid in the world.

One comes under the spell of India immediately upon arrival. I loved it and think back with fondness to every occasion we stopped at any of its ports. Upon reaching Calcutta, the ship berthed about two hundred feet from the Howrah Bridge, over which half of humanity seemed to pass on its way to the inner city in the morning and out again in the evening. There were other spectacles, all involving human beings who live in a density unequaled anywhere. Many live in the streets and roll out a mat on the sidewalk to sleep on at night. The heat was oppressive, but it can be surprisingly cold in winter, as I experienced during subsequent visits. The best entertainment, for me at least, took place just over the side of the ship where one could observe life as lived by Indians who tended all manner of river craft. Most of them were housed in rabbit hutches erected on the stern of a vessel where they cooked, raised children, and idled away the hours babbling in the rapid and rolling style of Hindi. Moving about the streets took some resolve, probably because one is intimidated by the huge crowds, but we did get around on occasion by taxicab and found the city had entertainment well worth attending. We saw a movie which played in a theater resembling Radio City Music Hall and, during intermission, were impressed by the faultless beauty of many of the women in the audience. It was in this city where, of all places, I happened to be introduced to a concert by a symphony orchestra, which made me a lifelong lover of classical music.

One day during our stay, we were warned that a tidal bore was likely to travel up the river and were advised as to its estimated arrival in Calcutta. While it caused obvious commotion all around us, none equaled the excitement which took hold of the crew, and we became aware of the acute anxiety the captain labored under when he came under stress. A tidal bore is the remnant of a tidal wave originating at sea as a result of a volcanic disturbance. It floods the area where it comes ashore but where there is a gap, like the mouth of a river, it continues upstream as a bore. There were predictions of dire consequences such as ships colliding with each other or, worse, being dumped on land, and the engineers were ordered to have the engines on standby while deck personnel lowered the bow anchor and then produced another one which was lowered at the stern—the only time the crew had ever seen one used in this manner.

One person I did not mention as part of the crew was the radio officer, who was an employee of Radio Holland, an independent contractor providing licensed operators for all Dutch vessels. Once the ship reached land, he could only listen to his radio and had therefore not been able to ask questions about the impending disaster. As he and I stood within earshot of his receiver and watched the feverish preparations from our vantage point on boat deck, he expressed his doubts about the whole affair. As it all turned out, we never noticed anything unusual until the next day when all sorts of debris came floating down the river, including dead animals. We never felt the ship move an inch, and no explanation was offered as to what actually happened.

Departure from Calcutta after about a week's stay was as interesting as the arrival had been. It required that the ship be extricated from a seemingly immovable mass of all manner of craft jammed together in the harbor before the tugboats were able to turn it around in midstream. It turned out to be no problem at all, and we were soon moving down the Hooghly River somewhat lighter and therefore higher out of the water.

The next port-of-call was Madras, two-thirds down the east coast of India and two days sailing through the Bay of Bengal. It has a man-made harbor, a beautiful promenade along the waterfront, and was far cleaner than Calcutta. We didn't stay long and got a better look at the place on a subsequent occasion. Colombo on the island of Ceylon (now known as Sri Lanka) was next. It was once a Dutch possession and even earlier belonged to the Portuguese. It is chiefly known for its tea and was until not long ago a coaling station for ships traveling the great eastern routes. Passenger ships traveling between Holland and the Indies always made a stop there. It is a pleasant place, much like Singapore, and affords great opportunities for sightseeing.

Three days and nights sailing brought us to Bombay, the second largest city in India and gateway to the subcontinent. The ship berthed in Saint George's Docks, which are situated in the inner city and are reached through a system of locks. Toward the end of the world war, an ammunition ship blew up just a short distance where we were docked, and the effects were still very much in evidence. The catastrophe was a closely guarded secret until war's end, and casualties numbered in the thousands.

To the utter consternation of everyone, a ship either loading or unloading behind us, keeled over and fell toward the dockside so that its masts came to rest on the roof of a warehouse. Had it gone the other way, it would have capsized and could even have gone belly-up with—depending on the depth of the harbor—great loss of life. Not only that, but had such happened in front of us, it could have blocked our exit for no telling how long.

Within a few days after our arrival, all cargo brought from the United States and points in between had been unloaded, and the ship had completed its 115th voyage. There had been much speculation as to where our next voyage would lead us since the vessel was overdue for a turn in dry-dock. It still carried a gun emplacement on the stern, its passenger quarters needed to be returned to their original state, and its two diesel engines were in need of a complete overhaul. The question was whether the work was to be carried out in Holland or in the United States. As it turned out, the captain found his orders in the usual letter from the owners; hence, we loaded for another trip to the west coast of North America where we were scheduled to enter dry-dock in Vancouver, British Columbia.

June 1946

News that we were going back to North America was welcomed by most of the crew. The end of a voyage meant closing the books and sending them to headquarters in Rotterdam, a task which kept me busy.

Bombay turned out to be a great place and its railway station, which was in walking distance from where we were docked, was a fascinating place, where I spent much time watching trains come and go while walking up and down the platforms and wishing I could board one. While a few of them looked quite luxurious, most were packed solid, with some even carrying people on top of the carriages. At dusk, the city's sidewalks became virtually impassible as the homeless began staking out their sleeping spaces. I was particularly careful not to lose my bearings while walking through what seemed to be a labyrinth where one could come upon some strange scenes. One was a large wire enclosure built in the corner of a dark alley where about a dozen women were locked up, some carrying infants. As I approached to take a closer look, they tried touching me through the wire, or simply held out their hands, from which I surmised that they were beggars locked up as a public nuisance. Next day I was talking to our agent's representative about what I had seen and was told that these creatures probably were victims of the illegal practice of *suttee* in accordance with which widows were expected to throw themselves on the funeral pyre of their husbands. Not having done so rendered them outcasts from society. I recalled the indignant discussions of the subject at school about how the British had failed to stamp out the practice completely, and it just never occurred to me that such might have been what I blundered into.

A gruesome pair one was apt to encounter was that of two small children dressed in rags—allegedly brother and sister—one whose eye sockets were empty and who did the talking, while the other had no tongue and could lead the pair around begging. There were other not-quite-so shocking varieties of beggars to be seen who were chased away by storekeepers and police. Whenever they could sneak past the guard at the gangway (which seemed to be no problem), all sorts of entertainers would spontaneously put on a show on deck before being ordered to get off the ship. Many were clever fortune tellers, expert at dumbfounding the uninitiated (me included) with their seemingly uncanny knowledge of a person's background. One sold me an amulet which I was supposed to wear when sleeping, and we all had a big laugh when one of the engineers forgot to take one just like it off before coming to breakfast one morning. And then there were the inescapable snake charmers, some of them good enough to cause a work stoppage as stevedores crowded around to watch a show. They would have several bags with snakes in a basket while they held a mongoose on a string tied around its stomach just in front of its hindquarters. To attract attention, a charmer would casually fish a snake out of a bag and release it on deck. It would promptly head for the scuppers with the mongoose in hot pursuit. Just before he grabbed him, the snake would coil up and a struggle ensued, but the mongoose would soon get a hold of him behind the neck at which point the charmer would jerk him away and shove him back in the bag. If collections turned out to be promising, a cobra would be produced while the mongoose would be put back in a bag. Spectators would respectfully retreat into a wider circle as the charmer began playing his flute, which mesmerized the snake. If enough money found its way into the cup, the snake would be snatched up to be replaced by a king cobra, and this forced most spectators up whatever stairs were nearby. An extremely aggressive snake, the snake still responded to the charmer as well as any other. Only once, on a later visit, did we get to see a cobra tangle with a mongoose. It is not a pretty sight to see—two animals in a death struggle—which, fortunately, did not go all the way.

Time to depart came before we knew it, and our first destination was Cochin on the lower west coast. Also located in Madras province, it was earlier settled by the Portuguese, captured by the Dutch, and then by the British. It was small, a gem of a place to take a walk in the early morning, the way a wealthy tourist might do while on a world cruise. We stayed a couple of nights before heading back to Calcutta to pick up a new load of passengers. Next came Singapore, and then we were back in Jakarta.

"How's the old sea dog?" was the first thing everyone would ask me back in Jakarta. There was no room for the ship at dockside, and we anchored in the harbor roads. Every evening I would take a boat to shore and ride home with my brother-in-law. They were still singing the same songs and getting just as drunk as before, and it was a relief to set foot back on board the ship each morning. The sea breezes, even in the tropics, were like a tonic, particularly when the ship got underway again and the sailors set to work scrubbing and hosing down the decks. One would faintly hear the soothing sound of the ship's bell striking the half and whole hours, and the rumble of the engines would bring sleep in an instant.

Surabaya, only a day's sailing to the east, was the next port of call. It had always been the naval base of the Indies but the ship stopped just long enough to pick up two lighters (called barges), which were placed on the aft deck while an LCT (landing craft tank) was placed across the ship directly in front of the bridge. These were to be used in less developed parts of the Indonesian archipelago to bring copra from shore to ship. We now headed into some truly isolated parts of the world, the kind tourists shell out a fortune to visit. On approach, they looked like idyllic retreats, until one went ashore to find nothing more than a bunch of native huts at the water's edge. Coconut palms were everywhere, and these produced the fruit which was husked, chopped and dried in the sun. This was copra, and thousands of hundred-pound bags were brought out to the ship on the lighters, pulled by the LCT, which itself was loaded and which served as a tugboat at the same time. Copra is the kernel of the coconut which yields the oil from which they make soap and margarine, among other things. Along with the cargo came millions of tiny beetles, which got into everything, including our food. They would not disappear until we got rid of the host material.

Most of the passengers were missionaries going to the United States on leave. A couple of them were priests who spent an inordinate amount of time in the company of a voluptuous young lady of British-Indian heritage who was going to America to study. In keeping his daily vigil, the second engineer soon concluded that the parties had dishonorable intentions. There was also a handsome, middle-aged American couple who had come aboard in Singapore. The lady was a gregarious type who liked to take her exercise walking the length of the ship on main deck, and she had soon befriended every member of the crew. The cook got into serious trouble with her on account of, of all things, a pet duck which had been brought on board by a drunken sailor in Surabaya. The lady just went wild over the creature, and the attraction was obviously mutual. When the menu called for Peking Duck one day, the cook carelessly left trimmings lying on deck just outside the galley which plainly suggested that he was preparing such a dish. It just so happened that the pet duck was busy somewhere else and, in passing, our lady anxiously inquired if those were the remains of her friend. Although it wasn't his nature, the cook irascibly answered in the affirmative, and she became terribly upset. What to do next? Well, lots of suggestions came from the sailors, one of whom came up with the idea of soaking a bandage with Mercurochrome and winding it around the duck's neck. On her walk before dinner, the duck came waddling up to the lady and she went into hysterics, which scared everyone to death. The captain got to hear about it and personally apologized for the "disgusting" behavior of his crew. He even included a full account of the incident in his monthly newsletter to the owners—just in case!

We were so far removed from civilization that only the radio owned by the chief steward still picked up short-wave broadcasts from Europe, just as clear as if it were next door. It was a prewar model made by General Electric. I later combed radio shops whenever possible to find the same model but without success because they had quit making them. I had just come face to face with one of those remarkable Yankee products which seemed to have an eternal life and were of unsurpassed quality. Once upon a time, "made in the USA" really meant something!

Life while roaming through these regions, while intensely boring, retained its normal quality, thanks to the crew's discipline. Dress code was never relaxed for a moment, cleanliness was up to standard, and food was as satisfactory as ever. However, everyone was glad when the final load of copra came on board, and the ship sailed away without the LCT and the lighters, which were left behind for use by another ship. A few days before that, things got a little out of hand—some might even say festive. The ship must have been located offshore of one of the outermost islands because there was a noticeable swell. The water was beautifully clear, and some of us decided that a dip in the ocean would feel good for a change. The gangway was lowered and a lookout posted to watch for sharks. About a dozen of us, both crew and passengers, dove in, and it felt so refreshing that I just swam and swam as if at a beach. When I turned around to survey the scene, the ship looked so enormous, and yet so far away, that I was almost overcome by panic and couldn't get out of the water fast enough. Nearly everyone had stayed close to the gangway, and few had wasted any time getting out. We never engaged in this kind of recreation again.

Word had gotten around that the shore, which looked so serene from a distance, could be a very lively place after dark and the sailors decided to go and investigate. One evening after dinner, while Sparks (the radio officer) and I were sitting at our usual spot on the boat deck, we were approached by members of the crew who wanted to know if we would do them a favor.

"So what might that be?" asked Sparks.

"Would you consider taking us to shore in the LCT and pick us up later?"

We looked at each other as if to say: "Hell, we can't run that thing! Besides, coming after dark? No way!" But they persisted and would show us how easy it was. The craft was gently bobbing up and down, and we could step into it right off the gangway. It had a huge Chrysler diesel engine with no fewer than twelve cylinders, and the ride to shore took about twenty minutes. It all looked so simple, and any doubts we had about the adventure quickly evaporated. We promised to be back by 10:00 to pick them up and made them promise to be there waiting for us. Sparks was going to steer, and I would operate the throttle and gear shift.

"Ready? OK, let's go then," and I shoved the lever forward while simultaneously opening the throttle wide, just as they had shown us. For some reason, a light wood frame had been installed around the top of the well in which I was standing. Part of it protruded over the side and, as the LCT responded, it got hung up behind the jetty, causing a pincer action which could have easily cut me in half if it hadn't slipped free. What was a little mishap? We sped back to the ship without giving it a further thought. Sparks aimed straight for the gangway where they had left a mooring rope dangling to make our return easy but, try as we would, we never managed to grab it. After several approaches, we desperately began watching for someone to come to our rescue, but there seemed to be nobody around. Boy! What now?

"What's going on down there?" we heard over the noise of the engine. Leaning over the railing on bridge deck stood the captain with a megaphone in his hand. It was the first time I had ever seen him wearing a T-shirt.

"We can't seem to tie up, sir," Sparks shouted back.

Suddenly the captain was gone, and we were hoping that help would soon be on the way. It was! In a minute or two, the boatswain came staggering down the gangway, followed by the carpenter, both obviously under the influence. We were told to come alongside starting from the rear, staying as close to the ship as possible without bumping it (which we did, anyhow) and when we reached the gangway, both old men unerringly jumped aboard, as drunk as they were. One pass by the experts and we were tied up, glad our adventure was over. But word awaited us that we were wanted on the bridge immediately.

Being the senior man, Sparks was requested to explain what in the world we were doing on the LCT and who had given us permission to fool with it.

"Well, nobody really, but we presumed . . ."

"Presumed nothing!" the captain cut him off.

"But, sir, when a whole bunch of people request to be taken ashore . . ."

"What the hell do you mean. What bunch of people?" and he looked puzzled. At this point, it occurred to Sparks that perhaps the captain didn't know that half his crew was partying ashore, and when that fact sunk in, he went into a rage.

"Both of you get out of here!" he screamed. We were supposed to leave the next day, and the deck officers had been looking forward to a quiet evening. They were all summoned to the bridge where they were chewed out for the better part of an hour. When it was over, some of them seemed amused but others were furious. When the chief mate got back downstairs, we asked him who was going to pick up the fellows ashore since, after all, we had promised that they would be picked up by 10:00.

"Nobody in his right mind goes into that hole after dark; we'll wait until in the morning." That was it!

It so happened that nobody needed picking up because, shortly after midnight, a sudden commotion occurred on deck. Some of the revelers had returned, and the rest were on the way. They had paid some of the natives to bring them back to the ship in a couple of outrigger canoes—a rather risky venture in the middle of the night—and they were mad as hell at being left stranded. The boatswain was mad too. In fact, everybody was mad, and it looked as if a fight was about to erupt when the chief mate strode into their midst and ordered them all back to quarters. All of this was being observed by anxious passengers, who didn't know what had caused the commotion.

I got up the next morning wondering if it would be safe to go about my business. The chief seemed amused and sat down to tell me about the days of coal-fired ships when it was often necessary to round up stokers in the pubs ashore, haul them aboard, and leave Rotterdam only to drop anchor at the mouth of the Rhine River (also called the Waterway) to let them shake off their stupor before getting back to shoveling coal.

We entered Manila Bay five days later. There was no room for us, and the ship dropped anchor just inside the harbor's breakwater, a good distance from dockside. A day or so later, everyone got to witness an historic event when a large US aircraft carrier entered the harbor no more than a ship's length in front of us. It was returning President Quezon's remains to the Philippines with all due pomp and circumstance. It was the largest vessel anyone had ever seen up close. Except for a barely audible humming of its machinery, the towering mass glided past us while hundreds of men in dress uniform were lined up on deck. On the hangar deck below, a hearse was visible surrounded by what was presumably an honor guard.

For a long time after the war, ports in the Far East—particularly where war had raged—were congested to a point that a ship could count on being delayed, sometimes for weeks, and Manila was no exception. It had suffered severe damage in contrast to either Singapore or Jakarta, which were easy conquests for the Japanese. Reconquests required greater effort in the Philippines which was in the path of the United States advance toward Japan.

War seems to have left one indelible mark on Manila in the form of minibuses which evolved from jeeps left behind by advancing US forces. They replaced a common oriental means of conveyance: a pony-drawn cart capable of transporting five persons, including the driver. The jeeps were originally makeshift affairs, and pictures of Manila today show far more refined models, somewhat larger but more garishly decorated than before. The town was a mass of confusion, and, besides the arrival of the aircraft carrier, the only other memorable event was our first sighting of a jet-propelled craft, which came roaring over the bay at low altitude one morning, preparing to land somewhere close by. Instead of wheels, it seemed to have skids, and people on board had seen similar contraptions during the German occupation of Holland.

The ship's next destination was Cebu on Cebu Island. Why it had first gone north and then backtracked four hundred miles escapes me, but there must have been some valuable cargo awaiting transportation. There was another delay of several days, of which some of us took advantage by making a sightseeing tour by taxi of the interior. They advised us not to do so because guerrilla warfare had erupted on the island, which we chose to ignore. Communists? Why, the couple of communists we had on board were probably far more dangerous than theirs.

Early one evening, our second engineer was needed to render advice in connection with an auxiliary engine they were overhauling, but he had gone ashore. For some reason, I was always the one sent out on missions to find missing persons, among other things. They told me that he could more than likely be found in one of the whorehouses, and I was too shy to let on that I didn't know the difference between a regular house and a whorehouse. After a diligent search lasting about an hour, I found a promising place where some scantily dressed Filipino ladies were sitting on the front steps, and I made discreet inquiries as to whether they might have seen a bald-headed old man. Why, yes, he was in the back—please come in! He was there all right, dressed in his underwear, drinking beer and playing cards with the madam while two half-naked women were looking on. He was most unhappy to see me and even less so with the message I brought him.

The day of departure for Los Angeles finally arrived. As the ship weighed anchor just after dark, something went wrong with the capstan. It was always operated by the carpenter while the boatswain looked over the side to keep an eye on the procedure, to alert the bridge to any problems. The anchor was halfway out of the water when something snapped, and the capstan began letting out chain faster and faster while those standing nearby scrambled for safety. Suddenly, all was silent and the boatswain matter-of-factly called out, "Anchor gone, chain gone, everything gone, captain!" Great consternation reigned on the bridge for, although ships carry two of them, the loss of an anchor is no insignificant event. It required a long telegram to headquarters, and the loss was attributed to equipment failure.

USA and Canada

The trip across the Pacific Ocean took the better part of three weeks, and the weather was perfect all the way. I worked six hours a day, from eight to twelve and from four until 6:00. After lunch and a short nap, I sunbathed on top of a raft carried above the engine room and soon picked up a deep tan for which I was to pay with recurrent skin cancer in later life, but lying in the fresh breeze while the ship gently pitched and rolled in the giant swell of the Pacific was simply irresistible.

The fourth mate and I were chess partners and played at least one game every evening after he came off watch. We were equally good at it (and equally bad losers), and he must have spent many a night fuming after going to bed because of having made some mistake which caused him to lose a round. That was particularly tough because he had to be back on watch at 4:00 in the morning, but we managed to remain on good terms.

It began to get cooler after we passed the Midway Islands, and I worried about not having any warm clothes to wear. The only wool garment I had was an army officer's shirt someone had bought for me (illegally) at an auction of a deceased man's belongings during the war. Everyone offered to lend me warm clothing, but it was summer in the northern hemisphere, and I planned to take care of the problem as soon as we reached Los Angeles. Excitement mounted noticeably as we neared our destination, as it always does after a long passage at sea. A couple of nights before we made landfall the passengers held a farewell party, which we observed with much amusement. The person most intensely interested was the third engineer, a lanky fellow by the name of Rienks, who hailed from a town called Stiens in the Dutch province of Friesland. He was an old-fashioned family man who was kind of a father figure to some of the crew. He was in the habit of proudly handing me a letter to mail home which was addressed, "Rienks, Stiens, Holland." To my knowledge, it never failed to arrive, no matter where it was posted in the world.

Mr. Rienks, as he was called by everyone, had differed with the second engineer over the relationship between the two priests and the young lady from India. Although by no means a religious fellow, he believed everyone was behaving quite properly, until one evening when evidence began mounting to the contrary. Several of us were sitting on boat deck watching the passengers becoming quite drunk when a sailor came running up and urged us to follow him. Halfway down a passage on main deck beside the passenger quarters was a bathroom window in which someone had carelessly left a crack in the blinds. In passing, the crew member had been unable to resist the temptation to peek inside and, knowing about the running disagreement between the two engineers, immediately sounded the alert for others to come and have a look. In just a few minutes, half a dozen of us were crowding around taking in a scene which vindicated the second engineer's prognostications. Since the cook was a devout Catholic, someone decided to cruelly haul him out of bed and told him to look through the crack. The poor man was devastated by what he saw and actually began to cry. Everything did calm down at a fairly decent hour, and when we awoke the next morning, we found that the ship had stopped and was waiting for the local pilot to come aboard.

There is nothing lovelier than the coastlines of the United States on a bright and sunny day and San Pedro was no exception. However, upon arrival, problems beset us at once. Not only did the passengers disembark but, except for the officers, almost the entire crew jumped ship. This, in addition to some of the most recent events (such as the loss of an anchor) caused the captain to have a nervous breakdown, and he was taken away, never to be seen again. That first night we all got rip-roaring drunk, which was a first and only time for me because the hangover was awful and definitely not worth it. Fortunately, we remained in Los Angeles about ten days before moving on to San Francisco.

In those days, San Pedro was recognizably the harbor, while Los Angeles was some distance away, separated by open countryside where oil wells were pumping away. What remained of the crew spent much of its free time ashore in Long Beach, where there were two dance halls on opposite sides of a street, featuring Jimmy Dorsey and Tommy Dorsey and their respective bands.

Customs and immigration officials were strict upon arrival, and they snared one hapless sailor who on the previous visit had fallen in love with an American girl whom he had promised to marry. Except for the officers, the crew was unceremoniously examined for venereal disease by means of a procedure called "presenting arms" and, sure enough, our friend wound up being quarantined. He was the only sailor we salvaged—the others all deserted. He never even got to see his sweetheart and was later sent back to Holland upon our arrival in Vancouver. The company flew out a retired captain from Rotterdam while a new deck crew was hired locally, which turned out to be the biggest bunch of hooligans ever assembled. Most of them spoke hardly any English and we knew no other language in which we could communicate with them.

The ship steamed under the Golden Gate Bridge at 2:00 in the morning, and one of the quartermasters kindly woke me up in time to take in the awesome sight. Up until this time, I had given scarcely a thought to America, but San

Francisco changed things. Everything about the place was appealing—the climate, the scenery, not to mention the food. Late each afternoon, a fog bank rolled into the splendid bay and remained well into the evening. All that would then be visible from our vantage point would be the masts of other ships and here and there a smokestack. The mournful bellowing and clanging of navigation buoys added a special touch to the mood of the surroundings. We spent another ten days unloading and I was left wondering why the crew chose to run away in Los Angeles instead of waiting for San Francisco.

A minor emergency arose while we were anchored awaiting space at a wharf: the ship suddenly started drifting toward one of the pilings of the Oakland Bridge, possibly because we were minus one anchor. But the engine room was at the ready, and we were able to move to a safer location without the use of a pilot. As soon as the ship had tied up at a wharf, the entire bunch hired in Los Angeles was fired because the captain had decided to go on to Vancouver with a skeleton crew. It would be a three-day trip, most of it over open water, and the weather forecasts were favorable.

Canadian customs officers gave us a hostile reception and searched us as if they had been expecting a ship loaded with contraband. My office was literally turned upside down and, once in my cabin, they insisted that I empty all drawers on top of my bunk. Some of the crew members had engaged in petty trading such as buying bicycle tires in Bombay, then selling them in Indonesia, where they bought bags of black pepper, which they thought would bring a nice price in Canada. The whole thing had started when they bought large quantities of cigarettes at the beginning of the last voyage in Los Angeles on their way out to the Far East, and it had tied up a respectable amount of their money. The customs officers wound up confiscating all the pepper and one would have thought that this was a lesson for them. But no, they started all over again next time out.

If customs officers were unpleasant, Canadians in general made up for it by being extra friendly. Not long after we were docked, a convertible with two lovely young ladies drove up alongside and asked us if anyone would be interested in coming to a party. Well, yes, as a matter of fact, we wouldn't mind at all, but how many of us would they like to have come along?

"Oh, about three or four."

"Why, of course!"

They took us to a house in a lovely neighborhood, where there was a party in progress in the basement. It was the home of one of the girls, and we were welcomed by her parents. How nice an evening that turned out to be. We learned something about British Columbia, and they seemed genuinely interested in what we did for a living. There wasn't the slightest suggestion of improprieties, and they brought us back to the ship shortly after midnight where they thanked us for coming and said goodbye. We never saw them again.

There wasn't much cargo left to unload and the ship was empty in a couple of days. It was also the end of the 116th Voyage.

Tugboats moved us across Burrard's Inlet to a shipyard in North Vancouver. Right next door was a ferry slip which enabled us to cross over to the main city in fifteen minutes all day and most of the evening.

First thing on the agenda was deratization of the entire ship. Cargo holds, the engine room, and all living spaces were sealed off to be fumigated, which required that everyone leave before 7:00 on a Sunday morning and not return before 10:00 at night. This was no problem in a place like Vancouver, which has all sorts of attractions, and we were dead tired upon returning, only to be greeted by a noxious smell of chemicals, which persisted for several days. All our friendly little living companions had vanished, and I particularly missed two inquisitive jumping spiders which had watched me shave every morning.

For the better part of two months, the ship was overrun every day by outfitters who restored the passenger quarters to their original splendor, removed the huge gun emplacement from the stern, and overhauled the two diesel engines. Additional crew members decided to jump ship, and requests for manpower replacements from Holland had to be repeated several times. The company would have been better off if it had flown out a whole new crew and sent back the old one. On Dutch ships, all crew members are permanent employees, and union membership is optional. In those days, promotions were based on seniority, and most officers would get a chance of occupying a top slot in their specialty before reaching the mandatory retirement age of fifty-five. Except for the occasional misfit, human relations were quite civilized, and the word career really meant something. Our new captain, however, turned out to be a nasty character and, oddly enough, I was the only one he treated with some civility, probably because he never had the luxury of someone doing the onerous task of keeping records for him.

We had lost all our Indonesian service personnel in Los Angeles, and they were replaced by six Dutch stewards. The thing we had looked forward to most was the reinstatement of the custom of being awakened each morning by someone who served us a cup of coffee with a smile. Not only did the new stewards smile, but they laughed at us outright. They never had the slightest intention of performing any such service, even for the passengers! After that, we considered ourselves fortunate to have our cabins cleaned up.

Just as certain places bear a close resemblance to hell on earth, Vancouver must be the closest thing to paradise, and this feeling was reinforced during a visit almost half a century later. Now a metropolis of almost two million people, it is a place of extraordinary beauty where everything works and where people have managed to remain courteous and friendly. What is now called Gas Town was the main downtown area in 1946. The place across Burrard Inlet where the work on our ship was done is still in business, although the area around it has been built up and the dry dock is plainly visible only from the ferry as it approaches its slip in North Vancouver, which was a mere village at the time. The matter of staffing continued to bedevil the ship's command since quite a few members of the crew recently sent out from Holland simply walked away. They, too, obviously recognized paradise when they saw it, and it was a tempting thing to do, but the penalty for illegal entry was deportation, and we never heard how these people made out.

Upon completion of the repair work, the ship entered dry dock where it was cleaned externally and painted. There are several kinds of dry dock; ours was the floating kind, a U-shaped vessel with two open ends. With tanks full of water, its bottom sank far enough to let a ship enter from either end. Hundreds of square wooden blocks would support it as water was expelled from the tanks causing the dock to rise and lift the vessel so that work could be performed on its hull to remove barnacles, which had impeded its speed. When all work was finished, surveyors made an inspection of the entire ship prior to certifying its seaworthiness.

All the time the ship was in dry dock, the crew was restricted to using washing and toilet facilities ashore. The galley was closed, and they furnished all of us a meal allowance. Once the reconditioning job was completed, the ship became the object of public admiration as it lay in full view across from the ferry slip in North Vancouver. One of the newspapers carried an article on its history and pointed with justifiable pride to the work done by the local shipyard.

Tugboats returned us to the wharf in Vancouver, where we began taking on a load of cargo. The process took at least two weeks. Most of us would like to have extended our stay indefinitely and, as the final weekend arrived, we gleefully learned that several box cars had been shunted to the wrong railroad spur, which would delay us for several days. Passengers had come on board on Saturday morning at the appointed hour and seemed to be equally pleased that they would be given a chance to explore the beautiful city and surroundings. However, we had failed to take the captain's fickleness into account because, shortly after noon, he abruptly decided to leave whatever cargo was contained in the railroad cars behind for the next ship and issued orders to prepare for departure at 4:00 that afternoon.

Most of the crew had made plans for one final fling ashore and frantically tried to get in touch with newfound loves to commiserate with them over the utterly tragic turn of events. Amidst much gloom and doom, we cast off precisely at 4:00 and, as we approached Lions Gate Bridge, we noticed a small group of women—some with small children—forlornly waving good-bye from shore at Stanley Park. It was almost dark, and a cold drizzle was falling which didn't help matters at all.

Vancouver is shielded from the ocean by Vancouver Island, and the ship had to travel about one hundred and fifty miles to reach open sea. Although it was not to reach the Pacific Ocean before dawn, a lot of frantic activity was taking place on deck such as battening down hatches, but inquiries as to the reason therefore were dismissed with a curt explanation that things were proceeding as normal. During the night I did wake up several times and noticed that the ship seemed to be laboring and that a stiff breeze was blowing. So far, I had been a fair-weather sailor, and nothing had prepared me for what awaited us as we came to the end of the Strait of Juan de Fuca, set for the Philippines. For the next ten days we sloshed through water, often up to our knees, while at the same time trying to keep from being flung against the wall due to the violent motion of the ship. Winter in the North Atlantic may have the reputation for terrible weather, but the Pacific is just as bad, if not worse. The swells were frightening, and life aboard was plain miserable. It also became quite cold as we skirted the Aleutian Islands on the great circle route to the Far East.

1947

Where he ordinarily wore an expression as if he was suffering from acute dyspepsia, the captain was now grinning and mercilessly bitched at the deck officers. Nothing they did could please him, and he treated them with the utmost disdain. Passengers were a mere nuisance to him, and he might show up every third night or so for dinner, hoping that they would all still be seasick. The stormy weather did not abate until we passed the northernmost part of Japan.

The ship crossed the international date line early on a Sunday morning, and the crew was ordered back to work because it was actually Monday. Those who would have had to work anyhow lost their double overtime pay. The mates swore that the old man carefully planned it that way, just for the hell of it. And hell he got, which only seemed to make him happier than ever.

There wasn't much cargo for Manila, and our first big load was destined for Makassar on the major Indonesian island of Celebes (now known as Sulawesi). On our approach to the latter port, the captain decided that he had run into a minefield and abruptly ordered the engines reversed, after which the ship backed out seemingly for miles. Many of the crew watched the proceedings with a great deal of trepidation, while others walked around shaking their heads. Upon picking up the local pilot after his second approach, he blessed him out and ordered him to stand aside while he personally brought the ship into the harbor without a hitch. The latter was, of course, his prerogative since he alone was responsible for the safety of the vessel and all on board. Later, he had a violent argument with the harbor master and ordered him off the ship. About three days or so later, just after lunch, a Navy PBY (Catalina flying boat) circled the harbor before landing several hundred yards away. Directly a signal flashed out of the cockpit. Sparks translated it as, "Send boat, we wish to come aboard." It took about twenty minutes to lower the one lifeboat equipped with a motor, and half an hour later three naval officers marched up the gangway, demanding to see the captain. The chief mate escorted them to the bridge, and he later recounted how, after proper introductions, the captain was informed that they had come to relieve him of his duties and would he please come with them. After he had gathered some of his belongings, command was officially turned over to the chief mate, and the party left for the plane which shortly cranked its engines and departed. Nobody had ever witnessed such a spectacle nor even heard of anything like it. A new captain was waiting when the ship arrived in Jakarta, and the crew was later informed that the old one had been diagnosed as suffering from arteriosclerosis and was retired on account of such a disability.

By the time we reached Jakarta, it was early 1947, a year after I came back from Australia. While things had improved materially speaking, the political situation decidedly had not. A military stalemate existed, and Indonesian troops participated in providing security which was of doubtful value. Some of the Dutch who had earlier been evacuated were beginning to return, while others were getting a chance at enjoying a period of leave in Holland on a rotational basis. The company's one remaining passenger ship, first placed in service in 1929, was busy going back and forth, packed to capacity. A new ship, which would have been in service long ago had it not been for the outbreak of war, was in the process of being completed. Its keel was laid in 1939, and it was intended that she be named *Batavia*, after the capital of the Netherlands Indies. The story went that the president of the company, Willem Ruys, ordered her sunk for which the German occupiers had him executed. Named after him instead, she made her maiden voyage late in 1947. No longer needed after the Dutch abandoned the Indies, it later served as a cruise ship for a while before being sold in 1964 to an Italian company, which remodeled her and renamed her *Achille Lauro*. She was on one occasion hijacked by terrorists while cruising in the Mediterranean, and a handicapped American citizen confined to a wheelchair was rolled overboard to his death. Some years later, the ship burned in the Indian Ocean east of Africa and sank.

In Singapore I finally managed to get in touch with an old school mate whom I had missed the last couple of times because he was out in the field dealing with a communist insurrection. He was a police lieutenant and showed me the town like nobody else could have done. For this, he enlisted the aid of a Chinese businessman, reportedly the richest in the Far East, who saw to it that we had a grand adventure.

Calcutta was in a sad state of turmoil because of communal strife. Many dead had never been collected and a nauseating stench permeated the entire city. Late one afternoon, when I was amusing myself while feeding scraps of food to seagulls, I failed to keep an eye on the dozens of vultures roosting on the ship's antenna stretched between the fore and aft masts. Just as I pulled my arm back to throw another morsel, one of them swooped down and snatched it out of my hand leaving a nasty scratch which bled profusely. The agent ashore had to find a doctor (it was after normal business hours) who dressed the wound and gave me a tetanus shot.

It doesn't take long for one to reach the conclusion that, upon returning to what seemed to be such an interesting place, it loses some of its appeal and quickly becomes just another spot on the face of the earth. A huge amount of cargo had to be unloaded, and shipboard life had become tedious due to a number of factors. I had discovered a club for merchant marine officers and decided to spend nights there in the comfort of its guest quarters. The place was practically deserted, it had excellent food, and one did not have to endure the suffocating heat and constant din of a ship in the process of unloading cargo throughout the night. My audacious behavior must have raised more than just eyebrows aboard ship, but I could not have cared less. Besides, I thought, why not savor the life of the privileged while one has the chance.

In Madras, the third mate and I attended an Indian theater performance and quietly occupied seats in the last row of the house. Suddenly, we became alarmed when we were invited by two men standing in the aisle who asked us to come with them. They took us all the way to the front row where two seats had obviously been vacated for us. It was a hospitable act indeed, except for the fact that we had been turned into a captive audience, and good manners forced us to sit through an interminable show of which we understood nothing at all.

Another voyage came to an end when the ship reached Bombay, where the news was waiting that it was to proceed to Indonesia to pick up a load and then head for Holland.

In addition to run-of-the-mill cargo, we picked up a couple of hundred drums containing sulfuric acid. They were placed on deck and covered with tarpaulins. Hazardous materials, I was told, were always carried on deck unless a ship was specially equipped to carry dangerous cargo. In addition to the acid, they also loaded a keg of phosphorous, which was placed on a wooden platform hung immediately behind the stern. In the event something happened to the aquatic solution in which the material was suspended, all they would then have to do was simply cut the cable and jettison the whole affair. These surplus chemicals had been accumulated during the war and were destined for Singapore. They were carefully watched during the days ahead.

About three days after we left Bombay, a leak of acid was discovered. It had eaten the asphalt deck covering while the steel underneath had already begun to corrode. All the drums were immediately uncovered, and it was found that the tops of quite a few had begun to bulge, some to the point of bursting. The ship had to travel another five or six days before it would reach its destination and it was realized that a dire emergency existed. Hoses were rigged up to cool the drums with a steady stream of water which was to carry any leaking acid overboard, but this did not seem to help much since more drums began to leak. They wired for advice as to what to do next and the answer was, "Get rid of any drums which even threaten to leak." A boom and tackle were rigged up, and a party began selecting likely candidates which were swung over the side and dumped. As one of the quartermasters was positioning a sling around one of the drums, it exploded without warning and drenched him with acid. Most of it hit him full in the face which was to cost him his eyesight. They immediately hosed him down thoroughly while taking all his clothes off on the spot and the accident put a stop to the dumping operation. As we approached Singapore, the pressure of the emergency abated somewhat since it was expected that local experts could cope with the situation, but that turned out to be wishful thinking. The evening before arrival, authorities warned the captain not to enter port and to take his dangerous cargo elsewhere, even though it was destined for Singapore. They wouldn't even allow us to drop off the injured sailor and we continued full speed ahead toward Jakarta, three days farther sailing to the east.

Upon arrival, the ship anchored offshore, and a motorboat delivered a detail of Japanese prisoners under the command of one of their own officers who resolutely set to work dumping all drums overboard while the crew stood by with hoses. A couple of the mates stood on the bridge with rifles and shot holes in them as they drifted off and we saw most of them disappear before they got too far away. The shipment of phosphorous was the only dangerous cargo which survived the trip intact. A good deal of damage was done to the asphalt covering the main deck but, overall, the continuous hosing proved to have been effective.

After a brief stop in Jakarta, we again headed into the remote areas of the Indonesian archipelago. This time we had on board several native deck passengers, who were migrating to other areas under a continuing program of relieving pressure on the overpopulated island of Java. One of these people came down with a case of the dreaded smallpox, which gave us a bad scare although every one of the crew had been vaccinated against the disease. However, in one place I discovered a swimming pool and took a refreshing dip, which was to yield some unexpected results. We had gone upriver in the southern part of Sumatra when I began to feel dreadfully ill. A doctor at the Shell Oil Company hospital didn't know (or probably didn't care to know) what was wrong and, by the time we had moved across the river to pick up cargo at an American refinery, I had developed a rash on the inside of my lower arms. Everyone diagnosed it as another case of the smallpox, and an ambulance was sent out by the hospital to pick me up. They rigged up a stretcher with which they were going to hoist me overboard, but I summoned up enough strength to walk down the gangway. The nurse on duty at the hospital opened my pajama top and announced that that was the grandest case of red measles she had ever seen. Other than the penicillin, which was pumped into my rear through enormous needles, I was treated well and was thankful that I had broken out while berthed at the American refinery rather than the Dutch one. It was the second childhood disease I picked up in a swimming pool, and I have tried to avoid the nasty things as much as possible ever since. As an aftermath of the illness, cracks appeared in the corners of my mouth, and the doctor told me that such was actually the beginning of scurvy due to a vitamin deficiency. Vitamin C tablets made them disappear almost overnight.

While we were loading for the homeward journey in Jakarta, I seriously considered giving up the job and making another attempt to settle in Australia, but was convinced by everyone that I should at least go and visit what was after all the motherland. My sister promised to ask her parents-in-law to let me stay with them upon arrival in Holland until I could find a suitable place to live.

Once we had made the customary stops in Singapore and Colombo, the sights were new to me. I began looking forward to going through the Suez Canal. In the Red Sea, I learned the origin of the expression "posh," a colloquialism for luxurious surroundings. It is a contraction of the term "Port side out/Starboard home." A ship traveling from Europe to the Far East would get the afternoon sun on its right side, or starboard, and pity those who occupied cabins on that side. Conversely, a ship traveling back to Europe would get the sun on the left side, or port. To avoid the unbearable heat late during the day, travelers would seek accommodations on the port side going out to the Far East, and on starboard for the journey home to Europe, hence the word "Posh." Both my cabin and office were on the correct side that first trip through the Red Sea.

Just before sunset one evening, a flock of thousands of tiny birds landed on the ship, totally exhausted. They appeared to be migrating and got caught over open water with no place to land. We gently brushed them out of harm's way wherever we walked—they were either too tired or else very tame—and the next morning most were gone when we awakened, leaving countless dead behind.

About one hundred miles south of the Gulf of Suez are a couple of rocks called "The Brothers." Passing ships used these as a convenient reference point to establish the actual speed at which they traveled while engines were turning at a given number of revolutions per minute. Most of the time, a captain is interested to see if his ship can still reach top speed. Having recently been in dry-dock, our speed was precisely sixteen knots per hour—fast for a cargo ship in those days.

The Gulf of Suez is about 175 miles long and ten miles wide, but both sides seemed almost within reach at some points, and ship traffic was heavy at times. Upon arrival at "Port Taufiq" at the southern end of the canal, the ship dropped anchor to wait for the next convoy. There were two a day in each direction, one traveling in the daytime and one during the night. The actual formalities took place with customs and immigration, and soon a small rowboat was hoisted aboard with its one-man Egyptian crew. It is used in the event a ship must be moored to let others pass or for any emergency. Mishaps do occur but are usually corrected. Nevertheless, the rule is that if a ship blocks the canal for over a day, it can be blown up and, indeed, at one point there were large remnants of a hulk lying on the banks which, it was said, were parts of a vessel which met this fate during the war.

Ships travel at a very slow speed through the canal and stay about a quarter mile apart. Fifteen miles north of Suez one passes first through the Little Bitter Lake and then through the Great Bitter Lake. About halfway on the trip is another smaller lake with the town Ismâiliya, where the British presence was quite evident from the beach packed by sunbathers and people swimming in the azure water. Finally, after about twelve hours, the ship reached Port Said, which, had it not been for the Suez Canal, would never have existed. Getting ashore there is facilitated for persons on passenger ships in that a gangway is rigged up for them. Those on other ships either remain on board or take a small boat for about fifty feet. A wide variety of merchandise is offered by Egyptian hawkers, who spread their wares for all to see on so-called "bum boats." Few tradesmen are allowed on board for security reasons, and those who are generally are representatives of the best-known local establishments. At that time, it was Simon Artz. One man by the name of Said was known to the crews of all Dutch ships passing through. He had full run of each ship and spoke Dutch and Malay as well as a smattering of French and German. He would make his rounds to find out if anyone needed anything and could arrange for excursions to the pyramids if time permitted, which was seldom the case.

At the northern entrance to the Suez Canal stands a statue of Ferdinand de Lesseps, its builder. Once a ship passes that point, one instantly feels the refreshing breezes of the Mediterranean Sea, which is one of the most beautiful areas of the world. The weather there is seldom disagreeable—which is not to say that things can't get rough at times—and the journey from Port Said to Gibraltar at the other end takes the better part of a week. Excitement mounted among crew members every day they came nearer to home. Some had not seen their families for nearly two years during which children were born, relatives had died, and all sorts of noteworthy events had occurred in their hometowns.

As we passed the Rock of Gibraltar, we were met by several schools of porpoises which were attracted by the ship's noise as it moved through the water. They frolicked just in front on both sides, and I hung halfway out of an opening above the anchor to watch them scratch their backs against the bow and then become small as a herring when they receded into the depths to race ahead and leap out of the water, squealing with delight. The moment we passed Cape Vincent on the southwest corner of Spain and turned north, we came upon two floating halves of a Liberty ship which had broken apart. Hundreds of these vessels had been built during the war, and a similar fate awaited many a one. To speed up construction, prefabricated sections (including parts of the hull) were welded rather than riveted together making a rigid whole which tended to snap in extremely rough weather. One salvage tug was already on the scene, and another was on the way.

A couple of days after passing the Bay of Biscay, the ship reached the New Waterway—the mouth of the Rhine River—and picked up a pilot for the trip to Rotterdam, some ten miles away.

So this then was the motherland, or fatherland, or whateverland, and everything seemed as strange to me as it would have been to a Turk or a Chinaman. Lots of policemen with their prewar black uniforms, knee boots and peaked caps resembling the ears of a German shepherd dog made me feel uneasy whenever I saw one strutting around with his hands behind his back. My shipmates were totally preoccupied with their own affairs and seemed to have adopted the same indifferent attitude as that of the horde of strangers flooding the ship, demanding this or that. A sickly-looking middle-aged man came slithering into the office wringing his hands and begged for cigarettes. He turned out to be a gofer from the accounting department and I thought that a few packs of Lucky Strike might grease the skids. He almost went berserk with joy and, less than an hour later, didn't even recognize me. Suddenly, the lights went out and a strange stillness set in. Directly, they came back on again, but it remained strangely quiet. I soon discovered that all auxiliary engines driving pumps and generators had been stopped and that electric current was now fed through a huge cable from ashore. Since it was time for lunch, I decided to get ready and eat, but the dining room was dark and empty. Nobody had bothered to tell me that when a ship reached home port, shore personnel took over and the crew was expected to vacate all quarters as quickly as possible. When I got back to my cabin, all bedding and linens had been removed and no water came out of the faucet. But all of this was just the beginning, for I had not even begun to run the bureaucratic gauntlet ashore before I could leave for Hilversum, where I thought I was expected. In one department they told me that the company no longer needed me and to go and pick up my final paycheck. However, that turned out to be the wrong department, and in the next one they treated me like a most valuable employee, telling me to enjoy my well-earned leave and that they had already picked out a ship for me when I returned.

The inner city of Rotterdam was a difficult place to negotiate because it had been obliterated during a German air raid, which supposedly claimed the lives of 40,000 innocent men, women, and children. Streetcars appeared to be aimlessly wandering through a moonscape where small groups of people stood waiting for them. Getting on one was not entirely without hazard, as I soon found out while on my way to the Maas railroad station. A buxom lady smacked me on the side of the head with her purse in which she seemed to be carrying a brick; she cursed me like a seaman would have, even though I had every intention of letting her get on board ahead of me.

The Germans had appropriated all railroad rolling stock for military use, and all that remained after the war was substandard material which had been retrieved from junk yards. Trains were made up of creaky wooden carriages which, as far as temperature was concerned, were tolerable in the summer, but were either blazing hot or freezing cold in the winter.

I arrived at my destination late in the afternoon and took a cab. My sister's parents-in-law were living in a lovely place owned by an aunt who lived downstairs. Yes, they did receive my telegram and that, incidentally, was the first they had heard of me coming. No, they had no room, but I could spend the night in a small room in the attic if I wished.

After that warm reception, I spent the next day in Amsterdam desperately looking for suitable quarters which simply were not to be had. There seemed to be plenty of rat holes, but that was all. A widower uncle on my mother's side lived in a depressing walk-up flat and was of no help. Dejectedly, I returned to Hilversum and was surprised to find my hosts in an entirely different mood. They wished to know if my stay in the attic had been comfortable. Of course it had; the room was about as big as my cabin on board the ship, had a dresser in it, and had a window overlooking the driveway; it was actually quite attractive. Well, then, if I wanted to, I was welcome to stay. Hence, what was an inauspicious beginning promised to turn out all right after all.

Holland

The summer of 1947 was just around the comer, and I had earned almost two months of leave during the past year at sea. Hilversum is a twenty-minute ride southeast of Amsterdam and it is the radio and television center of Holland. Except for the shortages of food and goods, it seemed untouched by the war.

My new hosts appeared to have been initially put off by the idea of taking in a young man who they could only have remembered as being of questionable character, but they appeared lonesome and were probably ready to try anything to improve their lot in life. We were to become good friends, and I wound up having a real home to come to any time I was in Holland afterwards.

Food was rationed, but Mr. Heesterman received generous quantities of dairy products because he was recovering from a bad case of tuberculosis. Even though black marketeering was severely punished, it flourished nonetheless. At odd times a man dressed in overalls would come by, always after dark, in a tiny delivery wagon with which he transported all sorts of food items. He would first reach deep in a secret part of his clothing to produce ration coupons which he would sell and then take back in exchange for particular items. We supposed that it was his way of keeping things straight because, had he been caught, he might have had to face a firing squad. He was particularly leery of me at first but got used to seeing me around.

Mrs. Heesterman was a fabulous cook, and I enjoyed running daily errands for her at the butcher, the milkman, the bakery, and so on. The second floor of the house had a combination living and dining room, which had a picture window overlooking a terrace and a well-tended garden full of flowers. There were two bedrooms, a bathroom, and a kitchen, while a narrow stairway led up to my hideaway in the attic. For heat, there was a potbellied coal stove which I would tend whenever I was there during cold weather. Gas was rationed, and I was at first allowed one bath a week. When I convinced my hosts that I used hot water sparingly, they mercifully allowed me to take two baths per week.

My hosts both happened to be members of interesting and well-to-do families. Mrs. Heesterman had three sisters; the one who owned the house was a widow and lived downstairs and owned a well-known furniture store. Her oldest son was a veterinarian who had migrated to Canada. The youngest son had recently married, and he and his wife were living in an old homestead deep in the forest about an hour's train ride away. Another sister lived in The Hague and was married to a man who owned a trucking business. I spent a couple of weeks in their home once, during which I often hitched rides on one of the trucks and got to see a good bit of the country. At other times I went canoeing with the son's fiancée, an intelligent and sweet young lady who eventually became his wife. We would launch a canoe in a ditch behind the house and gradually proceed until we reached a canal and sometimes even open water. Once we ventured onto a busy waterway and almost got run over by one of those enormous, motorized barges. Yet another sister, also a widow, had been the wife of a steamship company representative and had lived most of her life abroad. Their last post of duty had been Hong Kong, where her daughter still lived. Everyone called her "Aunt Riek," and she lived until the impressive age of ninety-four. She visited us every other day and brought life to the household. A shipboard artist had once given her husband a large oil painting of the flagship of the company he represented. The company's president had begged her to sell it to him so he could hang it in his office, but she told him that he could have it after she died. Her stories about wartime experiences were most informative. Because bed linens were unavailable during the war, she vowed that she would never run short of them again; she had piles of sheets, pillowcases, and blankets stashed away in a closet. She told me that hot weather was uncomfortable at worst, and that cold weather was pure misery. She detested the sister whose house we lived in and accused her of hoarding food while her neighbors were starving toward the end of the war.

My friend the radio officer and I occasionally spent an evening in Amsterdam, which in those days was considered the Paris of the north. It was really a pleasant city where many eating establishments had live orchestras and where one could comfortably pass the time while sitting either inside or on the sidewalk outside. No word exists in the English language comparable to *gezelligheid* in Dutch or *gemütlichkeit* in German, but that was the atmosphere in Amsterdam until the city was discovered by the hippies in the late 1960s; they liked to roost on the monument across from the royal palace on the Dam not far from the railroad station. Members of the marine corps took it upon themselves to clear the area once during the early seventies, but to no avail. The city has steadily deteriorated since that time to become a magnet for all sorts of criminal elements.

A few days before my leave ran out, I was notified to report for work in the office in Rotterdam until I was needed on a ship. This was probably the main reason for later deciding to leave Holland for the natives to enjoy. The atmosphere in the office was stultifying, and I was assigned to help an elderly first mate who had been disqualified for sea duty because of health problems. We sat across from each other in a cubicle checking overtime sheets, which came in from ships all over the world. He was a real nitpicker but saved the company a lot of money because he knew the tricks of the trade. He brought his lunch with him every day and was taking an art course in his spare time, something he wanted me to do as well, but I had enough trouble just existing.

My living quarters were a joke; all I had been able to find was a walk-up flat which consisted of a big room filled with overstuffed, ugly, old furniture in the middle of which I had to sleep on a fold-away cot. The place to take a bath was three flights up in the attic and consisted of an ancient tub standing amid piles of junk. I still shiver to think how anyone could possibly have stood the howling wind coming through the cracks during the winter months. It took fifteen minutes to draw less than a quarter tub of water and I was charged a hefty fee up front each time I took a bath. The woman running the establishment, a boarding house, seemed puzzled about why I took so many baths, but she served a pretty good breakfast and dinner. The other guests looked and acted more like ghosts than human beings. Fortunately, my confinement ashore was short and one day I got a phone call to tell me that my ship had come in. It was the *Kota Baru*, the oldest ship in the fleet. It had been converted to carry troops to Indonesia and was bringing back evacuees on return trips. By the time I got on it, movement of people was beginning to be reversed; hence, we were to take a load of male civilians to the Far East and bring troops back. It was generally agreed that the ship must have survived the war because the enemy didn't want to waste a torpedo on it.

Trip on the Main Line

The *Kota Baru* bore a close resemblance to the old tramp steamer in the movie *Exodus*, and even more so by the time it had taken on its passengers, except that they were all male and were returning to Indonesia in advance of their families. We were a perfect target for interception by the British, who were trying to stem the tide of Jewish migration to Palestine; in fact, trouble promptly started when we were entering the Mediterranean Sea. As the ship slowly made its way past the Rock of Gibraltar, a bright light suddenly sprang from the summit and demanded in Morse code, "What ship, where bound?" The captain, who happened to be a testy fellow, elected to ignore the signal, although courtesy dictated that he respond. The British had stood guard over the entrance to the Mediterranean during the war and had routinely greeted passing vessels in this manner. Directly the signal was repeated, this time seemingly with some urgency. The captain ordered the radio officers to signal in reply: "Kota Baru, Batavia . . . what ship, where bound?" That impertinence must have created consternation at the command post on the Rock, and no more signals were received. Neither were shots fired across the bow, but it wasn't long before a spotter plane appeared on the scene and began circling the ship at low altitude. Its occupants were cheered by our passengers who by then knew what was happening. The Dutch flag, which had hastily been hoisted on the stern, displayed an anchor as an emblem which indicated that the ship was under the command of a naval reserve officer. This obviously satisfied the spotters because the plane abruptly disappeared behind the Rock. During the trip across the Mediterranean, we were repeatedly buzzed by military aircraft while a couple of times a naval vessel would close in. This went on until it was clear that we weren't heading for Palestine. However, more problems awaited us at Port Said.

The Egyptians had mounted a sympathy campaign in support of the Indonesians' effort to rid their country of Dutch oppressors. All passengers were therefore requested to cooperate and stay out of sight, which meant that they had to remain in inadequately ventilated quarters below deck. Once underway in the canal, the rule was relaxed somewhat until we reached Port Taufiq at the other end.

Nowadays we are accustomed to abrupt changes in temperature as we jet around the world, but the difference between the Mediterranean and Red Seas was rather debilitating. Fortunately, conditions weren't too bad for those poor civilians going out to the Far East. The vessel wasn't overcrowded, and the food was excellent. The ship ordinarily carried twenty passengers, but the cabins were occupied by additional crew. Hence, it carried a full complement of radio officers who maintained a twenty-four-hour watch. There was a sizable staff of medical personnel, the purser's office carried a staff of four and, finally, there were assorted crew members not normally found on a freighter.

Our office was located directly below the bridge in what used to be the lounge. The purser, we soon learned, was in line for the coveted job on the soon-to-be-completed, new flagship of the company. He was an arrogant fellow, and an atmosphere of fear existed in the office. Things he took exception to were unbelievable. For example, we were in the Indian Ocean, and during a lunch period I happened to catch a whiff of smoke drifting into the office out of the hallway. Fire aboard a ship is the last thing anyone would want, and I immediately went upstairs to report the matter. The captain's sitting room was at the head of the stairs, and I could see through the open door that he was entertaining some people. I knocked on the door and he looked up to ask, "Yes?"

"I beg your pardon, sir, but I smell smoke downstairs."

"Thank you," whereupon several people dashed down the stairs to investigate. There was indeed a smell of smoke, and they searched all afternoon for the possible source without finding one. In the meantime, I was severely berated by my boss for having had the audacity of knocking on the captain's door; he felt that I should have reported the matter to the officer on watch on the bridge. I asked him if he really meant what he said, at which he turned crimson with apparent anger, which made me realize that I was dealing with a nut. Before I let my temper get the best of me, I excused myself and went to my cabin. For the next three days we communicated with each other through third parties and for the rest of the voyage we treated each other with disdain. In the end he seemed to have realized that he had exceeded the bounds of reason, perhaps for the first time during his aristocratic existence, and the incident was never mentioned in my evaluation report at the end of the voyage.

We made the trip from Suez to Jakarta without stopping anywhere, which was really quite a tribute to the way the ship was provisioned because it was slow, and the overall journey lasted thirty days. For the homeward journey we were ordered to proceed to Singapore and take on a load of British troops bound for Southampton.

Many changes had occurred in Jakarta, and most of those people staying at my sister's home had gone elsewhere to new assignments. My brother was about to be discharged by the air force, and he and his wife were making arrangements to return to the United States. He had been unsuccessful in getting a flying job with the airlines, probably because he lacked experience on four-engined aircraft. Both he and his wife urged me to consider joining them as soon as they were settled, and I tentatively agreed. Fighting had resumed and this time the Dutch occupied the capital of the republic which had requested the United Nations to intervene.

Once the British troops were on board in Singapore, main deck looked like it was crawling alive with ants. Quite a few of us had to vacate our cabins to make room for a number of women auxiliaries, or WACS for short. They put me in what looked like an animal cage hung over the rear corner of the engine room; it contained a bunk and a washstand, but it had a door and a window and it was one deck above where the crowds were.

The WACS turned on their female charms to the maximum extent and, when catcalls became too persistent, would coyly retreat to their cabins alongside a hallway at each end of which an armed guard was posted twenty-four hours a day. In the afternoon they liked to climb on top of a pile of life rafts above the bridge to take a sun bath and would either be wearing swimsuits or shorts with a halter top. Once they laid down, they were invisible, but soon a couple of halter tops would be tied to the side of a raft to flap in the breeze for all to see. A pitiful moan would promptly rise from the masses on main deck, and hundreds would maintain a vigil for hours in the hope of catching at least a glimpse of something or other. When one of the girls wearing a swimsuit would get up for a leisurely stretch, the multitude below would howl like a bunch of wolves.

We in the purser's office had little or nothing to do and our only contact was with the relatively few military officers who occupied cabins, four or six to a room, on the opposite side of the ship where the WACS were quartered. We had difficulty keeping our distance since, as on any other ship, only the most senior officers were allowed to socialize with the passengers and, having no access to alcoholic beverages, they tried to befriend us in order to get at least a bottle of beer. Our bosses kept a sharp lookout for any violation of the rules.

The troops were unhappy with the food, particularly breakfast; they wanted bacon and eggs, which is not normally part of a continental menu. They had plenty of eggs but no bacon. Well, what about sausages? Sure, they had plenty of delicious knackwurst about the size of wieners, so they tried feeding them that. No, that wouldn't do at all! By sausages they meant tiny English link sausages. Upon reaching Port Said, we consulted our Egyptian friend Said about the matter. Sure, he could get us all we needed—anything else? Within an hour, a whole pallet loaded with boxes containing a seemingly fly-blown substance was hoisted aboard under Said's supervision. The chief cook wanted to know if you boiled them. Well now, Said only knew where to find them but, being a Moslem, couldn't eat pork and didn't know how to cook them.

"Pork . . .? That's pork?" the cook wanted to know.

About that time the chief steward walked up and brusquely ordered them to "put the stuff away . . . we'll figure out how to fix it!" Buying sausages in Egypt seemed a risky venture, but the troops lapped them up and nobody died.

For undisclosed reasons we were to stop in Algiers, of all places to come to with a load of British troops, who cheered enthusiastically when they heard the news. Poor fellows! We never found out if it was their commanding officer or the French authorities who wisely forbade all shore leave. A few of us managed to pay the town a quick visit but we were cautioned to avoid a section of town called the Casbah, which was considered unsafe. It seems that this was actually an old fortress in the Arabian section, and after just one brief foray into one of the alleys we heeded the advice. The then European section had nice wide streets and a shady park overlooking the harbor. We stayed just half a day, probably to take on fresh water, and were out again by nightfall.

A couple of nights before the ship reached England, the troops put on a most entertaining variety show to which all of us were invited. Musical instruments materialized out of nowhere, and the participants were obviously quite talented. It was the first time I had an opportunity to go downstairs in what was normally a cargo hold. Those were tough quarters to spend three weeks in, or one day for that matter, but they had somehow rigged up a stage in the eating area, and everyone enjoyed the show.

The day we docked in Southampton, they settled a maritime strike which had delayed the departure of the *Queen Mary*, berthed just around the corner from where we were moored. They announced that she was to leave at 4:00 that afternoon, and I took my camera to record the event. I was amazed at its size as I walked past it from one end to the other a couple of times. No visitors were allowed on board, so I went across the inlet to get a better look as it prepared to leave. The most unforgettable thing was the sound of its foghorn that announced departure was at hand. Its deep rasping sound felt like it was vibrating my teeth. Three tugboats pulled the giant into the roads where, almost imperceptibly, it began moving ahead under its own power and then quickly disappeared into the foggy night. I had seen the vessel once before off the coast in Western Australia during the war and have had the privilege of boarding it in Long Beach, California, where it serves as part hotel and part museum.

As I returned to my ship, I had the shock of my life because it was no longer there! It wasn't supposed to depart until the next morning, so what on earth happened? As I frantically walked up and down the quay, I spotted a uniformed guard and walked over to ask when the *Kota Baru* had left.

"You wouldn't be talking about that troop ship, would you now?"

"Yes, I sure would; when did it leave?"

"It hasn't left; you're looking at it."

The tidal changes in Southampton were something I had never experienced before. It was low tide and only a small portion of its superstructure was visible. Having looked at the *Queen Mary* for several hours, I thought I was looking at az tugboat when I saw my own ship.

By the time we arrived in Rotterdam a day or so later, we had been away seventy-two days, and winter was approaching. My hosts in Hilversum were glad to see me, and I happily took up residence in that tiny room in the attic once more. This time their daughter was staying with them, and she was expecting a child. Her husband, a coast guard officer, had just left for Indonesia. The household had become very lively, and I was to stay just a little less than a month.

Trip to South Africa

My next assignment was on the company's one remaining passenger ship, which was scheduled to leave just before Christmas in 1947 to transport emigrants to South Africa. I had to work ashore again for a couple of weeks, this time in the payroll department, and commuted between Hilversum and Rotterdam by train every day, about an hour and a half each way. In those days, most of the larger railroad stations had full-service restaurants, and I enjoyed some of the fanciest meals in my life in either the one in Utrecht or Hilversum when I was running late some evenings.

The chief purser turned out to be the family friend who got me interested in going to sea almost two years earlier. The motor ship *Sibajak* had been in service since 1928 and, while old, still retained many of the features of a luxury liner. All the company's other passenger ships met their demise during the war. Besides the chief, the office staff included an associate as well as an assistant purser, two clerks (of which I was one), and a baggage master. The latter was my roommate, and we were assigned a comfortable cabin on main deck a few doors down from the office. We came aboard about a week before departure in order to attend to countless minor details.

There were some real characters among the service staff, not the least of which was the chief steward who had the official title of restaurateur. He was a jolly, fat fellow and had been a longtime shipmate of the purser during the war years. He had suffered a nervous breakdown when the last ship they were on was torpedoed off the North African coast and then bombed by the Luftwaffe while they were trying to beach it with hundreds of troops aboard. The man never made much sense to me, and I learned to deal with his immediate assistant instead, a very dignified maître d' type who insisted on addressing everybody as "mister" or "sir" and who never cracked a smile.

The departure day of a passenger ship is one of extreme confusion. We took aboard 1200 men, women, and children with destinations all over South Africa. Many were refugees who had a hard time proving their identities after having wandered about Europe trying to keep out of the way of fighting armies. The assistant purser and I had our desks at the counter, and I had to get used to answering questions in four languages. The lack of practice in French and German had taken its toll, and it took a while before it started coming back to me.

Just before departure, a porter came running up to the counter and handed me a ring wrapped in a piece of paper addressed to one of the passengers. A lady had left it lying on a shelf in a bathroom ashore and her husband had retrieved it for her. Would I please see to it that she got it because it was rather valuable? I assured him that it would be taken care of and placed it in the back of a desk drawer.

The ship pulled away from the quay just before noon, and the orchestra played the national anthem amidst a sea of tears before breaking into a cheerful tune. Ah, yes, the orchestra! It was to be the source of much amusement to us in the office. It consisted of a group of about ten talented musicians, each of whom played several instruments. They could perform collectively, in small groups, or even singly, and could give excellent renditions of both classical and popular music. The leader was a long-haired individual who managed to raise the ire of the purser each morning when he came in to get his instructions as to where and what they should play that day. The chief got particularly upset when he had seen a musician accept drinks from passengers during the previous night. As he put it, he didn't want any souse-heads slopping all over the bandstand. The meeting always ended with a question about when the leader was going to get his hair cut?

We were kept busy the first couple of days, so busy in fact that I failed to notice what repeated conversations about a passenger in the sick bay were all about. Late on the second afternoon out, the purser asked me to take a telegram to the radio room for transmission to the head office in Rotterdam. Needing a break and a breath of fresh air, I took the long way around and while on the way casually glanced at the message to be sent. Having to negotiate several stairways, I was able to read only parts of it at a time. It was in reply to a query as to what happened to a valuable ring which had been lost by one of the passengers. I was about to reach the radio room when I suddenly remembered the porter who had handed me something wrapped in a piece of paper which, he said, was a ring. Panic set in—what to do now? Without going into the radio room, I slowly retraced my steps, all the while thinking about possible options. The package was still in the back of the drawer, and I stuck it in my pocket to take to my cabin to examine it. It did contain a ring, but I had no way of knowing how valuable it was. Perhaps I should throw it overboard, deliver the telegram and act like I didn't know a thing. Yes, of course, that was the thing to do. (In retrospect I have often liked to think that that would have been an average twenty-one-year-old's decision.) I stuck the ring in my pocket and upon reaching a quiet spot on deck, was about to throw it overboard when something told me not to. Instead, I returned to the office, walked up to the desk of my boss and, while pulling the ring from my pocket, asked: "Sir, would this be what the telegram is all about?"

"Aha, the ring! Dammit, let me call the hospital so they can tell that crazy woman we found it."

I told him how a porter had handed it to me just before the ship was about to leave and had forgotten all about it. He told me not to worry about it and that he would take care of the matter—case closed!

The weather quickly warmed up as we headed south. The ship called at Las Palmas in the Canary Islands to replenish its fresh water supply. Older passenger liners lacked desalination facilities, and everybody had to bathe in salt water which required special soap to work up a lather with. One rinsed with fresh water which came out of a small spigot by pressing a button.

Compared to a journey to the Far East, South Africa seemed just around the corner. Less than two weeks after leaving Rotterdam, we woke up one morning and there was famous Table Mountain. We entered the harbor of Cape Town as most people were still having breakfast. A busy day lay ahead and the last of the passengers were not to leave until shortly before dark. The first to come on board after the gangway had been installed was a military police detail commanded by a captain who wished to see one of the passengers. In a case like that, one looks up his or her cabin number and then finds a steward or stewardess serving that section of the ship; they are more than likely to know the person on sight. They had no trouble finding the man; he was a German, slightly balding and very nice. When we entered the office, I introduced him to the police captain, who thanked me and then asked the man if he was mister so and so, alias somebody else, to which he politely answered in the affirmative.

"Sergeant, arrest this man," he ordered one of the detail; then turning to the purser he said, "Sorry, sir, but we have information that this man has engaged in war crimes and will not be admitted to South Africa. We will hold him in custody until the ship is ready to sail and then bring him back on board."

We were all dumbfounded, and even the purser remained speechless as the prisoner was handcuffed and marched down the hall toward the exit. At departure time, the same detail came marching back in and saw to it that the man was locked up in the brig. It was our business what we did with him, but he was not to be released until two hours after the ship had cleared the harbor entrance. The captain must have decided to keep him under lock and key because we never saw him again until the police in Rotterdam came to fetch him.

The ship had a public address system, which was controlled from a small storage room behind the first-class dining hall. It was my job to make all announcements in English while one of the assistant chief stewards made them in French. Passengers were processed by immigration and customs according to their destinations. They could then walk straight off the gangway into trains which were waiting to take them to such exotic sounding places as Bloemfontein, Pretoria, Durban, and so on. Everything seemed to be extremely well organized, and I even had a tinge of envy at not being able to join them. However, my thoughts often go back to all these people who seemed delighted to have found a new home—and a glorious one by any standard. The last few years, thousands have left to go to other parts of the world and, lately, the word is that many are seeking refuge in their original homelands.

Of all Europeans, the British were the dominant element in Cape Town, which is spectacularly located at the foot of Table Mountain. The city was nothing extraordinary in those days and reminded me a great deal of Brisbane in Australia. I took a ride to the top of Table Mountain in a cable car, probably one of the oldest such attractions in the world. The view from the top was unbelievably beautiful. While Afrikaans is an offshoot of the Dutch language, it was hard for us to understand because it is kind of like Pidgin English is to English. There were bilingual signs everywhere cautioning the public not to spit. In Afrikaans it said, "Nie moe nie spu nie," whereas in English the caution was "no spitting allowed." Had it been in Pidgin English, it would likely have read, "No spittie spittie."

For the return trip we had the crew of the MS *Brastagi* (sister ship of my old MS *Bantam*) on board. While traveling down the east coast of Africa, they had somehow managed to set it on a rock when the third mate was on watch, as was the case with the Exxon *Valdez* almost a half century later in Alaska. Someone had taken a picture of a man standing under the ship's bow, which he seemed to be supporting with one arm. Salvage crews from Holland were attempting to refloat the vessel, but we later learned that they were unsuccessful and had resorted to stripping everything of value before abandoning the hulk. The captain, one of two brothers holding such rank, was put to work ashore, more than likely checking overtime sheets as I had done.

We were back in Rotterdam on January 5, seventeen days after we left. I had hoped that all the rivers and canals were frozen so that I could at least experience those scenes commonly depicted in Dutch paintings. It was cold all right but never long enough for everything to freeze up and remain frozen for skating.

1948

Being a fresh air addict, I slept with the window open and for the first time noticed the stillness of the night in the temperate zone. The city of Utrecht is about eight miles south of Hilversum. As I lay in bed, I could hear the last train approach at night, when it crossed the yard switches and came on the main track headed in our direction. I could follow it all the way until it disappeared behind the buildings in town. The colder the night, the clearer the sound.

For some time, I had been suspicious of the nature of a nagging cough I had developed. The doctor said that it was nothing to worry about and advised me to quit smoking or at least cut down from the two and a half packs a day. After the third consultation, he finally consented to send me to a pulmonary specialist who, like most physicians, practiced at home. The waiting room was packed with people still suffering from diseases they had contracted during the war. After a two hour wait, my name was finally called, and as I entered the room I found a female doctor sitting behind a fluoroscope; she had on a lead apron and was wearing a pair of dark goggles. I was told to strip to the waist and sit down on a little stool where I had to wrap my arms around the machine while facing her. No sooner had she switched it on, she flipped it off again, and snatching off her goggles, demanded, "What are you doing here?"

Well, what was I doing there besides getting my lungs examined, I thought, but before I could answer, she barked, "There is nothing wrong with your lungs! Listen, I have a room full of very sick people who need help and . . ." Anyhow, she practically kicked me out of the room, and I hastily got dressed in the ante room and took off. However, there must have been something wrong, unless I picked it up during the long wait among those sick people because, many years later, a physician called my attention to a small, calcified area indicating past disease which my body had overcome without treatment.

Holland in wintertime was cozy, although there were many inconveniences left over from the war. My main contribution to the household this time was to keep the potbellied stove going, shaking the grating early in the morning, and filling the thing up with coal out of a tall fluted container. My leave was short, and they put me to work ashore again, which meant much commuting as before. New rolling stock was beginning to appear on the rails, and travel seemed to take a lot less time.

My brother, Jan, wrote that he and his wife were in Singapore waiting for the arrival of a ship belonging to our competitor which was to bring them back to America. I later learned that, desperately short of money, they were staying in a Chinese hotel which was something that, in those days at least, no westerners would consider doing.

The MS *Sibajak*'s next assignment was to transport mostly women and children to Indonesia and bring back a normal load of passengers. We again reported for duty about a week ahead of departure in order to attend to countless details. The nature of the job was quite different due to the kind of passengers we were to have. They were the regular clientele, who required handling with kid gloves.

The captain and the purser spent an inordinate amount of time in conferences to decide who was to sit where in the dining room. As always, the captain's table was the most sought after, followed by those occupied by the chief mate, chief engineer, and the purser. In the second class, the top dogs were the second mate and second engineer, as well as the adjunct and assistant pursers. There was a third class safely tucked away toward the rear of the ship and kept mostly out of sight. An officers' mess was located way upstairs behind the bridge, but I ate with a select group of service staff (sort of like downstairs in the popular TV series *Upstairs, Downstairs*) in a tiny mess which had a large window overlooking the promenade deck.

Seating arrangements for passengers was very serious business, which could generate unbelievable controversy if not properly attended to. The passenger list showed the husband's occupation, and seniority was determined on a case-by-case basis. Those with titles such as counts, barons, lords, and sirs headed the top of the list, and we, in the office, had to be very careful. Our friend Said in Egypt was to create a minor uproar on this very trip concerning a matter of title. He had the habit of flippantly addressing a passenger by a phony title and sometimes invented some really fancy ones, like calling a lady *Baronin von Habenichts*, which translated into "baroness-of-have-nothing." It just so happened that he was talking to a real baroness who appeared to be experiencing hard times and who took offense. She came traipsing into the office to complain to the purser about the insult, and he called Said in to tell him that he would have to behave or get off the ship.

We left on Friday, February 13, 1948, at 13.00 hours with 1300 passengers on board. The first thing that went wrong was the fire drill, when heavy steel doors slammed shut automatically, causing children to be separated from their mothers. The racket caused by the various alarms only exacerbated the hysteria, but things were soon under control again.

Before the war, a ship would leave Rotterdam with relatively few passengers, many of whom would be tourists on a cruise to Marseilles, where the full load would come on board after having traveled by overnight train via Paris. This would give people a little more time in Holland before having to return to the Indies, and they could also avoid the usually nasty weather while crossing the Bay of Biscay, which happened to be quiet on this trip. Old hands told the story about this ship's maiden voyage during the 1920s, when a grand piano came loose from its moorings during a storm when crossing the Bay and crashed through the glass enclosure of the grand staircase to come tumbling into the dining room several decks below. They had to send out an army of ship outfitters to Marseilles to repair the damage before the ship could continue its voyage.

Among the purser's duties is that of acting as the ship's postmaster. As we neared Port Said, an auxiliary post office was opened in the second-class saloon, which I manned for two hours before lunch and again between 2:00 and 4:00 p.m. each day. Selling stamps is one thing, but taking all kinds of foreign currency in payment is another, not to speak of the whimsical behavior of some of the passengers. One Englishman sat a few feet away from the counter playing cards all morning and, when I started to close up shop to go to lunch, decided that he needed some stamps. When I told him that I would be back in the afternoon, he became loud and abusive and threatened to go and see the captain. If he did, I never got to hear about it. Upon reaching Port Said, we had about ten sacks of mail to go, most of it going to Europe. All postal documents had to be prepared in French which, at that time, was still considered to be the international language. On arrival there were just as many sacks waiting for distribution. One batch never reached the addressees, which seemed to be concentrated in one area of the ship. It later turned up in the personal closet of a steward who got tired of handing out mail and, presumably, intended to dispose of it by throwing it overboard when the opportunity presented itself. He was later fired.

Our passage through the Suez Canal was again during the day and, except for the occasional *fellah* standing on the canal bank exposing himself for the benefit of the ladies, was uneventful. Just after departing Port Taufiq, there was an explosion in the engine room, sending a thick column of smoke into the air after which the ship coasted to a stop. The slender smokestack looked like a palm tree with twisted pieces of metal protruding out of the top. After drifting dead in the water for several hours, we felt the ship beginning to vibrate again, and we resumed our voyage without further problems, at least insofar as the engines were concerned. They never told us what happened.

The purser had begun giving me assignments in public relations such as assisting the beautiful and talented social directress with organizing games such as horse racing, a popular diversion on ships worldwide. He told me that he had big plans for me and that he wanted to be able to recommend me for the job of assistant administrator. Ill at ease in any social situation, I was afraid I must have disappointed him, although he never gave up trying. My reluctance obviously must have had a tendency of relegating me to the lower rungs of the ladder and to develop a distorted view of society in general. And yet, did it really? I seem to have had plenty of company in life, most of whom have done pretty well.

Predictably, the shipboard routine, however luxurious, was making the passengers restless, often even combative. Stories began circulating about trysts involving some ladies and crew members even though they were rigidly segregated. One of the third mates whom I later came to know well as a second mate on another ship related how he had come off watch one evening during the current trip to find a naked lady occupying his bunk. He politely requested her to get dressed and leave. Unbelievable? Hardly! His taking advantage of the situation would have been unbelievable because such were the standards among officers in those days.

There was a round-the-clock fire watch maintained by three men who had come from the ranks of ordinary seamen. It was their duty to see to it that passenger areas remained clear of intruders, although they could do little or nothing about the presence of passengers in areas which were off limits for them. The places where they were discovered in compromising situations were ingenious and caused unlimited gossip. A longstanding practice among young people starting careers in the tropics was for the man to go out ahead of his fiancée and, once he was settled, for the two to marry by proxy. One of the ladies on board who had recently become betrothed in this fashion apparently misbehaved to such an extent during the voyage that her husband sent her back to Holland with us. Nobody had any idea who informed on her, and everybody felt sorry for her because she seemed to be such a nice person.

The first stop in Indonesia was the port of Sabang, situated on a small island a short distance north of Sumatra. The ship had reached the harbor entrance before daybreak and was drifting outside while waiting for the pilot to arrive. Most people were still slumbering when there was a thunderous jolt, which seemed to lift one out of bed about half a foot. Mines left over from the war continued to be a hazard for quite some time and practically everyone, including the people on the bridge, thought that the ship had hit one. The hall outside our cabin immediately filled with people most of whom were still in night attire, but no alarm was sounded. Shortly, word came down from upstairs that they were as puzzled as everybody else as to what had happened. It was later decided that we had experienced a sea quake, which the dictionary defines as a submarine earthquake. Several passengers disembarked and a short while later we moved on to Belawan-Deli, the port of Medan on the east coast of Sumatra, where my sister now lived. Her husband had only recently been appointed general agent for this place, but there was no time for visiting.

During the last days of the journey, complaints were received from the chief steward that enormous quantities of silverware were disappearing, which made serving meals extremely difficult. While not sterling, hotel silver was valuable because of its weight and quality, and all of it was engraved with the company's logo. Besides eating utensils such as knives, forks and spoons, bigger items such as sugar bowls and cream pitchers, even large platters, were disappearing. It was concluded that people were taking these things to set up housekeeping, and company representatives in Jakarta were asked to engage the help of customs inspectors to retrieve the material. Upon arrival, all baggage was carefully checked and virtually everything was recovered and brought back on board in pillow slips. Next time out, we found that dime-store utensils had prudently been substituted for the silverware until more propitious times, if ever. Few indeed are the places nowadays where one finds a table set with old-fashioned hotel silver.

The night prior to arrival in Jakarta they held the last of a series of festivities which had begun with the captain's dinner a couple of nights before. We had been working in the office until the early morning hours getting everything ready. When we were finally dismissed, I went looking for a snack in the pantry. Afterwards, I took a shortcut to my cabin by going through the cooks' quarters, located way below the waterline, where astonishing activities were taking place. Naked women were cavorting up and down the hall with equally naked males in hot pursuit. I quickly turned around and went back the long way, through the dining room and by way of the elevator, hoping that nobody had noticed me—as if it mattered!

Turn-around time in Jakarta was about a week, and, without my sister there, I came to see the place through the eyes of a casual visitor. There wasn't much to see, and I was looking forward to departure. This time we were to have a normal load of men, women, and children. One woman managed to board in an advanced stage of pregnancy and gave birth to a child within a matter of days after we left. Each passenger was entitled to a free baggage allowance of one cubic meter and her husband came into the office that same day to request a partial refund of the excess baggage charged to the family upon embarkation. He came to regret his greed when he was presented with a bill for delivery and hospitalization, a service ordinarily provided free of charge as a courtesy.

Halfway across the Indian Ocean one morning, a young engineer was discovered dead in his cabin. The cause of death was determined to have been a heat stroke. Engineers work in engine room temperatures of 130 degrees Fahrenheit, or more, and must take salt tablets as well as drink copious amounts of water to guard against dehydration, which this man apparently had failed to do. At noon the next day, the ship stopped, and a number of crew gathered just in front of the bridge where a platform had been erected at a forty-five-degree angle on which a flag-draped coffin rested. The captain delivered a short tribute, a hymn was sung, and the coffin slid over the side.

It had holes in it and was weighted so that it quickly disappeared into the depths. The engines came to life and the funeral was over, but then unexpected complaints came in from a group of passengers. It so happened that the coffin had been stored somewhere below the second-class dining room, and a detail of sailors had come to fetch it during the lunch hour the previous day. They had dragged it through the dining room in a most irreverent manner, which had greatly upset the eating passengers. Fortunately, this wasn't a problem for the purser, who referred the matter to the chief officer.

In the Red Sea, we passed the new flagship of the company going in the opposite direction. Such an occasion requires some preparation in terms of flag displays as well as the plotting of a safe approach since ships pass each other a couple of hundred feet apart, in this instance at an aggregate speed of nearly sixty miles an hour. At the height of this tricky maneuver, each vessel emits three long blasts of the horn to wish the other "bon voyage" while the passengers whoop and holler, which was totally inaudible because of the wind. Several years later, the unimaginable happened when the flagships of the company and its competitor collided during such an event, also in the Red Sea. They came too close at an even higher rate of speed, and hydraulic suction brought the sterns together, disabling both vessels.

While in the Red Sea, a crew member lost his balance as he was cleaning a navigation light on the side of the bridge and fell overboard. He was fortunate that the officer on watch saw what happened and instantly ordered the helmsman to turn hard to starboard, on which side the man had fallen, thus swinging the stern and one of the propellers out of the way. I was selling stamps in the second-class saloon again and heard people running on the promenade deck shouting "man overboard" and soon noticed that the ship had slowed down and was making a wide turn. The sea was smooth as glass, and we could see in the distance smoke which came from a canister attached to the life buoy which had been tossed overboard. The man was able to reach it and cling to it until a lifeboat picked him up. He had injured his back but was soon on the mend. It was amazing how pitifully small a human head looks at a distance. Had the sea been the least bit rough, and had he not been able to reach the life buoy, they would never have found the victim.

Working in the purser's office on a passenger ship was like working in a travel agency, and we were making travel arrangements for passengers with destinations in Europe and beyond. I made a sad mistake not signing on as a crew member when the ship continued for a two-week cruise to the Scandinavian countries. It was springtime, however, and people had urged me by all means to see the tulips in bloom, and I wasn't disappointed.

The Mediterranean was as delightful as ever. On top of the ship's stern was a spacious area called the poop deck, which was reserved for members of the crew. It was where we gathered in our spare time to sunbathe, talk, and occasionally dance at night, when some of the musicians volunteered to play for us after having performed for the passengers. It so happened that the moon was full, and it was difficult not to think of this period without some degree of nostalgia when the time came to abandon my career at sea.

Despite the hard times which still prevailed, I was beginning to like Holland. I inquired about continuing education and found that this was feasible, provided I first prove my proficiency in the Dutch language. The latter was undergoing a change in spelling, a process initiated just before the war and which has confused me ever since. The prospect of finding work ashore looked none too promising, not even with the steamship company which offered a position at a ridiculously low salary. About a month later, I signed on for another trip on the same ship, really for lack of having something better to do.

During the three-week voyage to the Far East, my boss, a heavy smoker, continually suffered from a sore throat, leading us to suspect that he was afflicted with something more serious than a mere infection. We had to carry on more and more without him. One exalted member of our staff with the rank of associate purser was quite useless in the day-to-day operations of the office and he strictly did public relations work. He had flunked out of the naval academy and had obviously been hired on account of his social connections.

We continued to have trouble with the stewards over tip income. The Dutch government rigidly controlled the supply of foreign currencies, and the company had introduced a cashless economy aboard ship by selling books of coupons with which passengers could pay for incidentals such as drinks, haircuts, and tips, just to name a few. The stewards didn't like having to disclose their earnings for, after all, it was a well-known fact that one of them was able to keep two children in an exclusive boarding school in Switzerland. Endless meetings continued to be held concerning the problem for which there did not seem to be a solution.

The ship made an unscheduled stop in Aden at the southern tip of the Arabian Peninsula. It was then a British protectorate and was until recently the People's Democratic Republic of Yemen. Arriving early in the afternoon, we were to depart after midnight. It was seldom that a ship of the company called at this port, and I was the only one who got a chance to go ashore in order to make monetary arrangements with our agents. The place looked like the end of the world, and vehicular traffic in the streets consisted mainly of carts pulled by camels. The ship had anchored in the bay, probably because they didn't want to turn loose so many passengers in an area which was more or less hostile territory. Later in the afternoon, the ship was overrun by peddlers trying to sell a large variety of duty-free merchandise, but they refused to accept anything except British pounds or US dollars in payment. Our agent had only been able to supply Indian rupees, and the purser called in all the money changers wandering around and spent a couple of hours swapping currencies. He somehow managed to make a tidy profit, which he later distributed among us in the office for working until 3:00 the next morning and then coming on duty at the regular time as if nothing had happened.

Upon arrival in Jakarta, which ship should I see in the harbor but the MS *Bantam* on which I had started my career at sea two years earlier. Many of the old crew were still on board and when I heard that they were about to finish loading for the east coast of the United States, I instantly made up my mind to ask for a transfer. I asked the captain if he needed a purser. Well, of course he did, but he wasn't at all sure if they would authorize him to have one. My old friends ashore proved instrumental in making the necessary arrangements, and official approval from Holland came the next day.

With the office on the *Sibajak* shorthanded, I felt guilty about leaving, and the worst moment came when I had to say good-bye to the chief purser. He lay ill in bed, almost unable to speak. He became emotional, and I realized that he was a dying man when he confided that he had been diagnosed as having cancer of the throat.

The Nedlloyd Line

Being back on a freighter was like getting a breath of fresh air. The work was entirely different, and I was given complete freedom to bring order—which had been totally neglected—into the administration. However, I never quite gained the captain's confidence until we reached New York and cleared customs and immigration in record time because all documents were presented in such as a fashion as to merit effusive compliments from the boarding officials. After that, I could practically do no wrong.

New York in 1948—what a place! We docked in Brooklyn just a few hundred yards from the Brooklyn Bridge. Upon awakening, the first thing I saw out of my cabin window each morning was the lower end of Manhattan. A subway station was scarcely a block away and, even though we were in the middle of everything, the city's noise was muted aboard ship.

On the morning of arrival, I was the first one ashore to head downtown for our office on Broadway to pick up $30,000 for payroll advances. For the occasion I carried a briefcase scarcely big enough to contain the amount, which consisted mainly of bills of small denomination. On the way back to the subway station, I stopped to purchase a radio and when the time came to pay, placed the briefcase on the counter to get some money out of it. The salesman almost had a seizure when he saw all that cash and, had it not been for the fact that I was wearing a uniform, likely would have notified the police. He told me that people just didn't walk around New York with that kind of money and insisted that I take a cab back to the ship. The subway was just a nickel and the cab cost almost two dollars for the ride back to Brooklyn, but I was glad that I took his advice. Later that day it became apparent why people became so excited over a little money. We had carried gold bullion from Jakarta to New York, and I remembered the day it was delivered to the ship in an open truck guarded by a single native policeman riding along in the cab. Bullion is carried in a special chamber located at the base of a ship's front mast so that, in case it sinks, divers can readily locate it if the wreck is at all accessible. But what a contrast when they came to get it in New York. An armored car arrived on the scene which had been preceded by a police van carrying a dozen officers who stood guard on both the ship and the dock area where the pallets came to rest after having been hoisted overboard in a steel net. Once the entire shipment was put in the armored car, it left under escort of the police van.

The first morning after we had docked, someone excitedly called everyone's attention to a spectacle which was to become a daily matter of intense speculation. We must have been located close to where a sewer emptied into the harbor because, when we looked over the side, we saw that we were floating in the midst of a zillion condoms which, by midmorning, would all have disappeared.

Overlooking Times Square on Broadway was the Astor Hotel where, on the second floor, there was a Dutch Club patterned after a USO facility. It must have been a holdover from the war, and it was staffed by very nice young ladies every night. On quieter evenings, the place to visit was a seamen's club in Brooklyn, run by the Catholic Church. It was roomy and tastefully furnished and had a nice reading room. Several priests on duty were always ready to strike up a conversation, and some spoke several languages.

Our boatswain had discovered the Bowery, where he managed to lose his wallet, which contained his passport, in addition to his money. After eliciting a vague description of where he had been hanging out—drunk, of course—the chief mate sent me in search of the place. It turned out to be a bar which looked like dozens anywhere in Rotterdam. His belongings had been left on top of the counter, and the bartender had put them away figuring that the owner would come back looking for them. It didn't teach the boatswain anything because he somehow missed the ship when we departed after a two-week stay. He was put on a train with a tag around his neck (he spoke little or no English) and we found him patiently sitting on a bollard on the dock when we arrived in Galveston where we started loading oil drilling equipment destined for the Persian Gulf. We later moved up the ship canal to Houston where we tied up in the boonies not far from a huge mound of sulfur. Day and night a hot breeze dusted us with the stuff, almost choking us to death as we groped about with watery eyes. It was the only place in the United States where they ever warned us that walking about the shipyard after dark was risky, but we nevertheless went into town once, which was enough.

New Orleans was our next port of call. In those days, it was the busiest port in the US after New York. The place was obviously thriving, and Canal Street with its trolley cars and fancy stores was the shopping center for a large region. The French Quarter was wide open, and *les bontemps* were really rolling. My brother was standing on the quay as we moored; he and his wife had settled in her hometown in the Mississippi Delta. We hadn't seen each other in a couple of years, and he proudly showed off his new car (a Kaiser), which he had bought only a week earlier. They were visiting his wife's brother, who was an ex-GI student at Tulane University and who was living in veterans' housing on campus with his wife and two children. It was the first time we had an opportunity to discuss the prospects of me coming to join them and how I should proceed to apply for admission as a resident alien. There were lots of suggestions all around, but nobody seemed to have any knowledge about the requirements under the law. One had to have a sponsor—that, everyone knew—with sufficient means to ensure that a prospective immigrant would not become a burden on society. It was furthermore concluded that I should prepare myself for some field of endeavor which would make finding a job easier.

"Accounting!" everybody shouted, "that's where the future is," but when I asked how many among the friends gathered in the living room were studying the subject, there wasn't even one. Nevertheless, everyone insisted that it was the thing to do, particularly since one could even learn it through a correspondence course. An outfit of some apparent renown in Chicago by the name of LaSalle Extension University existed which taught accounting, but nobody knew how to get in touch with them in New Orleans. However, they assured me that they were bound to have representation in New York, and I resolved to try there. First thing, though, I should get an English dictionary (having gone to school in Australia they apparently didn't consider me literate), and someone brought me one the next day. I still have it after these many years, well-thumbed but intact.

During our stay, a hurricane visited New Orleans, dumping torrents of rain. I was unable to get back to the ship on time the next morning because the streets were almost under two feet of water. When I did finally make it, I was severely reprimanded for not returning on board before the storm struck. Had we been in a port located directly on the coast, the ship could well have left for open water to avoid being dumped on dry land. I apologized for my ignorance but did not remember any warnings being issued the previous day about severe weather. It seemed that they were upset about having been caught off guard and having had to endure some anxious moments during the night while everyone ashore was peacefully asleep, including their purser, who didn't know better.

Traveling down the Mississippi River takes much less time than going upstream against an eight-mile-an-hour hour current. I hated to leave, but there was much more to see in the days ahead. The next port was Baltimore, where the chief steward and I took a train early one morning into Washington to go sightseeing. We wore our uniforms and had no difficulty entering the visitors' galleries in either house of Congress, where debates were in progress. Restrictions came years later. Washington was beautiful then as it is now, but it is a tiring place to visit even under the best of circumstances. Each time I have been back, even for a week at a time, I found that there was never enough time to see much of it.

Unless one is on a passenger liner, getting a haircut is a trying experience. When we reached Philadelphia, I decided that I could no longer go without one and visited a barber shop in a local neighborhood not far from where we were docked. Things didn't look encouraging at all when I entered, but I was not prepared for what I had to endure the next two or three hours. I must have been fifth or sixth in line in the one-man barbershop where a lively discussion was going on concerning the latest ball game. Everyone was participating in the debate over which the barber was presiding. He would snip a hair here and there, and then lecture his audience for five minutes as to how the ball should have been hit, all the while gesticulating with comb in one hand and scissors in the other. More people kept entering the shop, and only a few did not participate in the discussion. When my turn finally came, I sat in the chair almost forty-five minutes while the barber pranced around me flailing his arms and narrowly missing my face with his scissors. I never did get a real haircut, but he did a little trimming here and there for which he charged what seemed to be a small fortune. He kept on talking as I handed him the money, never making any eye contact, and didn't even bother to say thanks. I often think about this introduction to a perfectly absurd sports mania, particularly when the addict happens to be an Italian with poor command of English.

Back in New York, we wound up in the same general area as before, but I did not get back my splendid view of the lower Manhattan area. LaSalle Extension University did have an office downtown, and I signed up for their accounting course. The first lesson reached me before we left, but it proved to be rather difficult after that to keep material flowing in both directions. Company personnel in our New York office were wonderful in forwarding it to different parts of the world, something they didn't have to bother with at all. The course turned out to be a lifesaver in the years to come, and a whole career was built on what it taught me.

After the ship finished loading, twelve passengers boarded with destinations all the way to Malaya. Among them was a US State Department officer, who soon managed to get his nose into everything we did and who might as well have been a member of the crew. He was to leave us in Karachi.

Stormy Weather

Something seemed wrong the second morning out from New York; I could feel it in the ship's motion. The North Atlantic was not supposed to be that smooth unless there was fog. I got up, dressed, and while I was shaving, the mirror above the washstand suddenly hazed over as if somebody had breathed on it. That was strange, more so because the door and window of my cabin on boat deck were open to let in the fresh air. It was then that I noticed that the air outside had turned warm and humid while the sea was glassy smooth. In the mess hall, everyone seemed unusually quiet during breakfast until someone said, "Well, by this evening we should be standing on our heads."

"What are you talking about?" I asked.

"Big hurricane—haven't you heard?" was the reply, and my heart skipped a beat. Before we left, the newspapers had mentioned a hurricane coming up the east coast, but we had paid little attention to it. As a matter of fact, most of us didn't seem to know what a hurricane really was all about, other than just a lot of wind and rain like we had earlier in New Orleans. Shortly, the first mate stuck his head in the door to announce that the captain had called a meeting of all deck officers at 9:00, and we anxiously awaited the result as we gathered for coffee later that morning.

The hurricane we had all but forgotten about had changed course during the night and was headed for Sable Island, about 600 miles northeast of New York. The meeting had been called to decide whether we should change direction or proceed on course. The ship was loaded to the limit, and a correct decision was critical. Latest reports indicated that the storm was to pass equidistant between us and the shoreline and that the worst that could be expected would probably be rough seas. After the deck officers were polled, the captain ordered to proceed on course. In the meantime, the wind had picked up and white caps had begun to show as the sky became overcast. Deck hands set about the task of battening down the hatches, rigging up lifelines on open deck, and stowing away anything that could wash overboard. Inside the ship, similar measures were taken, and passengers were informed as to what was happening.

Weather reports showed no change all morning and everyone was beginning to breathe easier. I observed my usual siesta and took a shower prior to going back on duty at 4:00. I did notice that the sea had become considerably rougher and during afternoon tea, someone coming from the bridge reported that things had changed during the last hour or so; the storm appeared to be heading for a point where it would intersect our path, and it looked like we might stand on our heads after all. By the time dinner was served, we were having difficulty keeping everything on the table, and by 8:00 that evening we were in it beyond any doubt. It turned out to be one of those monstrous storms which occur in the North Atlantic Ocean periodically. And what did it feel like? I was terrified!

First of all the wind! It moved through the ship's rigging with such velocity that the resulting roar made it impossible to hear yourself shout to someone standing inches away. Then the water: enormous waves began breaking over the ship. I learned firsthand why ships built for the North Atlantic had much smaller cargo hatches—they didn't cave in as easily. Water was sloshing around knee-deep everywhere on open deck, no matter at what level of the superstructure one happened to be. I was shown why all doors to the outside had those high thresholds and learned why both interior and exterior walkways had railings for people to hang on to because, without them, one could be tossed about helplessly. The utility of safety ropes strung between deckhouses became apparent when I saw several persons negotiate these open spaces disappear in a wall of water for a long time. General crew quarters being in the stern, the boatswain came into the officers' mess to ask for a cup of coffee because he was too exhausted to go to his own. He looked worried and had little to say. The ship shuddered and objects in the pantry came rolling off the shelves. For a moment it looked like we were submerged because water came squirting between the heavy doors and facings on both sides of the mess hall. We figured out later that it must have been the moment that a wave smashed against the superstructure head-on, breaking several cabin windows below the bridge. As the occupants scrambled to safety, everything not tied down came through the doors and washed down the stairwell. Suddenly the wind stopped blowing, and we could hear the thundering sea which sounded like confused surf pounding a beach. Word came from the bridge that we were in the eye of the storm, and we were warned to stay put because things would probably get much worse. The ship labored heavily, and several times both foghorns mounted on the smokestack began blaring staccato fashion. The cables that activated them ran between the rear of the bridge and smoke stack, and they stretched when a wave lifting us reached midships, leaving bow and stern suspended in the air. Propellers raced as they momentarily cleared the water, and I didn't like the expression on the boatswain's face as he sat huddled in a corner, looking up at the ceiling as if in prayer. Several of us mustered up courage to go and see what the eye of the storm was like. Looking straight up, we saw the stars shining brightly, and as we ducked back inside, the last ones were soaked by a sudden wave. One of the apprentices came in to fill up thermos flasks with coffee, and all of us wanted to know what things were like on the bridge.

"Well," he said; "the captain has wedged himself into the port side comer of the bridge house and doesn't seem too worried. He did tell me to warn everybody that the backside of a hurricane is the worst." The minute after he told us that, a violent gust of wind hit us which started the rigging to howling again. The sea, confused while we were in the storm's eye, rapidly became organized and broadsided the ship several times before they were able to pull it around. Most of the damage later discovered was attributed to these moments.

The logbook showed that the ship's course during the hurricane resembled the shape of a pear because the bow was kept heading into oncoming seas, something only one of the quartermasters had been able to accomplish. He was an older man and, like the boatswain, had a tendency of getting into trouble. He was later declared unfit for duty, but we considered ourselves fortunate that he was with us at that time because several ships in the vicinity got into serious trouble. The *Queen Mary* was in the neighborhood and was delayed forty-eight hours arriving in New York.

We remained in rough water until we reached the Strait of Gibraltar, and the first port of call was Alexandria, in Egypt, where an initial damage assessment could be made of the cargo. Number two hatch (the one right in front of the bridge) contained half a dozen automobiles packed in crates bound for Kuwait in the Persian Gulf. They were stowed on lengths of oil pipe and had come loose to start sliding from side to side. One crate, containing a Cadillac convertible, had broken open. Parts of the contents were scattered all over the cargo hold, where bits of the vehicle's roof kept showing up months later. Other custom-designed vehicles sustained damage to varying degrees.

Arabian Days

The ship had dropped anchor in the harbor roads of Alexandria and from time to time a sleek, brightly colored speedboat came skimming past us with a roar. They said that it was King Farouk at play, and he waved back at us whenever we waved to him. Several men were with him, presumably his bodyguards, who looked at us menacingly.

There was a lively night scene ashore and we were fascinated by the belly dancers who, once they zeroed in on you, conveyed the feeling that they were trying to seduce you with their eyes. We stayed only one night and moved on to make the usual trip through the Suez Canal and the Red Sea before stopping in Aden. This time I had a chance to go ashore and really look around. The natives seemed friendly and didn't mind posing for pictures. Luxury items in the tax-free port were dirt cheap, and I bought a much-needed watch, which was to last me a long time.

Instead of going southeast as usual, we headed northeast into the Arabian Sea and three days later entered the Gulf of Oman, which is separated from the Persian Gulf by a spur of the Arabian Peninsula. At the end of this spur is a rocky outcropping that is divided by a narrow channel barely wide enough to let a ship through. Unless thoroughly familiar with the area, no mariner in his right mind would attempt to take a short cut through the channel, but our captain seemed to have been there before because he headed straight for it. We shortly sped past towering rock masses practically a stone's throw on either side of the ship and entered the Persian Gulf. It must have been an impressive bit of seamanship because it startled the first mate, who was working in his state room, when he saw a wall of rock slide past his porthole. "Damn, I don't believe this!" I heard him say through the open door behind me. We had been in heavy traffic for two days and were continuously overtaking slower ship, although a few were obviously leaving us behind. The shortcut put us ahead of the pack, and we arrived at the island of Bahrain the next morning to drop anchor among ships of all nationalities. The usual boarding officers representing customs and immigration didn't come aboard until the next day. The news as to when we could expect to start unloading was not at all encouraging; they couldn't even provide the captain with an estimated waiting time. And so, the days passed as we dolefully watched other ships move alongside the single wharf—a long one, to be sure—until somebody spotted one going in which had arrived days later than we had. It was at that point that we learned about the time-honored eastern custom of *baksheesh*, which prompted the captain to submit a discreet inquiry to headquarters in Rotterdam if the prohibition against it could possibly be waived under the circumstances. "Absolutely not!" came back the indignant reply, which was followed a few days later by a more timid inquiry as to how much would be involved. Our agents said that the going rate was $6,000, and they were instructed to pay it. We were alongside the wharf the next day. Two weeks had gone by, and it cost almost as much per day to operate a ship which wasn't going anywhere. On top of that, our fresh water supply was dwindling, and we were unable to find a safe source of replenishment so that the emergency desalination equipment had to be put into operation. We watched with a great deal of fascination and relief as potable water trickled through a glass vial. They told us that it required a ton of diesel fuel to provide a ton of water and were asked to use it sparingly.

After Bahrain came Kuwait, destination of the fancy automobiles, which initial inspection showed to have incurred some damage. Unfortunately, it turned out to be far worse than expected, and not one crate came through unscathed. Besides the convertible, which had been badly battered, a limousine was virtually demolished after its crate had burst open and loose parts were scattered throughout the cargo hold. One wheel was never found. The sheiks communicated their intense displeasure, and a great deal of static was to come from headquarters during the following weeks. I could guess at the degree of the owners' annoyance from the volume of additional information supplied in letters to them and even had to reproduce several pages from the logbook including detailed drawings of the ship's course before, during, and after the storm. The captain took all of this stoically; nothing ever shook him up.

About fifty miles northeast of Kuwait lies the mouth of the Shatt al-Arab through which the waters of the Tigris and Euphrates empty into the Persian Gulf. It is navigable by oceangoing freighters as far as Basra, the port city of Iraq. Halfway up the waterway, on the Iranian side, lies Abadan, where the British Petroleum Company operated the largest oil refinery in the world. This was our next destination, followed by Khorramshar, also on the Iranian side, with a short distance further north. It was where we finally managed to replenish our fresh water supply, although extraordinary measures had to be taken to purify it. It had been shipped in two railroad cars all the way from Tehran.

One of the crew members was a fourteen-year-old boy who was serving as an apprentice seaman under the personal tutelage of the boatswain, who was more or less his guardian. His duties consisted primarily of keeping the crew's quarters in the stern of the ship clean and to fetch food from the galley. He had been rather ill lately and arrangements were made for him to go on sick call at the refinery's hospital. They asked me to accompany him and act as his interpreter. A British doctor examined him and, after several blood samples had been taken, diagnosed his problem as a severe case of syphilis, so severe that a purulent discharge was coming out of both his ears. He told me that it was a Turkish strain prevalent in the Middle East and that the boy should be repatriated without delay for intensive medical treatment. He was put on a plane to Amsterdam, and the event made quite an impression on the rest of the crew.

Wandering in and around Khorramshahr, we came upon a family washing Persian rugs in a water hole. Several were hung out to dry and were for sale, but they were too big to take along even if anyone could have afforded to get one. They had smaller and more reasonably priced ones in stores in town, and some of the fellows bought them to take home. They are very popular in Holland where people use them as tablecloths—unsanitary perhaps, but they are durable and colorful.

It was early fall, and temperatures in the region had begun to moderate. Although primarily desert, the area is quite beautiful, and a sense of history pervades it. Regretfully, we missed visiting Basra and resolved to see it next time.

The ship stopped in Karachi, Pakistan, a bustling city with a large harbor. It was the destination of several of our passengers, including the US State Department employee. He seemed to hate leaving us and was probably concerned that we couldn't find our way around without him. On the way to Bombay, we made a brief stop in Porbandar, birthplace of Mahatma Gandhi. It wasn't much more than a village on the sea, but I thought I recognized it years later in a movie about him.

Details of one's first visit to a place are usually remembered, whereas those on subsequent visits routinely fade from memory. So it was with Bombay and Calcutta, except that we found the latter to be surprisingly cold; it was also where our voyage ended and the ship was ordered to proceed to Malaya and Indonesia to pick up cargo for European ports.

Besides picking up copra, we were to transport its derivative, palm oil, in tanks located in number three hold amidships. These were equipped with heating coils through which steam was run to prevent the contents from coagulating in cold weather. The tanks had to be cleaned first, a job carried out in Singapore by several hundred Chinese workers at a cost of thirty thousand dollars. Obviously, the tariff for transporting this commodity was rather steep.

After having made the customary rounds through the Indonesian archipelago, the ship made a brief stop in Jakarta to pick up passengers before returning to Singapore to load palm oil. The two- or three-day journey wasn't entirely without peril. The empty tanks caused an unstable condition. Before leaving any port, the chief mate determined the ship's center of gravity which, in this instance, was way out of the safety zone. This meant that we had to proceed with extreme caution, making only gradual changes in course, lest the ship capsize. Had we encountered rough weather, we would have had to seek shelter in some port along the way or, in an emergency, the bottom tanks would have had to be flooded and then cleaned all over again. The ship rolled in an alarming manner, sometimes in such a way as if it were not going to right itself. This would stop conversation in midsentence, while a fork lifting food to someone's mouth would hover half way, until we slowly recovered our balance. But we made it, and everyone breathed easier as we entered the harbor in Singapore. From the moment palm oil started flowing into the tanks, it was just about all the engineers could talk about. They were the ones responsible for maintaining it at a required temperature, and they became particularly edgy the moment we came out of the Mediterranean into the Atlantic where it started getting cold. About half the stuff was delivered in Liverpool, and the rest went to London.

One of the passengers had brought along a German shepherd dog, which had become somewhat of a mascot to the crew. He would tirelessly retrieve a stick while his owner looked on anxiously to see that he wouldn't pursue one carelessly thrown or carried overboard by the wind. However, nobody had thought about the possibility that he might jump on an open hatch once we were in port, and that's exactly what he did in Liverpool and wound up in a tank full of hot palm oil. Fortunately, the engineer who had supervised the opening of the tank was just an arm's length away and was able to grab him by the collar to pull him out. Nothing floats in oil and a tragedy was narrowly averted, but they sure had a mess on their hands cleaning up the poor animal.

Liverpool was a run-down old town even in those days, yet we had fun ashore. A dance hall we visited just the one night we were in port was filled with pretty girls, many of whom we had difficulty understanding because of the kind of English they spoke. It was a mystery to us why practically every one of them made elaborate excuses about her presence in the hall because it seemed a perfectly innocent place to be. In London we never even got off the ship because the dock area was too far from the center of town, and word was that the place was even more dilapidated than Liverpool. Well, perhaps it may have been at that time; twenty-five years later, Ruth and I found it to be a perfectly nice place to visit.

Arriving in Holland, I found my sister staying with her parents-in-law. She had been there six months, and her husband had just flown back to the Far East to resume his duties. She had a little girl less than a year old whom I hadn't seen yet. It was midwinter, and we had a chance to visit for over a month before the MS *Bantam* left for the United States to resume service in the Nedlloyd Line.

1949

There were many new faces on board—younger men serving as second, third, and fourth mates—but the same captain was back. I struck it rich in that they assigned me the doctor's cabin on main deck in the passenger quarters. It was roomy, had a large built-in desk and a settee beside it, and there were no fewer than three portholes. The ship was traveling in ballast, which meant that it was empty, and we were heading straight for Galveston where we arrived two weeks later to pick up the first cargo for the Persian Gulf. The trip over was like a pleasure cruise, and as soon as the weather turned warmer, they rigged up a swimming pool on top of the number two hatch in front of the bridge. Few people knew that the ship was even carrying such a luxury item. It consisted of a frame of heavy planking in which a canvas liner was placed. The pool was about fifteen feet square and at least six feet deep. It was filled with sea water in no time at all and we frolicked in it like a bunch of schoolboys during the afternoon hours. They had to let the water out once or twice because of rough weather which put the swimmers at risk of being washed over the side and dumped on deck.

The ship had been provisioned for six months and upon arrival in Galveston, customs officers repeatedly brought visitors on board who just had to see all the sides of beef, mutton and pork in the freezer locker. They claimed that there was still a wartime shortage of meat, and Texans apparently loved nothing else more.

I was given permission to take time off and meet the ship in New Orleans a few days later, so I took a Greyhound bus for an all-night ride to arrive at my destination early the next morning. Jan and his wife, Virginia, met me at the bus station, and we all stayed at her brother's apartment at Tulane University, where I was afforded further introductions to life in the United States. We went out on the town practically every night and took a ride up the river one evening on that same craft which still seems to be in existence today. I liked what I saw and resolved to make application for admission as a resident alien.

The Dutch had an annual quota of 3,000 people, which was based on the number of immigrants during a peak year at the turn of the century. I had no trouble getting on the waiting list because most people trying to leave Holland at the time were interested in Australia, which was paying the price of their passage and even offered financial assistance in getting them settled. Interestingly enough, both a leading Dutch publication as well as Radio Holland alluded to the fact that many of these people retained their Dutch citizenship and intended to come home and retire.

The ship made its way up the east coast to New York, then Boston, and finally to Halifax to finish loading. There was foul weather outside Boston, and at one point, an engineer had to be rescued while he was repairing a winch on deck when a wave came over the side and froze him almost instantly. A dense fog came next, and the ship was delayed a couple of days outside Halifax. The recently installed radar showed that the harbor entrance was blocked by some sort of craft which was frantically sounding its horn in concert with those of other ships, including ours, and everything was at a standstill. After listening for two days to all this racket, the fog lifted and showed that the culprit causing all the commotion had been a tugboat trying to negotiate the narrow harbor entrance while towing two barges.

The people in Halifax were as hospitable as their fellow citizens on the other side of Canada, and four or five of us were invited one evening by a group of young ladies to come over for drinks and a snack. After departing the next afternoon, we immediately ran into a storm which accompanied us all the way to the Strait of Gibraltar.

The chief steward and I occupied identical cabins (staterooms, really), except that his was on port side while mine was on starboard. We both had shortwave radios which required rigging up outside antennas. Anyone putting up such an affair had to first secure the radio officer's approval, lest it interfere with his function. At any time he started transmitting, he would thoughtfully tap his Morse key to warn all listeners to turn down the volume on their radios so that the powerful signal wouldn't damage their equipment or their hearing. Whenever we were near land and the visibility was bad, he would be called to the bridge to take soundings with the radio direction finder. This required that everybody's antenna had to be lowered quickly by one of the sailors, and those not equipped with a rope and pulley would simply be cut down with an axe. The chief steward's antenna was one of the few which was fixed, and the reason why it had not previously been bothered was that it was right behind and below the bridge and apparently had not interfered with the direction finder. The radio operator, a cranky old man with many years' experience, was not the type to make any exceptions and had the ax-wielding sailor accompanying him chop down the whole installation and dump it on deck. Perhaps the chief steward resented an upstart like me invading his territory because he blamed me for the incident and our good relations were never restored. But then, dissensions of varying intensity had been making their appearance among members of the crew and it was hard to pin down their causes. It could very well have been that older and easygoing officers had largely been replaced by younger men among whom competition was keen.

One of the great amenities on board had been unexpectedly interrupted when our two Chinese laundry men jumped ship in New York. All ships were equipped with complete laundry facilities, operated by Chinese men who were paid a monthly wage supplemented by fees charged for laundering the personal garments of both passengers and crew. Fortunately, it was still winter and we were wearing wool uniforms when we were left to our own devices and the company did manage to have replacements for them by the time we reached Port Said. Laundry men lived in isolation among equipment contained in the laundry room under the rear mast. They cooked their own food and always seemed to be dressed in shorts, a tank top and wooden clogs, no matter what the weather was like. Nobody fooled with them because they were rather combative, and I remember one occasion when a fight had to be broken up between one of them who was wielding a hammer and an Indonesian steward brandishing a knife.

This time our first port of call in the Persian Gulf was Bandar Shahpur, a desolate place about fifty miles east of Abadan. Ever since the cabin boy who had syphilis left us, we had talked about playing soccer in our spare time, even if it was no more than kicking a ball around somewhere. Not far from where we docked there was an open space sporting goal posts (one couldn't possibly call it a football field since there wasn't a blade of grass in sight), but we were discouraged from using it because anytime we went ashore the guards at the gate house insisted that we leave our passports with them, something we weren't about to do. After giving the matter some thought, I fabricated a bunch of passports out of file folders, in each of which I pasted a picture accompanied by some text material cut randomly out of a magazine. Anyone wanting to play ball was given one of these with his name printed on the front in large letters, and the guards were perfectly satisfied with these official-looking documents.

The heat, usually between 115 and 120 degrees Fahrenheit, was unbearable but we survived and shortly we were able to identify enough talent to organize a team. Before moving on to Khorramshahr, we played against the crew of a British ship and were beaten 3–0, but that really wasn't fair competition because they wore football boots, while we wore tennis shoes and were afraid to be stepped on. By the time we reached Bombay, we had collected enough money to buy eleven pairs of boots. The captain was interested in our venture, and I suggested as tactfully as I could that perhaps the company should buy the boots because, after all, it would be cheaper than treating venereal disease, but he didn't buy that. However, upon reaching Indonesia, the company president came on board for two weeks to make one of his periodic inspection tours, and he was so impressed with the idea that he promised to look into the matter.

We were never so glad to leave a place as we were the Persian Gulf. The evening we sailed down the Shatt al-Arab, a good many of us gathered on the forecastle waiting for the first hint of a breeze. For two weeks we had not seen the temperature dip below the one-hundred-degree mark, not even at night. Only the latest passenger liners were air conditioned in those days, and then only partly at that, like the first-class saloons, dining room, and maybe a few of the luxury staterooms.

Soon after leaving, I began experiencing violent headaches, which ultimately were diagnosed as being migraine attacks. Unfortunately, not much was known about this affliction from which I was to suffer almost daily for the next thirty years. At first, I was convinced that strenuous activity in the intense heat had been the cause and I embarked on a series of visits to neurologists in India, Malaya, Indonesia, and Holland. They were all quite sympathetic but couldn't do a thing for me. The problem didn't go away until I was put on the drug Inderal to combat high blood pressure.

In Singapore I made the mistake of drinking a chocolate milkshake and came down with a case of bacillary dysentery within hours after departure. Jakarta was three days away, and before we arrived, I was passing nothing but blood. Upon arrival, I managed to reach the company infirmary under my own power. An Indonesian male nurse made the tentative diagnosis, which was confirmed by a doctor who was quite drunk when he returned from having lunch. A bottle of sulfa pills and drinking weak tea a couple of days took care of the problem. In the meantime, I had a chance to reflect on the miserable fate of the thousands of prisoners who succumbed to the disease while being forced to work on the Burma railroad during the war.

At some time during the trip, one of the older Indonesian stewards had fallen ill and had rapidly become incapacitated. The doctors in Bombay said that his problem was nephritis, and they didn't expect him to live much longer. The company offered to fly him home, but the man wanted no part of that and we later surmised that he had been afraid to die among infidels. He was moved to sick bay where he hung on to the barest thread of life until we reached Jakarta. He was buried in his native village.

The chief mate for this voyage had come to the company by way of a merger. Although an accomplished navigator, he seemed an unlikely candidate for the job if for no other reason than that he was grossly obese, dressed sloppily, and let his stringy hair grow out so long that his cap perched precariously on his head. He was an amateur psychologist and enjoyed analyzing his subordinates, myself included. He volunteered that I was inclined to be indolent, a trait which he thought usually afflicted those born in the Indies who were raised by servants. So far, his career had been confined to the uppermost reaches of Europe like Murmansk and Archangel, and someone suggested that his brain might have been frostbitten. It was his first trip to the tropics, and he was obviously uncomfortable, particularly when he had to negotiate the stairs leading up to the bridge, when he managed to look like a sea lion.

We were once again pulled out of the Nedlloyd service to return to Holland where we arrived in the fall, a good time of the year. We stopped in Marseilles on the way (my first time in France) to spend no more than a day. Whenever I read an article on body language wherein the usual clichés regarding ethnic preferences—or, rather, tolerances—in accepting living space are mentioned, I think of our company office in Marseilles, where staff members were packed like sardines in a can. I also had the wildest taxicab rides ever going to and from town. I was with Sparks who had orders from his wife to buy her some brassieres while in the States, which he had forgotten to do. Marseilles was his last chance, even though they didn't seem to be any better off in France than they were in the rest of Europe at the time. When we entered a shop, he had a hard time explaining what he wanted and finally had to resort to sign language. When asked what size, he explained: "pour deux grandes montagnes de viande" (for two large mountains of meat). They didn't have them that big, and the lady never even cracked a smile.

Late in October 1949, I signed on for what was to be my last trip to the Far East and back. It was kind of risky to leave Holland because I could have been called in at any moment by the US Consulate for a physical before being processed for issuance of an immigration visa, but I couldn't just simply hang around forever.

We had two canines for paying passengers, one a German shepherd and the other a greyhound; both were destined for owners in Indonesia. The captain took a liking to the German shepherd which found a luxurious home on the bridge for the duration of the voyage. Unfortunately, the dog had never seen a person with a dark skin before and almost tackled the Egyptian pilot upon arrival in Port Said. We were surprised upon arrival in Jakarta that his owner turned out to be an Indonesian. The greyhound was shut up in a cage beside the potato locker on boat deck. It was cold and the North Sea was doing its best to make things miserable. Being virtually exposed to the elements, the poor creature was shivering, and I decided to bring it to my cabin.

The Bay of Biscay was in a bad state as we ran before a storm blowing out of the northwest and, just before passing Cape Finisterre at coffee time one morning, a rogue wave smashed into the starboard side with a thunderous jolt, which even brought the engineers out of the engine room to see what happened. Both lifeboats on that side had been carried away. For the first time since the war, the ship had a doctor on board, and I was back in my cabin on boat deck. It was an uncomfortable feeling to look out and not see a lifeboat hanging in the davits between my door and the sea.

We stopped in Lisbon to pick up a group of Portuguese military personnel and their dependents (that's why we had a doctor on board), and these people were traveling with us to Jakarta where they were catching a ship going to Macau, a Portuguese colony off the China coast. Only a short stay was intended, but the harbor master would not let us depart without a requisite number of lifeboats on board and we wound up waiting several days before a ship arrived from Holland, dropping off a couple of replacements.

It quickly became evident that we were to have captain trouble on this trip. Ours was a weird bird, a stickler for detail whom nobody could please. Big and tall as he was, he was effeminate and very snobbish.

In Medan in northwestern Sumatra, larger ships still had to anchor outside the harbor of Belawan-Deli. Arriving there late one afternoon, we were welcomed by a dozen or more sharks which began circling the ship in a leisurely fashion, a bad omen as far as the seamen were concerned who are generally superstitious. It was the first time I had ever seen such creatures alive, and I promptly got the urge to catch one of them. I first collected a length of flag line at the bosun's locker and then begged the cook for a meat hook and a hunk of meat. One of the engineers fashioned an eye to the hook to which the rope could be attached and I was in business. As I was dragging all this equipment to the stern, which seemed a likely place to go fishing, the boatswain walked up to warn me that I had better tie the line to a stanchion because there was no way a person could control a shark fighting to free himself. I did as he suggested (fortunately) and tossed the baited hook overboard which, no sooner than it hit the water, was pounced upon by a group of the creatures before the biggest one of them all took off with it. Wearing no gloves, the rope chafed my hands and I had to let go to let it uncoil completely until it tightened with a jerk (thanks to the stanchion) and onlookers started hollering to pull him in. He came without much of a struggle until he was directly under the stern, and we were able to look each other in the eye. The meat hook was set firmly through the upper part of his mouth just in front where the jaw hinged.

"So what're you gonna do now?" asked the boatswain.

"Pull him aboard, I guess."

"Yeah, I'll bet; but watch out he don't pull you overboard," he added dryly as he turned and walked off.

As I returned my attention to my quarry, I saw him open and close his mouth a couple of times and then noticed that the line had slacked and no longer had the hook attached. The monster rolled over and took off. Never having fished before, I had failed to put a chain between hook and rope or, at the very least, always keep the line taut. Well, to pull him aboard without boom and tackle would have been impossible anyhow and, all said and done, it was exciting. The rest of the sharks had disappeared, and the older seamen seemed relieved.

As we departed Medan, we witnessed something nobody had ever seen happen before. Another ship had dropped anchor several hundred yards away and the captains, who appeared to be good friends, had gotten together for most of the next day. Ours returned just before we weighed anchor and they later reported that he was drunk. From a standstill, the engines were revved up to full speed after which the ship made two tight circles around the other vessel, heeling over more and more as we gained speed and blowing our horns as a farewell. That was when we found out the old man was not only a miserable individual but that he was crazy as well.

Traffic in Singapore had finally abated, and ships were no longer forced to drop anchor in the roadstead to load and unload. Of late, there was generally space available alongside one of the piers. A short time after we had berthed, our bow was brushed by a British vessel maneuvering to take up a spot directly in front of us. Little damage was done but our captain became hysterical and fired off a letter of protest which he ordered me to deliver to the offender. If they didn't accept it, I was to nail it to the ship's front mast and I wasn't quite sure if he was serious or just drunk.

The British captain turned out to be a pleasant, elderly gentleman who offered his apologies and said that the matter had already been brought to the attention of the insurers. Besides, after all was said and done, it was the fault of the "mud pilot," as those who maneuver a ship around the inner harbor are called. We wound up playing a game of soccer against his crew and were afterwards invited to come over for drinks. The next day I spotted a Russian ship in the harbor and, on a dare, went over to challenge them to a game. This was still in the days of Stalin and I could tell from the tone of voice as well as the general demeanor of the burly guard posted at the bottom of the gangway that he meant for me to move on.

1950

By the time we reached Jakarta, the Indonesians had achieved virtual independence from the Dutch. My sister had only recently returned to join her husband, and they were temporarily residing at the ever-popular Hotel des Indes. The future seemed uncertain, although nobody expected that within just a couple of years all Dutch citizens would be expelled. Many were laboring under the delusion that they would somehow be able to carry on with their lives as before.

Mil told me the incredible tale of how her two-year-old daughter had one day decided to take a walk and had been found a mile away. Just to reach the front gate of the hotel—which was guarded twenty-four hours a day—she would have had to walk a respectable distance and, to get to the place where she was allegedly found, she had to dodge heavy vehicular traffic of all kinds, including street cars moving in both directions, on double tracks, before crossing a bridge over a canal. It all sounded more like a case of kidnapping, but I didn't belabor the point. While reminiscing many years later, I brought up the incident and was shocked to discover that she did not remember it and had obviously blocked the traumatic event out of her mind.

On the return trip to Holland, our doctor had to have a tooth pulled while we were in Colombo, the capital of Sri Lanka. It developed into a nasty infection in a matter of days, and his intense suffering became a matter of concern to all of us. A huge swelling on his neck threatened to choke him and the captain offered to let another ship with a doctor only a hundred miles behind us catch up so that he could be treated, but he refused, insisting that he would have it attended to when we reached the Suez Canal. He somehow survived the ordeal although the swelling became as large as a football before it was over with and he confined himself to bed while living on morphine. The two ships arrived in Suez several hours apart and the other doctor came over immediately. He punctured the swelling, which caused puss and blood to squirt all over the infirmary, and then rode with us through the canal to attend to his patient who was practically back to normal within twenty-four hours.

One of the things required of a captain before a ship left port was that he advise agents at the next port as to how much cargo he had for them so that stevedores could arrange to have sufficient manpower on hand to handle it. As usual, the captain called back a letter I had typed for him addressed to our London agents because he wanted to add a postscript. The letter included cargo schedules and instead of inserting everything back into the envelope, he just handed all the material to me and walked off to see what was going on in the wheelhouse. Somehow, the all-important schedules didn't get mailed and wound up under some papers in one of my desk drawers. Halfway between Port Said and London we received an urgent telegram inquiring about the nature and quantity of cargo they could expect when we arrived. The captain went into a state of hysteria and (correctly) blamed me for the disastrous omission. When I found the schedules, I showed them to the chief mate (no friend of the captain), and all he did was look at me in disbelief before sitting down to stare at the floor for what seemed eternity. Suddenly he stood up, began tearing up the schedules, and asked me for a paper bag in which he stuffed the snippets.

"I'll take care of these," he said, adding, "the stupid bastard obviously forgot to enclose them with his letter."

That became the official story which only was to add fuel to a future fire. It earned me less than a satisfactory evaluation, as I was to find out upon reporting to the department chief at the close of the voyage. He asked me what in the world went wrong, and I referred him to the chief mate for details. He just grinned, because they had obviously already discussed the matter.

This last trip on the MS *Bantam* did have its pleasant moments. Among a shipment of wild animals destined for various zoological gardens were a tiger and an assortment of primates, which kept us occupied and often amused. One monkey managed to escape from his cage during feeding time shortly after departing the Far East and no amount of coaxing could get him back into his cage, so they decided to corner him by driving him to the bow of the ship. When all avenues of escape had been cut off, he shocked everyone by simply jumping overboard.

The tiger was sealed in a cage, which had been placed in a steel cargo net for additional security. At some time in the past, a tiger being transported escaped during the night and ambushed a crew member coming off duty out of the engine room. The latter was killed and partly consumed before someone came upon the gruesome scene.

The Bay of Biscay was turbulent as usual, and our tiger became seasick; he refused to eat and laid on his back with all fours up. Although he was adequately protected from the elements, they had to drape a tarpaulin over his cage and place an electric heater under it to keep him warm. Upon arrival in London, the usual contingent of customs inspectors descended upon us and one of them headed straight for the suspicious looking heap covered with a tarp. Our tiger had recovered and was in splendid form, greeting the man with an explosive roar. The poor fellow had to be escorted off the ship by two of his mates.

My four years at sea came to an end when we arrived in Rotterdam a few days later. Regretfully, it never occurred to me to keep a diary and all the foregoing has been from memory, much of which has faded over the years. I never could afford to purchase a decent used camera (even new ones were scarce after the war) and I have been able to come up with just a few pictures. I was able to reconstruct time frames from documents such as a passport and a seaman's registration book.

Going to sea was once a time-honored way for a young man to get his bearings once he matured physically. Aside from the fact that far fewer ships ply the oceans nowadays, there seem to be more exciting ways to engage both young men and women, but I doubt if any of them could be as interesting.

Herman Emanuel and Antoinette Smalhout, Erik's mother and father, in Batavia

Antoinette Van Uye, Erik's mother

Father hard at work

Father and his coworkers in Batavia Centruum

Herman Emanuel Smalhout's shop in Batavia

Mil and Erik in Batavia, 1927

Erik and Mil on vacation in the mountains of Java

Erik, Mil, and their mother on vacation in the mountains of Java

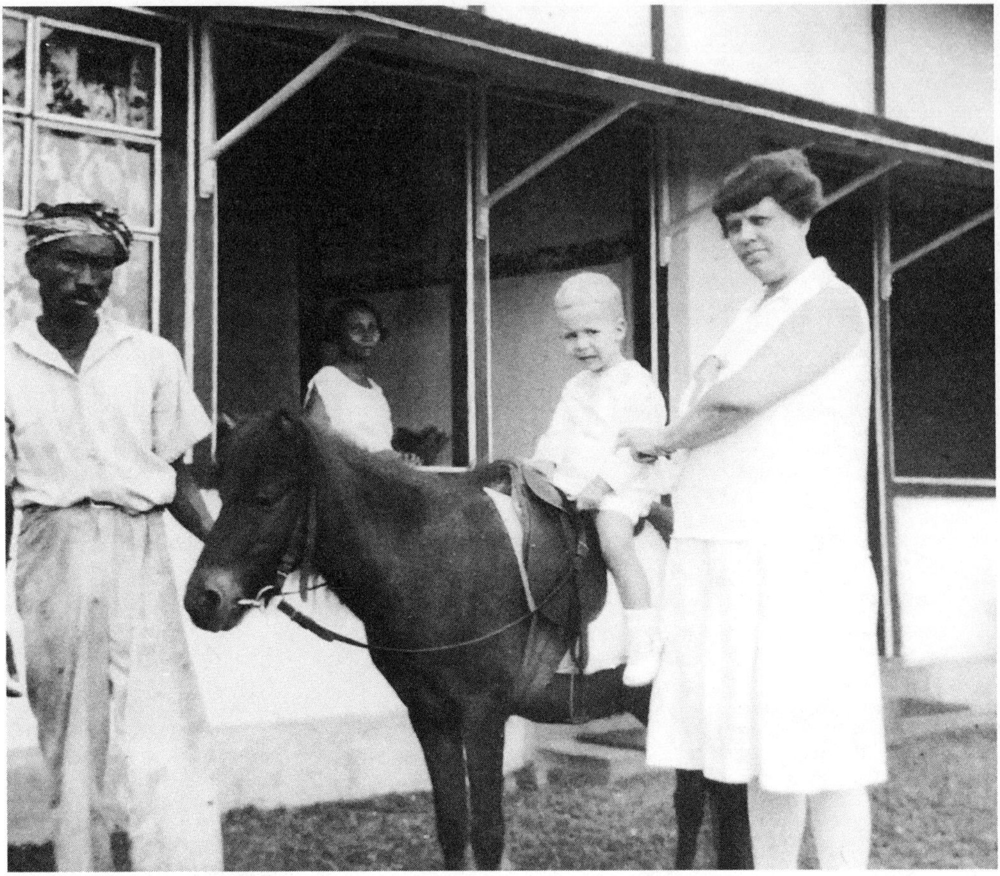

Erik and his mother on vacation in the mountains of Java

A page from the family scrapbook: Erik and Mil being cared for by their Tantje in Batavia, 1927

A page from the family scrapbook: Fun times in Batavia

Costume party in Batavia; Erik is seated in the front

One of the last photos of Erik and Mil with their mother

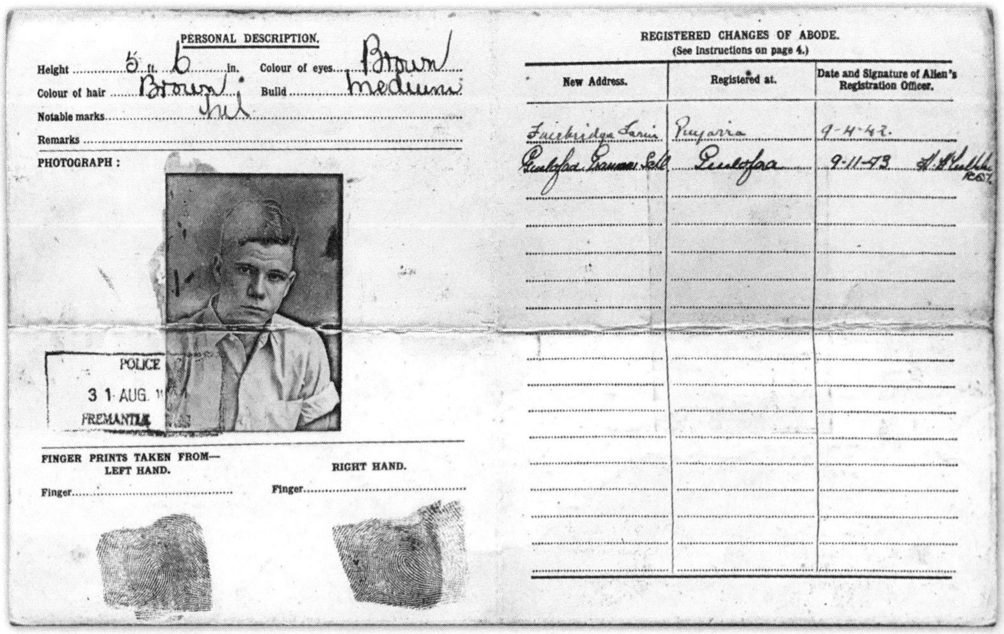

PERSONAL DESCRIPTION.

Height 5 ft. 6 in. Colour of eyes Brown
Colour of hair Brown Build medium
Notable marks Nil
Remarks
PHOTOGRAPH :

POLICE
3 1 AUG. 1
FREMANTLE

FINGER PRINTS TAKEN FROM—
LEFT HAND. RIGHT HAND.
Finger Finger

REGISTERED CHANGES OF ABODE.
(See instructions on page 4.)

New Address.	Registered at.	Date and Signature of Alien's Registration Officer.
Fairbridge Farm	Pinjarra	9-4-42.
Guildford Grammar Sch.	Guildford	9-11-43 [illegible]

Erik's alien registration during the war

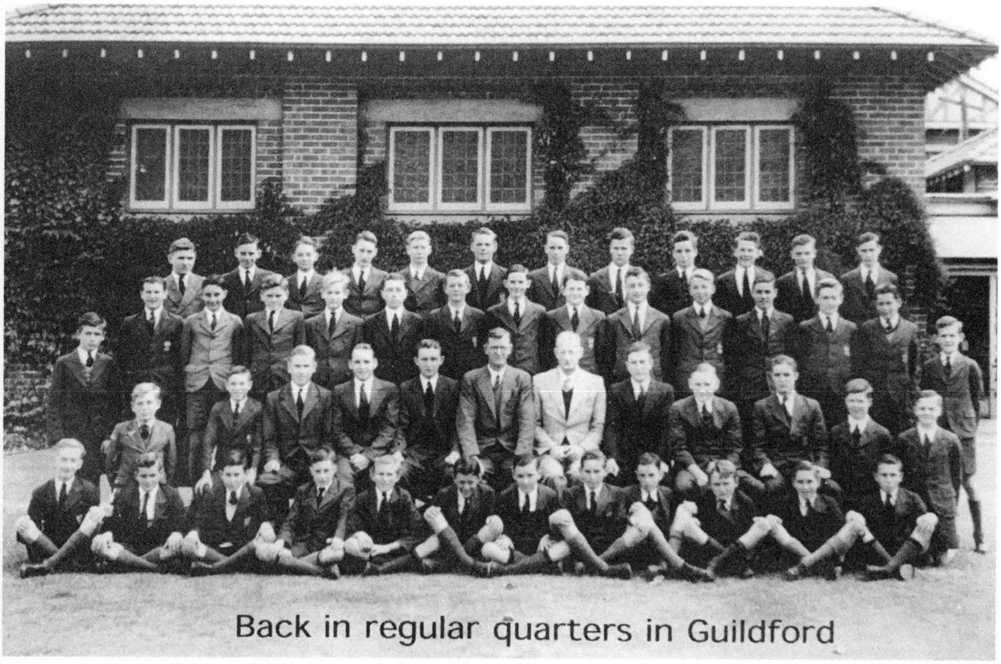

Class picture at Guildford Grammar School; Erik is back row, fifth from the right

Evacuations quarters in Fairbridge during the war; Erik is fourth from the right

OFFICERS and N. C. O's. 1944.

THE SWAN.

Back Row (Left to right): L/Cpl Beigel B. M., L/Cpl Bayley G. T., Cpl Harrold K. I., L/Cpl Smalhout E., Cpl Moss R. C., L/Cpl Lockyer R. P., Cpl Scott R. C., Cpl Tydeham D. H., L/Cpl Shepherd J. H., L/Cpl Gladstones W. H., L/Cpl Nichol R. W.
Middle Row: Cpl Robertson G. H., Cpl Chamier R. S. D., Sgt Jeffries P. R., Sgt Rhodes J. M., Sgt Riviere J. C., Sgt Maslen R. W., Sgt Tunstall N., Cpl Millar D. L., Cpl Grant A. D., Cpl Smith A. L., Cpl Ferrier A. N. E.
Sitting: C. S. M. Hamilton F., Cdt-Lient Caddy J. R. Cdt-Lieut Kiernan L. J., Lieut Milne D.A., Cdt-Lieut Davies J. D., Cdt-Lieut Robinson J. R., C. Q. M. S. Keogh J. W. S.

148

Cadets from Guildford Grammar School in 1944; Erik is on the back row, fourth from the left

AANMONSTERING EN BEËINDIGING VAN DE DIENST AAN BOORD

Datum van aanmonstering	Nummer monsterrol	Naam van het schip	Rang of kwaliteit	Termijn of aantal reizen	Ambtenaar van aanmonstering: Hoedanigheid	Ambtenaar van aanmonstering: Naam	Paraaf Ambt.	Beëindiging v/d dienst a. boord: Datum	Beëindiging v/d dienst a. boord: Plaats	Paraaf Kapt.	Paraaf Ambt.
28/8-47	699	KOTA BAROE	Scheeps...	1 r.	R'DAM		[illegible]	7/11'47	Rotterdam	[illegible]	
19 DEC. 1947	1043	Sibajak	—"—	1 REIS	W/S PLV R'DAM	G. BOOY	[illegible]	[illegible] IAN [illegible]	ROTTERDAM	[illegible]	
13 FEB. 1948	125	Sibajak	—"—	1 REIS	W/S PLV. R'DAM	G. BOOY	[illegible]	6-4-48	R'dam	[illegible]	
8/5-48	418	———	———	1r	W/S PLV. R'DAM	v. HAARLEM	[illegible]	15-6-48	Batavia	[illegible]	[illegible]
15-6-48	800	BANTAM	—"—	onbep	[illegible]	H. J. v. Dass[illegible]	[illegible]	15.1.49	Rotterdam	[illegible]	
20/2-49	156	———	———	1r	W/S PLV. R'DAM	v. HAARLEM	[illegible]	4-9-49	R'dam	B	
22-10-49	1050	—"—	—"—	1R	W/S R'DAM	v. SUCHTELEN v.d.H.	[illegible]	4.3-50	R'dam	B	

14 R 34141 15

Itinerary from Erik's seafaring days

The MS *Bantam* at anchor in the Straits of Malacca outside the Port of Pinang

The MS *Sibajak* and MS *Kota Baru*

Erik Smalhout and Ruth Gill on the eve before their wedding day, 1951

Erik and Ruth Smalhout on their wedding day, 1951

Erik with Antoinette, his first-born daughter, in 1953

Erik, his daughter Antoinette, and his half-brother Jan in Florida

Erik hard at work

July 1st

Dear Eric:

Congratulations for reaching the decision to finally retire from the rat race of combating a bunch of belligerent taxpayers. I am real sorry that it will not be possible for me to attend you retirement dinner but I am sure that your other associates over the years will attend and make it a gala occasion.

I know you are looking forward to the life of the country squire down on the plantation in Mississippi and I would like to wish you the best of luck in your retirement. I have found that I really stay busy most of the time, and have had a very enjoyable eleven years of retirement. I am sure tht you will look back on your years of service as being mostly enjoyable even though we were in a business that didn't make too many lasting friendships. I still hear that I formerly worked for IRS from some of my club members - but I don't mind since we know that it was a good and honorable profession, and in our days we were professionals!

Mary and I sond our best wishes to you and your lovely family.

Sincerely,

W. W. Jones

Life as an IRS agent must have been lonely: a letter from a former colleague

Erik and granddaughter Erika in 1987

Erik with his granddaughters Emily and Erika, at his home in Johns, Mississippi

One of Erik and Mil's final dinners together

Family reunion after Mil's passing, Johns, Mississippi, 1994

Family reunion in the Netherlands, 2019

Chapter 5

Home in the Mississippi Delta, 1950–1955

AMERICA

There was only a short interval between giving up my job and departing once more on a new venture. One had to pass a physical examination before they were issued an immigration visa, which was valid for only a relatively short time. This created problems in booking passage from Rotterdam to New Orleans. My old employer would have let me sign on as a crew member on any ship going to North America, but none happened to be going in that direction soon. I finally located a ship of the Waterman Steamship Corporation which was to make the trip within the official time limits.

Boarding the SS *Fairhope* was a new experience. In Rotterdam, many ships never come alongside a wharf; they are loaded or unloaded while moored to a buoy in the Rhine River. The travel agent informed me where the Fairhope could be located and instructed me to take a water taxi to the spot. When we got there, we found that no gangway had been lowered, and I had a hard time getting someone's attention on board. Finally, after much horn blowing, someone peeked over the side, disappeared and in a minute or so reappeared to heave a Jacob's ladder over the side which almost hit someone on the head as it unrolled noisily. They invited me to climb aboard, but what about my luggage? No problem: a rope followed the ladder with which to haul up my suitcases. All of this seemed to be a rather inauspicious start, particularly since I had never climbed one of those ladders before.

From the way things looked, the only reason the ship called in Rotterdam was to pick me up, and they were ready to depart as soon as I made it over the side. However, they had to clear immigration and customs first, and these people didn't show up until a couple of hours later. They were obnoxious and subjected me to a lengthy interrogation as to the purpose of my trip. Emigrants usually left in groups and were moreover sponsored by the government of the country of destination. Here was a person traveling alone, at his own expense, and on a freighter at that! Now, what could possibly be more suspicious? Fortunately, they were accompanied by a supervisor who had been chatting with people on the bridge and he reluctantly accepted the story of my life. They finally stomped out of my cabin, and I gleefully watched them struggle down the ladder while they almost choked on the acrid smoke emitted by the tugboat that had been standing by to turn the ship around and send it down the river.

The captain was a Spaniard and his first mate, or executive officer as they are called on American ships, was a Swede who had recently been laid off by a company in Stockholm. There were about ten other passengers besides myself who were headed for places all over the United States via New Orleans, the ship's destination. Dinner was served at 4:00 in the afternoon because the cook and stewards quit at five and were not allowed to put in overtime for any reason. There was one common dining room for all aboard and nobody seemed to observe the dinner hour because they came wandering in and out at random. The manner of dress was "optional," meaning T-shirts, tank tops, blue jeans or shorts, if so desired. Chinese flip-flops appeared not to have been discovered yet.

The food was bland and for the first few days the crew drank enormous quantities of milk. Extra supplies of milk were always bought in Holland, allegedly because of the superior quality. At the time, I had never known anyone not sick to drink the stuff. After the evening meal was over, the tables were gathered to form a buffet which was loaded down with platters of cold cuts, several kinds of bread, and huge chunks of butter. People snacked throughout the evening and probably the night as well. I found it all fascinating and was gratified that they took time to explain why things were done in this fashion. Everything was attributed to union rules; the union this, and the union that.

The ship carried nothing but ballast and was high out of the water. To avoid running into bad weather, a more southerly route was taken, which added to the crossing time. Accommodations were generally Spartan but comfortable. All interior steel bulkheads (walls) were painted seafoam green. There was a hint of a lounge consisting of a couple of plastic-covered sofas in the hallway in front of the dining room, and passengers would gather there to pass the time occasionally, but extreme boredom soon set in. I asked the executive officer if I could help him with some of his administrative duties. He was pleased when the captain gave his OK, and I was glad to get a chance to get an inside look at the operations of a US vessel. At the end of the trip, they wanted to pay me out of their own pockets but I refused and they gave me two cartons of cigarettes anyhow.

A couple of days before landfall, the captain received orders to put into Miami, and this caused much consternation among the passengers. A vessel not engaged in the coastal trade is prohibited by law from picking up passengers unless its next destination is abroad. Likewise, any vessel arriving stateside must discharge all passengers, regardless of their destination. With only fifty dollars to my name, I had no idea how I was going to reach Greenville, Mississippi. Several people were headed for California with all their household goods by way of either Mobile or New Orleans, and they were really upset. The company let it be known that they didn't much care and that the law was the law. To my regret I didn't get to see much of Miami until many years later, and I worried whether I had enough money to reach my destination. It turned out that I did; the bus fare was $42, which left me $8 for food and miscellaneous items. After arrival I wrote the steamship company and asked them for a partial reimbursement which was declined. I wrote them back to remind them that all ports had harbor masters and that the one in Rotterdam would quite likely be interested in my unusual experience. A check came by return mail.

The Trailways bus followed the Tamiami Trail through the Everglades to Tampa and thence via the west coast into Georgia and Alabama. We left Miami just before dark and, while waiting, I had an encounter in the men's room with a pretty young man who wanted to buy me a Coke. I declined with the most menacing growl I could muster, and he apparently went looking for more agreeable prospects. My European clothes were not exactly suitable for travel in the south in late April even though the bus was air conditioned. It made a lengthy stop in Montgomery in the middle of the night when all passengers had to get off with their luggage so it could be cleaned, and cleaned it was—spick-and-span! Arrival in Jackson was early the next morning, where I had to change to another bus. I took advantage of the time interval to have breakfast, after which I took a shower in the barber shop. That was about the nicest thing I had ever run across—a place to refresh oneself while traveling. The last leg of the journey went by Vicksburg and then to Greenville, where we arrived about lunchtime. Jan and Virginia were waiting and took me to their apartment, now in a run-down section of town but still very nice in those days.

Jan was manager of the camera department at Sears Roebuck, a job which he pursued with a great deal of enthusiasm. For me to be allowed to enter the country as a resident alien, I had to have a sponsor and he and his wife had taken this responsibility upon themselves. Immigration laws were not taken lightly in those days, as a matter of fact, very few people scoffed at any law. The Immigration and Naturalization Service kept tabs on noncitizens, who were duly impressed by the power of that agency.

After looking around a couple of days, my sponsors decided that it was time for me to go to work, and my hostess and I went over existing job possibilities. She did some calling and was able to arrange an appointment with an old friend who operated an aluminum awning business. The interview went quite well, so well in fact that the man hired me on the spot at fifty dollars per week plus commission to sell his awnings. He promised to furnish me with a new pickup truck, and I was to be trained for a week by a couple of his star salesmen. Both were war veterans, and the one I remember best had been a navy commander. He certainly acted like one and treated me like a little boy. The first thing he taught me was to get rid of what he deemed to be an irritating European habit of slightly bowing when shaking hands with people when being introduced.

"At least you don't click your heels," he said by way of encouragement. He also gave me some speech training, which I appreciated very much because, quite often people seemed to be puzzled by what I was saying (often they still are to this day, at least in the South), although they nodded in friendly fashion as if they understood every bit of it.

The news of my fabulous compensation obviously upset my sponsors who were existing on thirty-five dollars a week, and I decided to be generous with my contribution to the household. After all, there I was in America, had landed a job by just walking in and having a friendly chat with somebody, and on top of all that, I made the front page of the *Delta Democrat-Times*, which sent out a reporter to do a story on the new stranger in their midst. I proudly sent a clipping back to Holland and received a sarcastic comment by way of reply. They were probably just envious.

After a week of so-called "training," they turned me loose in that brand new pickup truck which had several samples of awnings mounted behind the cab. It was less than two weeks since I arrived in this giant of a country, and there I was, trying to sell strangers something they could perfectly well do without. Talk about a plunge! But I had no trouble selling whatever I had for sale, although I had a hard time catching on how to measure Venetian blinds, mainly because they were strange contraptions to me (I sold those, too). The people in the shop making them had problems figuring out the first few orders I submitted, and the boss had to come out to help me. That proved to be a lucky break and I learned more in two hours than I did in a week.

"See that thing out there?" he said as we were cruising down the highway in his Buick Roadmaster. "Let's go and sell them an awning." When we got to the place I couldn't quite see where he was going to put one, but that didn't deter him in the least. The sole occupant was an elderly black woman, and in less than fifteen minutes she had bought an awning costing several hundred dollars to be installed across the front porch. In the process of measuring the job, I became concerned how the dilapidated structure could possibly support anything, but the boss said, "No problem; the men will prop up the whole thing if necessary." The sale survived all credit checks and I looked at the job many times afterwards as I happened to pass by.

Having never had any personal contact with a black American, it was hard to get used to the fact that they lacked having a language of their own. At the same time, a black field hand in the Mississippi Delta was not likely to have encountered a strange animal like me. Nonetheless, I did have some interesting conversations, like the one I had with a black woman who was carrying around a beautiful white cat. When I asked her what its name was, she shyly replied, "Pickaninny."

The weather in the spring of 1950 was in a cooperative mood, and I spent much time simply riding around taking in the scenery. The cotton was just beginning to come up, and I was amazed at the large number of hands it took to weed the fields, or to "chop" cotton, as it was called. Shortly, I was to become intimately involved with agricultural enterprise when I was offered a job as bookkeeper in a tractor dealership. Not that I wasn't successful in selling awnings: on the contrary, I made my first month's quota in less than three weeks and had begun earning a commission on anything sold in excess of that. But I had spent much time preparing myself in the field of accounting, and the opportunity at the tractor dealership seemed too good to turn down.

LELAND, MISSISSIPPI

The company I went to work for was located in Leland, about ten miles east of Greenville. It was owned by a courtly gentleman who also was in the insurance business. After the war, the government encouraged the hiring of veterans by partly subsidizing their pay. Officially this was considered indemnity for the cost of their training, but everyone knew better and, by the time I came to work, quite a bit of criticism was beginning to be heard about the system. It cost an employer very little out of his pocket to hire, say, a mechanic or a parts man. In the case at hand, the first was an ex-Marine Seabee, while the second was an ex-fighter pilot. Working hours were from 7:00 a.m. until 6:00 p.m. six days a week, and after a full year's work one was eligible for a week's paid vacation.

Shortly after accepting the job, I began making my home with a middle-aged lady who lived alone in a large modern house on locally famous Deer Creek Drive. She had two daughters by different marriages and was on good terms with both. The daughters, on the other hand, didn't seem overly fond of one another. I had a luxurious room with a private bath in one wing of the house, and all meals were furnished. A maid and a cook looked after us, and the only problem was that dinner each night was always the same salad, steak and potatoes. It didn't seem to bother my hostess that I came home well after 6:00 each evening; in fact, she probably liked it because it gave her a chance to down that much more liquor. When I did get in, she usually was pretty well saturated and would be sitting in a rocking chair on the huge back porch futilely imploring me to join her for refreshments. She was old enough to be my mother and any designs she may have had were a waste of time on her part. She did try to pair me with a friend of the family who didn't appeal to me in the least.

Dinner never lasted more than half an hour, and the evenings were long enough to get into trouble if one were so inclined. The lady owned the latest model Buick Roadmaster, and she discovered that I loved to drive the thing, my own car being a modest 1937 Plymouth, which had been driven untold miles and on which the front wheels stood canted at almost a forty-five degree angle. And so then, each night for about a couple of months, I drove the car all over Washington County and surrounding areas, on paved as well as dirt roads, while she sat with one leg seductively drawn up, drink in one hand and one arm slung over the back of the front seat, offering juicy gossip about the local gentry.

The youngest daughter was with her husband who was attending school in Memphis learning to be a cotton buyer, a lucrative occupation in that part of the country. They would return home every weekend, and that was also the time that my landlady threw wild parties. Although Mississippi was a dry state, liquor was abundantly available and was delivered to the door by a bootlegger. While I declined to join in these affairs, I was nevertheless an involuntary participant inasmuch as guests, both men and women, would urgently beat on my door to be admitted to use the bathroom. It was explained to me that habits were hard to break. Well, perhaps they were, but it soon became evident that my presence was the subject of much discussion. There was a Pekingese dog named Toy in the house, and he liked to keep me company. While several us were playing croquet in the backyard one afternoon, the dog walked up to the son, raised his leg, and generously wet his immaculate white trousers. A merry chase ensued, first around furniture on the back porch, before moving indoors where it wound up with the dog crawling under my bed. That was the day that I found out that the son and daughter considered me to be nothing more than a freeloader. They unfortunately got me mixed up with my brother Jan who occasionally came by to join my landlady in a drinking binge. Anyhow, one night I ran into him in the local drug store where he called me aside to tell me that I would do well to cease my nightly forays into the country behind the wheel of a large Buick because he had even heard gossip about the matter in neighboring Greenville. Although entirely innocent, this deeply disturbed me, and I proceeded at once to cast about for alternative living quarters which appeared to be hard to come by initially.

On the whole, I found that my stay of about four months had been informative; it certainly gave me some insight into the social aspects of a planter's life, which was, and for all I know remains, distinct from that of other Mississippi residents. It is Memphis oriented rather than Jackson, a place which was regarded somewhat contemptuously. Money to operate plantations was borrowed in Memphis, entertainment was sought at the Peabody Hotel, people went to Memphis for medical treatment of any consequence; indeed, it seems doubtful that the fair city would be what it is today without the Mississippi Delta.

My state of euphoria of being in the United States continued unabated, and I was enjoying my work immensely. I had never had any experience in practical accounting other than the few elementary books I had kept on board a ship, and all that I had learned in my correspondence course was coming to life. The accounting system of a Ford tractor dealership was, even in those days, completely standardized, yet plenty of room remained for innovation. Then, too, I was more or less a jack of all trades, filling in one minute for the parts man, showing equipment the next, and so on. There were still shortages of new tractors, and we were selling all we could get. The owner saw to it that a plentiful supply of parts was kept on hand, and we soon found out why he was so insistent about it: he planned to assemble his own tractors for sale at a hugely inflated price. Such was strictly contrary to the distributor's rules, and we managed to put only about two or three in the field before they put a stop to it. He more than likely almost lost his dealership, but we had fun "manufacturing tractors," as we proudly called our activities.

Through a lucky break, the finding of new living quarters turned out to be easier than expected. A friend of Virginia's mother ran an old-fashioned boarding house where schoolteachers could find a safe haven, and I was offered to take the place of one of the boarders, the only male, who was getting married. Somehow schoolteachers have always intimidated me, and I was leery at first of moving in with them, but I decided to take a chance. Four nice-looking, young teachers were in the house, and in less than a year I was married to the prettiest one of them all.

Operating a boarding house used to be a respectable way of making a living and most of them have vanished over the years. The lady of the house ran a tight ship. Her husband sold sewing machines and helped her with the usual household tasks. An old black cook lived on the premises behind the main house but might as well have been one of the family because she was loved and respected by everyone. Besides the owners, there were a son and his wife and child, as well as an old, retired couple. Counting everyone, including myself, there were thirteen members in the household, which resembled one straight out of a Norman Rockwell painting. Board included breakfast and dinner Monday through Friday, nothing on Saturday, and midday dinner on Sunday. The morning meal was served à la carte in the breakfast room on a first-come, first-served basis. Dinner was at 6:30 in the evening and was quite formal, with the men wearing coat and tie. It would last an hour or longer, during which the affairs of the day were leisurely discussed. The house was a five-minute ride from where I worked, and I showered and dressed in record time so as not to keep anyone waiting. After dinner, it was time to play canasta in the quarters of the old retirees. It was the only time I ever played cards in my life, and, to be truthful, I saw it as an appropriate opportunity to pursue my wife-to-be.

There wasn't much going on anywhere after dark in those days. We had a movie house to go to, and there was an open-air theater on the outskirts of town, but it had so many mosquitoes that they had to rig up fans as big as airplane propellers to keep them at bay. In Greenville, ten miles to the west, things weren't much better, except that there were more shops, and there was the levee where one could observe activities going on in the harbor. The most popular hangout in Leland was Sam's Café on the highway. Coffee was served at a nickel a cup, and a penny tip brought a polite thank you.

Saturday night in a Mississippi Delta town was a joyful event for the black community. In Leland, the stores would remain open until 10:00, when the fire-alarm sounded as a signal to close up shop, but people would continue to linger in the street for a long time afterwards. If one wished to do more exciting things, there was a large dance hall halfway between Leland and Greenville, and there were several honky-tonks in the area where they ran a jukebox. Customers brought their own liquor wrapped in a brown paper bag. It was kept under the table just in case the sheriff's personnel raided the place. Notwithstanding the dearth of entertainment, people seemed happy enough while living conditions, at least as I experienced them, were splendid by any standard. Why so much scorn continues to be heaped on the 1950s era remains a mystery to me.

LOVE AND MARRIAGE

Fifteen months after arriving in the United States, I married that pretty schoolteacher and we spent our honeymoon in the Great Smoky Mountains. We managed to do it all—gasoline, food, lodging and souvenirs—for less than one hundred dollars and stayed gone a week. I had bought a late model secondhand car for the occasion, a 1949 Frazer, which was the luxury version of the Kaiser automobile produced by Henry Kaiser of shipbuilding fame during the war. It had previously belonged to a dentist and was about as well equipped as any car could be in those days; it had a long wheelbase and could be driven at high speed with little discomfort. There were no interstate highways, but traffic was a fraction of what it soon would be and we blissfully sailed along at eighty miles an hour whenever conditions permitted. We returned to the same general area from time to time and have watched Gatlinburg grow from a quiet village to a roaring tourist resort. Cherokee, on the other side of Newfound Gap, lagged for a long time but has done better in recent years. Upon returning home, we moved into an apartment, couldn't hack it, and begged our former landlady to let us return. She graciously consented and we were able to settle into a comfortable routine.

The tractor dealership was bought out by a Ford Motor Company block man with the support of a local financier, and work became more fun than ever. A block man was the territorial representative of the manufacturer and, in this case, happened to be a well-known former sports figure named Gus who had played football at Southwestern University in Memphis. He was a gregarious individual, intelligent, and utterly reckless in whatever he undertook, but he lacked business acumen and soon became prey for unscrupulous operators of all sorts.

Gus was soon taught to fly an airplane and soloed in a Piper Cup in no time at all, after which he announced that it was my turn to learn to fly and he would show me how. The first time out, we flew from Leland to Greenville where he made a perfectly smooth landing, handed over the controls and told me to take it into the air again. I swallowed hard and did as told but not without a good deal of yawing. Once airborne, I managed to do better, and Gus told me that I tried too hard on takeoff. He told me to fly around and line the plane up with the runway after which he took over to make another perfectly smooth landing. My next attempt was better, and we headed for the Mississippi River, where Gus promptly spotted the boat of one of his fishing buddies and took over the controls to take a closer look. Directly, we were circling a couple of hundred feet over the craft and Gus actually let down the window as he throttled back so he could hail his friends who responded enthusiastically. The Leland airport consisted of a grass strip, and I was invited to try my first landing. I didn't make it because I became too preoccupied with maintaining direction and almost caused the plane to stall. My instructor promptly took over, nosed down to gain speed and then pulled up just in time to go around and make another perfect landing. The man was a born aviator and later became pilot for an agricultural chemical firm. It was the last time I went up in a small plane because the man who had recently sold me an insurance policy heard about my adventure and cautioned me to refrain from flying in any aircraft other than one operated by a scheduled airline or by the military. I was forced to heed his advice but regretted ever afterwards doing so.

Gus was a unique individual in many more ways. He readily trusted everyone who worked for him and when things went wrong, as they often did, he shrugged his shoulders and bore no grudge. He was quick to praise and often was overly generous rewarding someone. One Saturday afternoon, an old black man accompanied by a little boy wandered into the office and asked to be shown some equipment. The one salesman on duty ignored him and continued to carry on a conversation with the parts man. I took him to see some used tractors but that was not what he wanted; he wished to see new equipment. Very well, so I showed him a new tractor, started it and showed him its features, but all he seemed interested in was how much one, plus two or three pieces of standard equipment would cost. I took him into the office and wrote down the particulars, but he was illiterate and was interested only in the total, which came to over three thousand dollars. He then wished to know if all the equipment could be delivered that afternoon. The delivery man had been given the rest of the day off and the shop would be closing down in a little over two hours. There were no volunteers, so I decided to do it myself and got the directions to his house. He told me that he would pay me upon delivery, and I loaded everything up to the accompaniment of much derision on the part of my coworkers.

The man didn't live too far out of town and the minute I saw his farm I began to wonder if I should just turn around and drive back but decided to go ahead and unload everything where he wanted it. When I handed him the invoice and the key to the tractor, he pulled out a wad of money and counted out thirty or more one hundred dollar bills into my open hand. Overjoyed, I raced back to the shop where the boss had just returned after playing golf. It was almost closing time and I sensed that he was highly irritated by my stupid venture. I asked him to sit down and began counting the hundred dollar bills which I placed in front of him on his desk. He took the last one, handed it back to me, said "This is yours," whereupon he got up and walked out the door.

The dealership's staff was actually quite small, and we had to be flexible to keep operations running smoothly. Had the monetary rewards matched our time and efforts, I probably would have been tempted to make a career out of it because the variety of the work, as well as the camaraderie, was most enjoyable. The boss was gone most of the time while either flying airplanes or cultivating prospective customers on the golf course. The problem was that our kind of customers didn't play golf whereas those who did were plantation owners who were generally interested in much larger equipment. Ultimately, this sales strategy, if that was what it could be called, caused the firm's demise, but not before a couple of exciting years had gone by which were probably the happiest ones of my life.

The world had recently reverted to its normal state of hostilities, and diplomacy by other means in Korea had exacted its toll to the extent that a pilot training facility needed to be reopened just outside of Greenville. The announcement caused enormous joy in the community, and one could see the dollar signs glittering in everyone's eyes, including those of my brother Jan. He and his wife took off on a lightning journey late one evening to Scott Air Force Base in St. Louis to apply for a flight instructor's job, and they returned full of expectations. Not long afterwards, they hosted a party for several people with similar aspirations. The guest of honor was some colonel who was closely connected with the enterprise. Much kowtowing took place that evening and most, if not all, were later successful in landing a job with the aviation company to whom the contract to train pilots was awarded. The company was located in Oklahoma and obviously paid well, judging by the abrupt jump in my brother's standard of living, which included the purchase of a new car. It seemed that relief came just in time because he had been desperately looking for ways to improve his lot. Some of the proposed ventures he considered were decidedly questionable, and I spent much time talking him out of first of one then another. Flying was in his blood, but not long after he had started his new job, he failed to notice that a student pilot had not lowered his landing gear and the pair came in for a belly landing. That was the end of flying, and Jan was fortunate to be given a job as academic instructor, a consolation prize which apparently destroyed his self-esteem.

It wasn't long before things locally (the infrastructure, in today's jargon) began showing signs of stress, and housing began to be in short supply. Then, just as suddenly as the initial flying school had been announced, the news broke that it was going to be replaced by a much larger operation run exclusively by the US Air Force. The civilian flying school was to be moved to Florida, and things in Greenville really began jumping.

AND SOON THERE WERE FOUR OF US

Shortly after the doctor announced that we were to become parents, we moved into a small house for which we had to pay an exorbitant amount of rent; however, it was furnished, no matter how poorly.

It was 1952, and we inevitably got caught up in the excitement of a presidential election. Everybody seemed to be for General Eisenhower, but Adlai Stevenson was more to our liking. Both of us often think back to this period with fondness since we led a secure and unfettered existence. As it must be wherever crops are raised, the weather was a constant topic of conversation, particularly because our livelihood depended on it. Tornadoes seemed to be a weekly occurrence that year, but we had not reached the state of madness of a NOAA radio show which compels us to remain glued to one of those devilish little one-station receivers to let a panting and often unintelligible announcer pump up our adrenaline. A storm did roar down our street one Sunday afternoon, scaring us half to death, but it must have lifted at the last moment, leaving nothing more than a huge cloud of dust. An unusual phenomenon which, according to the local people, occurs every so often was when hordes of crickets descended on the area. It was said that heavy rains following a drought up north flushed them out of cracks in the ground and sent them swarming like locusts. As we stepped outdoors in the morning, we crunched our way to the car while downtown the creatures would be piled up against doors almost a foot deep. They had to be removed with a rake and shovel and the resulting huge mounds of them created a horrible stench as they slowly rotted away.

Immediately next door to the tractor place was the town's only funeral parlor for whites, and the young undertaker who worked alone would occasionally call on us in emergencies. As I parked my car coming to work one morning, I saw him frantically motioning for me to come over and, when I got there, he asked me if I would please come with him. One of Mississippi's oldest paved roads runs seventeen miles along meandering Deer Creek between Leland and Hollandale. Long since replaced by a straight stretch of macadam further east, it was a murderous and narrow concrete road full of curves which regularly took its toll in human lives. That morning somebody had fallen off a scaffold while repairing a machine in a cotton gin and had fallen on his head. They called Billy (the undertaker) to take him to the hospital in Greenville and we went careening down the road at terrifying speed in a five-ton combination hearse/ambulance. Billy managed to turn the thing upside down not long afterwards while responding to another call but escaped serious injury. When we arrived at the gin, we found a badly injured fellow bleeding profusely from the base of his skull and screaming bloody murder. He was placed on a stretcher (no first aid in those days) and loaded him into the ambulance, where I was asked to take a seat next to him to keep him quiet. Had I had time to contemplate the situation I might have complied, but it was my first trip, and I froze at the sight of all that blood spurting out of the man's neck with every heartbeat. I meekly offered to drive, but that was out of the question, of course. Someone volunteered to ride with us, and we took off with a wailing siren. We had to retrace our route all the way to Leland before turning west to Greenville, quite some distance. Not far from the hospital in Greenville, a driver ignored our siren and emergency lights and continued backing his car out of a roadside restaurant parking place. He got clipped and his vehicle was knocked some twenty feet down the road across the sidewalk. The amazing thing was that we didn't even feel the impact. An elevator took us from the hospital emergency room to the floor where the operating rooms were located. Surgeons were winding up an operation and one of them came out to ask if we could please shut up our patient's hollering. Apparently they couldn't sedate him because of his head injury, and he was suddenly whisked away through a set of swinging doors, after which we didn't see him for over an hour. When they rolled him out, he was asleep, and his head was swathed in bandages. He had sustained a fractured skull, and we later learned that he was expected to make a full recovery. On other occasions I helped Bill pick up corpses around town, usually people who had died of old age. Contrary to gossip, people's remains were handled deferentially at all times, and Bill became the most popular undertaker in the area.

A frequent visitor at the tractor place was the Presbyterian minister, an affable young man who had befriended the boss and his family, who were members of his congregation. He came by most mornings, and again in the afternoon to join us for a cup of coffee in the hotel's restaurant across the street. Quite often he would have to play father-confessor when the boss had indulged in a tirade and discharged a stream of invectives concerning one thing or another. The worst such outburst occurred once when he was discussing delivery of a shipment of grain storage bins during a telephone conversation with the supplier, who happened to be an old friend and who probably had goaded him into such behavior. The two would carry on in an earthy fashion whenever they got together. He was a huge fellow who possibly weighed close to five hundred pounds and who drove a car which was specially equipped with heavy springs. The back seat had been removed so that the front seat could be pushed back just about even with the rear door enabling our friend to fit behind the steering wheel. On hot summer days he came staggering in, soaking wet with sweat (it was before the days of air-conditioned cars) using a bath towel as a handkerchief. The waitress in the coffee shop despised the man and would contemptuously plunk a gallon pickle jar filled with ice water in front of him so he wouldn't continually bellow for refills. He was perfectly capable of downing two of these in one sitting.

Someone sponsored me for membership in the Lions Club, which I attended faithfully if in a perpetual state of terror for fear of being called upon to make a speech. Once I realized that there were plenty of people like me, I enjoyed just being a "knife and fork member," as they called those who never got up to speak. It was a jolly bunch of people who met for lunch every Thursday in the basement of the Methodist Church. The police always cooperated by arresting a couple of unsuspecting motorists passing through Leland on US Highway 61 and bringing them to the meeting where they were treated to a meal.

The police chief was a shriveled up old man who maintained iron discipline among his force of two officers. City Hall was located practically across the street from the tractor place where, as we were coming out of the movie theater one night, we saw someone tampering with our car. We walked across the side street to ask the officer on duty at the police station to investigate and he came charging out, grabbed the man by his collar and pulled him out of the car. After a brief conversation, he twisted the suspect's arm behind his back and marched him off to jail to spend the night. He had been trying to jump-wire the ignition and broke the lock in the process. We were asked to press charges the next day but declined, and he was ordered to get out of the county before dark.

The town had two doctors, one a real professional type, the other a more relaxed and popular one who maintained a high profile and was present at all high-school football games as the team's physician. He charged two dollars for an office visit and delivered both our children for fifty dollars each at the local hospital. Blue Cross paid for everything without any of those loathsome deductibles or copayments. Insurance meant full coverage in those days. A female relative of the doctor murdered her mother with a pair of garden shears, and he purportedly testified during the trial that he considered her perfectly capable of committing such a crime. These were socially prominent people, and the affair attracted a good deal of notoriety, not to mention the discord it created among friends and relatives who took sides for one reason or another. The woman went to prison, and her husband and two teenage daughters circulated freely in public afterwards, because we saw them just about any time we ate at a popular local restaurant.

Then there was the case involving the son of the town's leading druggist; he had tossed a lighted firecracker into a fireworks stand run by a boy who came from a large and popular family of Italian origin. The stand blew up and grievously injured the boy, leaving him with a horribly disfigured face. He wasn't expected to live, and our doctor testified that he had named the culprit in a deathbed statement. It was presumed that these incidents were the cause of the doctor later moving to his wife's native Texas where he died of a heart attack, reportedly a broken man.

On Sunday afternoons a group of men would gather at a skeet-shooting range not far out of town. Driving out there once, I expected to—and did—find my boss among them, properly attired in fancy sportswear. Spotting us, he took time out to explain what the sport was all about, then thrust a loaded shotgun into my arms to try my luck at it. It so happened that I hit every single one of the clay pigeons which came sailing past on command. It stopped the crowd as I made a relatively rare perfect score twice in succession. Invited back the next Sunday, I hardly hit anything and retreated in disgrace, which was just as well since I could never have afforded to buy a gun, let alone shells.

MAKING PROGRESS

The senior partner of the accounting firm auditing the company's books continued to be highly complimentary about my work and implied that after a little more training, he would offer me a job. He recommended that I continue with my correspondence course and eventually sit for the CPA examination but that I should first try to gain experience by going to work for the government as an agent with the Internal Revenue Service, just as he had done.

Employment with the government required citizenship, something I had been working on since my arrival. Marrying a citizen reduced the qualifying period, and I was soon called in by the Immigration and Naturalization Service for an interview preliminary to appear in Federal court where a judge would confer citizenship, which was usually done on a group of people collectively. In time, all this took place in Clarksdale, some sixty miles north of where we lived.

An advertisement appeared in the newspaper for the position of office manager at the officer's club at the air base. Without really expecting a reply, I submitted an application and was shortly invited to come in for an interview. To my utter surprise, they offered me the job on the spot. My employer wasn't at all impressed with this development, but he accepted my offer to continue working for him if he would hire a secretary to handle the detail work and let me come in after hours to continue keeping the books. An older lady living in town happened to be looking for just such a job and came to work the next day.

The air base was still in the process of being organized, as was the club, which was part of an officers' open mess. This meant that the dining room was operated by air force personnel which served three meals a day. The rest of the building was being refurbished by a local interior decorator at a cost of $35,000, paid for by the members through individual assessments. The only time the place ever looked halfway decent was on official opening day when it was buried in flowers sent by local mercantile well-wishers. As soon as those dried up, much of the club became a dark, windowless dungeon reeking like a pub, except for the large dining room.

I had no trouble adjusting to the clientele, and the work reminded me a great deal of that in a purser's office of a passenger liner. The club officer was a captain who concerned himself mainly with the bar when he wasn't putting in the requisite flying hours to maintain his rank. On one occasion he took me with him on a trip to the Mississippi Gulf Coast in a B-25 bomber to pick up a load of seafood for a party. It was the first time I ever had to strap on a parachute, which was required of anyone flying aboard a bomber or fighter plane, or so I was told. Not long afterwards, the poor man came to work one morning wearing a sergeant's uniform, and he appeared to be in a profound state of shock. They no longer needed him, and he had to give up his reserve officer's commission, so he had enlisted as a noncommissioned officer. He apparently had been pleased with my performance because he arranged to have my responsibilities expanded to cover the NCO club's as well as the cadet club's offices. However, the NCO club turned out to be hazardous duty (I never did get along too well with sergeants) and I was more than happy to give it up.

The new club officer was also a captain, but he was a nonflying officer in charge of the base exchange, popularly known as the PX. It took quite a while before he got it through his thick skull that the officers' club was not a mere adjunct of his PX, but other than that, he did pretty well.

My working hours were from 7:00 in the morning until 4:00 in the afternoon with an hour off for lunch. They occasionally asked me to work at night when there was an especially big event taking place such as stag night combined with a casino operation, and somebody had to look after the money. The first time we had this, things kind of got out of hand and I didn't get home until almost daybreak the next morning. Although there was a large quantity of money on the premises, nothing got the old club officer's attention more than six bags, each containing five hundred silver dollars. The bags were gathered at the top and tied off with a short piece of twisted wire, leaving just enough cloth to be grasped with thumb and forefinger. Anyone who managed to carry a bag in such a fashion for twenty-five feet without stopping was entitled to keep it, but nobody ever succeeded. I had picked up the bags at the bank downtown while being escorted by two military policemen. When the night was over, we discovered that there was no room to store them, so I helped the club officer take them home where they were placed under his bed in which his wife pretended to be asleep.

The base commander was president of the club's board of governors and acted as its plenipotentiary whenever it suited him. As such, he brought in a club manager from somewhere in Florida. He was a German who personified the sleazy *ober*, a breed once prevalent in Europe. His hours were from 4:00 in the afternoon until closing time, which could be anywhere between midnight and daybreak. He turned out to be a thief and would have gotten away with a whole lot, had it not been for the eagle-eyed master sergeant in charge of the open mess. Occasionally, he would work during the day when important guests were entertained for lunch or when the officers' wives would throw a party. Other than that, I would see him only a short time each day as he was coming to work while I was preparing to go home. As a result, I would hear about his antics mostly from third parties. Because of him, we presented a juicy target for the base auditors.

The auditor in charge was a captain who was assisted by a lieutenant and a sergeant. The lieutenant was a certified public accountant—somewhat of a rarity in those days—and gave us no trouble. The sergeant was a fundamentalist type, rather dim-witted and full of suspicions. He easily got bogged down in useless detail, which kept him out of mischief. Captain Jones was a crusader and was at war with every section chief on the base. The poor fellow loved to come in for a drink during happy hour, but nobody would have anything to do with him. He must have dreamed up ways to avenge himself during those lonely sojourns at the bar. During our first semiannual audit, he charged us with about thirty "very serious" accounting discrepancies, none exceeding five dollars (under- or overvaluation of liquor inventory) and many representing differences of a few pennies. We were formally charged with these shortcomings during a meeting in the base commander's office where he only managed to further enrage the base comptroller, one of his bitterest enemies.

Just before Christmas, the board of governors expressed a desire to give all club employees a bonus of fifty dollars but was informed by Captain Jones that such was absolutely contrary to regulations. Word came down from the top to find a way to do it anyhow since, after all, the club was a nonappropriated function and the money came out of the members' own pockets. We wound up diverting part of the jukebox receipts and keeping these in a special container to which a couple of higher-ranking officers each had a key. Captain Jones couldn't wait until the next audit and came barging in the day after Christmas with a full crew. He had somehow found out that we had all received a bonus, and he was going to leave no stone unturned to find out how it was done. Before he finally gave up, I got a severe scolding and was promised that he "would get [me]!"

The officers' club had about six hundred members and continued to expand. Mindful of the distractions, we tried to downplay looks in the hiring of office staff but, despite this, one young lady rekindled a wartime romance with someone from upstate New York. He came flying in as commander of a C-46 cargo plane belonging to the National Guard. He hung around most of the day and was back again the next morning for a tender farewell. The two were engaged in intimate conversation when a telephone call came in for the major, who turned white as a sheet upon hearing whatever message they had for him. He dropped the phone and dashed out the door, leaving us wondering what had happened. Tired of waiting for his commander, the flight engineer had decided to warm up the plane's engines and, in the process, allowed it to jump the chocks. He was last seen running toward the rear exit as it headed for the control tower and, on the way, decapitated a mechanic who was servicing another aircraft. The plane slammed into the control tower where controllers were dealing with another emergency, that of a jet trainer in the air which had experienced a flame-out and was desperately trying to make it back to the field, narrowly missing the top of a water tank before it crash-landed in midfield. An official version of what happened was never released, but we got our information from eyewitnesses. We waited for the lightning bolt to strike our office, but it never came and assumed that it was realized that we were innocent. We never did find out what happened to the major.

Most of the club's activities occurred on Friday and Saturday nights, and we would catch up on the details on Monday. The dining room served as the ballroom, and they had a neat trick of clearing it out at closing time. The recessed ceiling fixtures all had high-wattage bulbs, and starting at midnight, they would commence turning up the rheostat controlling the light intensity a quarter turn at a time. The drunks were the hardest to disperse, but the bright lights would finally drive them away.

Much foolishness went on, not to mention the occasional brawl. We came to work one morning to find the road blocked by a sports car which, on closer inspection, was found to be straddling a big hole left by workmen repairing a waterline. A bunch of hell-raisers had picked up an MG and placed it over the hole, and the motor pool had to send out a crane to move it.

As time went by, the club began to bring in big-name performers for weekend dances. Some of the acts were paid incredible amounts of money and not necessarily because of the number of participants; sometimes just a one-man show would be paid more than a fairly large band. But they were all of a kind, much like the shipboard musicians my old boss the purser used to treat with so much contempt. Accompanied by two females, the leader of one group came by the office upon checking in on a Friday to receive instructions for the night's performance. One question was how far the ladies should go in their striptease routine, and the club officer answered, "As far as you're comfortable with!" It so happened that the father of one of the cadets receiving pilot training was a high-ranking chaplain (someone said that it was the chaplain general of the armed forces), and he and his wife were visiting the base. They were the guests of the base commander that Friday night and witnessed the act put on by the two women. It was said that the incident caused the removal of the base commander; if it did, they went to a great deal of trouble to achieve it. A group representing the inspector general came flying in unexpectedly one day to give the base a thorough once-over. The team's report must have been of massive proportions, judging by the section relating to the club, which dealt primarily with the bachelor officers' quarters, or BOQ for short. Like all correspondence, the report had a response date, which became the main topic of conversation, and we managed to collect bits of information concerning the overall efficiency of the base. It wasn't very high.

Before the commander was replaced (to go to war college), the base made a splendid impression on Armed Forces Day. Late in the afternoon, several senior officers decided to have some fun taking turns flying an F-86 Sabre jet with which they would make a low-level approach at 600 miles per hour to come thundering over the runway. Few people had ever seen a flying machine crash the sound barrier.

The new base commander had just finished a stint in Korea, and our German club manager immediately managed to displease him. "Who the hell was that clown jumping around us?" he wanted to know after the first dinner party. When told that the man was under investigation, he expressed the hope that we would soon be rid of him. He didn't have to wait long, for positive proof became available that he was stealing liquor and he was sent on his way as fast as he was hired. He later sent us a Christmas card from California where he had landed a cushy job in some country club.

Chapter 6

Home as a Pariah, 1955–1985

CAREER

The year 1954 brought upheavals in southern public-school systems which were mystifying to a newcomer in America. Most of the population in the Mississippi Delta was black, and the reaction of the whites to the Supreme Court decision in *Brown v. Board of Education* was one of profound shock. A speech by the superintendent of schools before the Lions Club, along with the defiance shown by the audience, was most disturbing. Then one evening not long afterwards, the high school went up in flames, bringing chaos to the school system. Even though we had two small children, Ruth had been pressured to resume teaching, and we were left to the mercies of a haphazard system of childcare provided first by one lackadaisical maid, then another.

Things were not going well at the tractor place, where they were financially strapped. The silent partner and source of wealth had died unexpectedly, and his surviving son and only heir didn't get along with the spendthrift manager. A buyer was found on the other side of the Mississippi River, and our free and easy times came to an end. One black mechanic, the lady bookkeeper, and I wound up as the sole survivors of the previous manpower pool as the new owner brought along his own staff from Arkansas, where he already owned a similar dealership. He was an illiterate former mule dealer who did most of the selling and who had to rely on his employees (some of whom were not much better off) to write things down. He was a phlegmatic sort, a slave driver who constantly complained that I was being paid far too much for what little I did. All things considered, I thought the time had come to move on, and I decided to follow the advice of the accountant in Greenville to apply for a job with the Internal Revenue Service.

One had to pass both a written and oral examination before being placed on the civil service register of qualified applicants. I was the sole applicant for the written test which lasted a full day and which I barely passed. The oral part lasted about an hour and was administered several weeks later by a panel of three IRS division chiefs in Jackson, Mississippi. What began as a polite exchange quickly turned into a heated discussion which abruptly ended when I was curtly informed that they would let me know if I was needed. As one of the panel members escorted me to the building entrance, he explained that they always tried to provoke an adversarial atmosphere to see if a candidate would stand his ground and that I had done quite nicely. And so I must have, because a notice came by mail a few days later that my name had been placed on the Atlanta register and to be prepared for an interview in any of the localities for which I had expressed an interest. It was early January 1955, and Ruth reminded me that she had a teaching contract; hence, I notified them that I would not be available until the end of the school year.

When this bit of excitement was over, we quickly returned to a normal routine and in time more or less forgot the episode. The base auditor called me one day and invited me to come and have a cup of coffee with him, which made me wonder what he was up to. He more than likely had been contacted as a character reference because he confided that he had been a revenue agent himself and just wanted to give me some free advice, which was not to even consider doing the same thing if I valued retaining my sanity. He said that his whole family had been subjected to harassment and finally could stand it no longer. In due course, I came to wonder if I should have heeded his advice.

The call to duty came via telegram shortly after school shut down for the summer recess. Would I accept a position as IRS agent in Goldsboro, North Carolina, and, if so, please advise if I would be available within ten days? In making up our mind, we tried to learn as much as we could about North Carolina by consulting our recently acquired encyclopedia (nobody we knew had ever been to Goldsboro) and found the decision to be a tough one to make, particularly since family income would just about be cut in half. Without any interview, I would furthermore not get a chance to look the place over but, in the end, we concluded that entering any career would probably require making some sacrifice, and I wired them my acceptance.

The first, and ultimately the last thing one learns during a government career—even one lasting thirty or more years—is that one is treated with some degree of consideration only during the time span between those two points and that at any other time one is devoid of status, unless one carries enough clout to make them sit up and take notice. Accordingly, I was summarily ordered to the Greensboro district office to be sworn in and was given precisely three days to get all my personal affairs in order.

My three employers were understanding enough and wished me luck. My landlady, on the other hand, could have killed me, but my biggest problem turned out to be passing a required physical exam administered by the only other doctor in Leland (of course, it had to be him) who was concerned about a persistent elevation in body temperature of half a degree. Returning practically every hour while holding a piece of ice in my mouth was of no help other than making it hurt. Two hours before my plane was to leave, the good doctor finally took pity on me and gave me a clean bill of health, stressing that he was doing so against his better judgment.

It was the first time I had to leave behind some people who were very dear to me, and it put me in a reflective mood, particularly in view of the two small children who couldn't grasp what was going on. The old DC-3s were still flying, and the girls seemed fascinated by them. It was late afternoon after we took off, and I was not to arrive in Greensboro until 10:00 the next morning after a three-hour layover in Jackson, one of four hours in Atlanta and, finally, an hour in Charlotte. Still alive, but limp, they swore me in immediately upon reaching the office, after which smiles and friendliness awaited me in whatever United States government office I visited during the next twenty-five years. Demolition of the civil service did not begin until 1980 and by the time I retired in 1985, nobody was smiling.

The man who was to be my group supervisor happened to be in the district office, and he took me to what was to be my post of duty by way of Raleigh, where his office was located and where I spent the night. He picked me up the next day, and we drove to Goldsboro, where I was introduced to the people in the office. Obviously far more prosperous than Mississippi, the state of North Carolina looked inviting in all respects. I discovered that I had lost all perspective of distance when planning a quick trip back in order to pick up my car and personal belongings. It happened to be Friday before the Independence Day weekend and traveling by train or by bus would have required about thirty-six hours. Since they expected me to be at work the following Tuesday, the only way to return was by air, which further depleted our meager cash reserve.

Looking out the window of my room at the Hotel Goldsboro, an old-fashioned, eight-story building in the center of town, I surveyed the scene at dawn of the first day of work and wondered how it all would turn out. The IRS had recently undergone a reorganization following the disclosure of scandals toward the end of the Truman administration, and my on-the-job instructor had only been an agent for little over a year. He was an exceptionally smart individual, a Duke University graduate as well as a certified public accountant. He, unfortunately, turned out to have prosecutorial tendencies and ruthlessly pursued his tasks, which, in time, caused problems for the Service and they had to dismiss him, but I benefited enormously from our association while it lasted. His attention happened to be focused on funeral parlors when I joined him for training, and we examined the returns of two of them before moving on to something else.

Before the reorganization, the Service was known as the Bureau of Internal Revenue and a great deal of effort was underway to change its image which, while seemingly appropriate, probably hurt it in the long run. People obviously respected it, and many even feared it, which was totally unnecessary. Thirty years later, it was the laughingstock of the wealthy and utterly despised by the general public.

My job was to review an assigned return, contact the taxpayer, and ask if I could come out to examine the material on which the information submitted was based. Usually, I was invited to come out right away. Only the more complex returns were sent out to the field while a far larger number were examined by office auditors through correspondence. Being a junior agent, the returns entrusted to me were those of small businesses, which included service stations, country stores, farmers, and furniture and appliance stores, to name just a few.

With a rapidly beating heart and a churning stomach, I ventured forth on my first visit to examine a furniture store. The owners were nice (most people usually were) and agreed that a couple of mistakes they had made should be corrected, resulting in additional tax. Every time we solicited an agreement—known as a form 870—we were required to explain that it was a consent by means of which a taxpayer waived the legal restrictions on the assessment of tax allowing him or her to appeal an agent's recommendations. The procedure is an extension of the voluntary system of taxation under which a tax can only be collected when a taxpayer agrees to pay the amount, just as he does when he files his return or after due process of law.

That first visit was the hardest, although one never quite gets over a certain uneasiness when approaching a person who is not particularly happy to see you. In time I found out that some agents with years of experience simply were unable to tell a person forthrightly that he owed additional tax. Toward the end of my career, I accompanied my immediate superior on a mission to inform the representatives of a large organization that they were about to be assessed a fifty-percent fraud penalty on an already substantial liability. We had been sitting all morning and part of the afternoon, in the opulent quarters of a Wall Street law firm, listening to my boss skirting the subject in a most embarrassing fashion, when a secretary interrupted the meeting to tell one of the attorneys that a client demanded to speak to him on the telephone. My boss badly needed to go to the men's room, which gave the company's attorney a chance to ask me if it really was the intention of the Service to apply the fraud penalty. When told that of course it was so intended, the meeting was for all practical purposes over, to the great relief of my boss who normally was not at a loss for words. He just could not look a person in the eye and give him unwelcome news.

My main concern that first month on the job was to find suitable living quarters, and I was able to rent a house close to a park which had tennis courts and all kinds of attractions for small children. It was unfurnished, and what little furniture we possessed had been temporarily dumped as a partial load by the moving company somewhere in the vicinity of Oak Ridge, Tennessee. It took almost a month before they were able to provide a firm delivery date, and, with that finally in hand, the family flew up to Raleigh. We came home from the airport to an empty house, but, miraculously, a moving van pulled up just before dark with our belongings. Nobody had told me that the driver would only accept cash, which a kindly old druggist in the neighborhood provided even though he had never seen me before. Needless to say, we were his faithful customers for as long as we lived in Goldsboro.

The year before I arrived on the scene, the area was visited by Hurricane Hazel, which, after moving inland at Wilmington, had passed just west of town, where damage was still very much in evidence. By the time I had barely gotten my feet wet, tax returns were coming in by the bushel for examination of large deductions on account of damage (real or imagined) sustained by taxpayers' property. It promptly got me into difficulties with several pillars of the community, which alarmed my supervisor in Raleigh. One case involved damage to all sides of a recently built, ranch-style house, which sat squat on a slab foundation, not all too common in the area, at least not in those days. All manner of cracks varying in size from hairline to half an inch were plainly visible, and the owner had deducted the difference in market value of his home before and after the storm. When I told him that it didn't look like storm damage to me but more like the result of a settling foundation, he became violent and had to be restrained by his wife, who advised me to leave. One of our engineers/agents came out to the field to look things over and agreed with me but suggested that we allow a token deduction to get rid of the matter.

Agents were chiefly judged by their ability to settle cases, but the reviewing process was very strict, and if there was even the slightest indication that an examination had been slipshod, the file was returned with a reviewer's memorandum, which was probably the worst demerit one could earn. Proving that the memorandum was unwarranted was well-nigh impossible because reviewers knew their business. Contrary to what the public was led to believe, we did have quotas, but they were generally reasonable and were resented only by marginal employees.

There were three agents and two collection officers in our post of duty. Essentially bill collectors, collection had the meanest job because they were the ones who stuck their hands in people's pockets, so to speak. In time, their jobs were to become increasingly dangerous.

The first six months were particularly rough on family finances. What little savings we had were rapidly dissipated, and poverty was staring us in the face. At Christmas we made a quick trip back to Mississippi, even though the children were ill and the trip took two days driving each way, which didn't help matters. Old records show that we were existing on twenty-three dollars per week after taxes, car payment and rent, and I had begun to wonder whether it was worth it all. A civil servant can be summarily dismissed the first year, while the first three years are referred to as "career conditional," which means that one gains permanent status only after that.

Fourteen months after coming to work, I received the first formal training at district headquarters. It lasted eight weeks, and I had to come home to an empty house on weekends because Ruth and the children were staying with family in Mississippi. Three senior agents instructed us in tax law and regulations, while visiting lecturers presented us with a comprehensive overview of the organization and our place in it. We were graded, and I don't recall any of us falling by the wayside, although the progress of individual class members varied widely over the years, most doing well, others not quite so well. We learned that special agents were fraud investigators and that they were the elite members of the Service, even though their grade structure lagged behind that of regular agents for many years. Also highly regarded were those agents who regularly referred cases for consideration by the special agents for possible criminal investigation.

Our bosses were generally respected if not admired. A few were truly outstanding individuals who would soon disappear from the scene due to retirement. Many of these people had been victims of the Great Depression and had been lucky to find employment with the Federal Government. I was fortunate to have had some of them as mentors on occasion.

The family returned by train at the conclusion of school, and they were treated to a spectacular show by Mother Nature, who had put on her coat of fall colors in the Carolinas. Trains were still running on time without derailing and noticeable among the rolling stock—at least to one who only recently had arrived in America—was the post office car on which mail was sorted after it was picked up on the way. Overnight delivery of a letter east of the Mississippi River was taken for granted and the cost was a mere three cents. While mail in the developed countries of the world was dependable, none matched that of the United States where the post office seemed to be a sacred institution. That it was eventually to be turned into a high-priced trash delivery system would have been unthinkable. So, too, would have been the tampering with mail or, worse, the actual confiscation of a personal letter with the excuse that a sorting machine had been the culprit. Some thirty years later, a letter I had written to my sister in Holland came back without an envelope in a little plastic bag supposedly due to such an accident. Postal inspectors were not even interested.

We returned to our regular duty with new confidence and were amazed by the results of our training. The variety of cases was immense and the organization we worked for never ran smoother.

The State of North Carolina comprises the Mountains, Piedmont, and the Coastal Plain. Of the three sections, we eventually found the last to be the most agreeable, although not necessarily the most progressive. War soon caught up with us once more as the Seymour-Johnson Air Force Base was being reactivated and quickly developed into one of the largest such facilities on the continent. It wound up housing a strategic wing of B-52 bombers, a fighter wing, and a "suitcase air force," so named because it could be rapidly deployed to any place in the world with a complete staff, led by a general, to assume command of units brought in from other areas. The B-52s routinely carried nuclear bombs, and one of them crashed during a rainstorm about ten miles north of Goldsboro while attempting to reach its base. This particular aircraft carried two bombs and only one was found in the rubble at the crash site, which was roped off for many weeks while they dug around with heavy equipment in search of the other one. Only the last of the five safety devices controlling the detonating mechanism had prevented it from blowing all those in the area into oblivion. As far as the missing bomb was concerned, it was theorized that its sheer mass had caused it to travel underground through mud, and it was never located. A book based on the incident was later published, but I never took the time to read it. However, some twenty years later, I had the pleasure of working with an agent who was a B-52 pilot at the time, and he provided the foregoing information which no one had ever heard before. Several persons we had known were either dying, or had died, from one form of cancer or another, which caused us to wonder whether the missing bomb might have affected the local water or food supply.

The opening of the base had little or no effect on our workload in audit. Most of the cases which did come in had to do with delinquent taxes owed by persons moving all over the place and who had managed to stay out of range of collection officers. One such case involved a captain who was paying alimony and child support to two former wives and who had married for a third time. Having personally experienced a bout of virtual poverty, I could only shake my head over the poor fellow's predicament.

Occasionally we would hear of peculiar military logistics like the arrival of a technical sergeant who came from the west coast. Aside from the considerable expense of transporting household goods across the continent, they had to consolidate two Capehart housing units in order to accommodate his large family. The man who he replaced was transferred to California.

The smaller the town, the closer we were watched by the inhabitants. Without always being aware of the fact, we were easily identified as *revenooers* the moment we ventured down main street, and the alarm would be sounded by telephone, as some of our citizen friends would later confide. There was even a case of suicide by a prominent businessman who had an office down the street from us and who apparently decided that one of our collectors was getting too close for comfort during a door-to-door canvass relating to employment tax returns. I recall examining the return of a successful businessman who happened to be a big-time gambler as well. He had a bad reputation with the FBI and, having heard that we were on the scene, one of their men paid us a visit to find out what was going on. While both of us knew full well that neither side could disclose anything, we wound up playing a friendly cat and mouse game. One morning I found the same person sitting bleary-eyed and unshaven in his car parked on main street and apparently startled him by asking, "Good Lord; is this a stake-out?"

"Shhh," he muttered, "keep going, I'll tell you about it," which, of course, he never did.

Anyhow, about our gambler, we hit him pretty hard in the pocketbook, and he listened stony-faced as I explained how much he owed. After leaving the usual agreement form for him and his wife to sign, I walked down a long hall to the front door and was about to open it when he yelled: “Hey, wait a minute, dammit!” Uh oh, I thought, here it comes, but it turned out that he only wanted to complain about the fact that we proposed to disallow all expenses associated with the operation of his wife’s Cadillac, a mere pittance when compared to the overall amount of the tax deficiency.

Not long after the agent who had been my on-the-job instructor was transferred, two fresh college graduates arrived on the scene. A promotion for me came about the same time and things began to look up. One of the new agents was to be trained by me while the other came under the tutelage of someone in the Raleigh office. Both newcomers either had, or were expecting, children, and our families got along very nicely with one another. Contrary to the popular belief, we worked hard and with a great deal of enthusiasm. Practically every Saturday morning one or more of us could be found in the office working on a case, sometimes for a full eight hours and often on Sundays as well. Overtime was not allowed and actually never even occurred to us.

District Directors were political appointees, and I don’t recall any employee dissatisfaction with the system. The one in charge when I joined the organization was replaced about three years later by a career man who happened to have political connections. He was a distinguished-looking gentleman with very formal manners who had the habit of making inspections by arriving unannounced at opening time in the morning. He need not have been concerned about us because we were either in the office or had already signed out for the field. While being strict with us, he was even more so with anyone on the outside who gave the Service any problems.

The division chiefs were all professionals with many years of experience. Ours, in examination, was a tough, no-nonsense individual who read every agent’s report before it was sent out to the taxpayer. He expected every one of us to come by and say hello anytime we happened to be in the district office, if for no more than a quick handshake and sometimes a pat on the back. Woe, however, to one who had committed some error, for he would be read the riot act in person. On one occasion I got it in the hall while waiting for the elevator.

“What the hell brings you here?” he demanded. Before I got a chance to tell him why, he cut me off to inform me about a call he had just received from Atlanta about an unusual way I had disposed of a case. When I asked what the outcome was of the discussion, he replied with, "Oh well, I told them that you were apt to do some weird things," whereupon he turned and walked away.

Quite often cases would drag on for a long time, and the statutory period during which tax could be assessed (three years after a return is filed) would have expired had we not secured a consent to extend the period of limitations. If the Service failed to do so, the taxpayer escaped having to pay any additional tax. The agent who had a return in his possession was responsible for securing a consent in time. Insofar as the chief was concerned, failure to do so was one of two reasons for dismissal. The other unforgivable was to gain public notoriety of any kind. To prevent these things from happening, the division had an assistant chief who kept up with every scrap of detail with a vengeance. We feared him even more than we did the chief because of his waspish tongue. Once he casually cut down a hapless middle-aged female employee who was somewhat long-winded during a meeting with, "Maggie, if you don't shut up, you'll have all of us coming out of here looking like you do." It shut her up all right, but it stunned everyone present. But one should keep in mind that years later, when everything was supposedly far more humane, the government lost a million dollars in a case where a district agent let a statutory period expire. They tried to hush things up and never did anything to the agent.

As my former on-the-job instructor continued to add to his reputation at his new location, cases began coming back for reconsideration at his old post of duty, and I began to get an inkling of some of the problems the man had created. More than one taxpayer told me that, if he ever saw him again, he would kill him. Another man started to demonstrate this by picking up a sledgehammer and walking around the desk to where I was sitting.

"Hold it please sir; you're talking to someone else now," I managed to say just in time.

The man seemed to be in a momentary trance, for he shook his head and was plainly embarrassed afterwards. Meanwhile, our agent in question continued to make his presence felt in his new post of duty until the bosses came swinging through on what appeared to be a sensitive mission, which turned out to be to relieve him of duty. But his crowning glory did not become known until some years later. He had participated in a fraud investigation which resulted in the incarceration of a taxpayer who served an eighteen-month prison sentence and who promptly filed a claim for refund of tax the moment he was discharged. This seemed to be an audacious act, and I became involved in the matter entirely by accident when I happened to be in the supervisor's office. He asked me if I could find the time to disallow "this crazy claim" he had just received. It shouldn't take more than a couple of hours, including a pleasant ride up the road. Intending to do just as I was told, I met the man, who turned out to be the most provocative character I had ever dealt with. From the very outset, he called me every vile thing imaginable, and the answers to my questions were accompanied by much cursing, but, curiously, he unfailingly compiled. A couple of hours turned into a couple of weeks during which I completely reconstructed his bookkeeping system, and he and his accountant convinced me that he was indeed due a refund. Well, what to do next, for this appeared to be a first, sure enough.

"Oh jeez!" was all my supervisor could muster when I went through the whole thing with him and after a long pause, he added, "You better pack up everything and go see the boss."

As usual, the chief was sitting with rolled up sleeves at the end of a long conference table loaded down with stacks of material awaiting his signature. He had already heard what I came to tell him.

"Do we owe the man a refund?" he brusquely asked.

"I'm afraid so, sir."

"All right—then give it to him," and with that I was dismissed. It was all I needed to know to face the gauntlet of inquiries which were bound to follow.

Whenever an agent suspects tax evasion (not avoidance, which is legal) he is required to interrupt his audit and refer the matter to the criminal investigators for possible prosecution. If the matter is rejected, he will subsequently be allowed to continue the examination and can then recommend not only a tax deficiency but also a fifty percent fraud penalty if such is warranted. Acceptance, on the other hand, brings about a full-scale investigation, which immediately puts a taxpayer on notice that the government is going to try to put him behind bars. On his first visit, the special agent will formally advise the taxpayer of his rights, and this usually prompts him to seek legal advice, which effectively puts an end to all cooperation. This particular taxpayer had sought counsel from someone who had previously been an IRS attorney and who everyone assumed knew his business. He allegedly advised his client to plead guilty after having availed himself of every appeals process. This was incredible and may have been in large part due to the taxpayer's poor attitude. Anyhow, the government wound up owing most of what it had collected, and the special agent never spoke to me again. After the case was thoroughly reviewed, I was called in to answer to a panel of senior criminal investigators as well as appeals officers, who conducted an inquiry into the merits of our recommendations. Quite some time later, I received a letter from the taxpayer in which he advised me that he had gotten his refund and he thanked me for my efforts on his behalf. The matter quite likely had an adverse effect on my career, but by then I had reached the highest grade an examining agent could attain and was able to serve the last two-thirds of it relatively free from financial worries.

Stories appear in the news with the regularity of clockwork about IRS abuses, but what is never explained is that most are based on incidents similar in nature to the following: on a Saturday morning there was an insistent banging on the office door which finally became so distracting that I decided—foolishly, no doubt—to investigate. Outside stood three huge African Americans, a father and his adult sons. They were very upset, and the old man loudly proclaimed that a collection officer had seized his bank account just before closing time the previous evening, making it impossible for him to meet his payroll.

"So, what do you expect me to do about it?" I ventured, having learned that attack often is the best defense. Before he could answer, I went on to point out that revenue officers resort to seizure only after all collection efforts have failed; that his predicament was undoubtedly due to his own stupid failure to pay any attention to past demands; that he therefore shouldn't come stomping in here on a day he knew the office was closed to disturb the peace, et cetera; that he should instead come in on Monday to make satisfactory arrangements so his bank account could be released.

"But how am I gonna pay my men?" he asked far more meekly.

"Can't help you with that—I sure don't have the money to loan you," and that sent them on their way.

Abuses of power do occur, but most are usually corrected before lasting damage is done. We once had a case of attempted bribery, which is always a serious matter. The examiner making the allegation stopped work and referred his case higher up. Such things are ordinarily handled by inspectors but for some reason a special agent was assigned. The two went out and just before reaching their destination, the special agent, who was equipped with a listening device, climbed into the trunk of the agent's car which was fortunately a large one or else he might have suffocated. The culprit was coaxed into the car where the agent tried to make him repeat the offer of a bribe. He more or less succeeded, and the team triumphantly headed for the US attorney's office. He listened to the tape and told them never to come back with that kind of crap again.

Inspectors are one way with which the government maintains control over its huge work force, and we were periodically visited by one dour-looking man who was feared by everybody. I spotted him coming down the hall shortly after the caper by the two in the bribery case and George—the agent who had been involved—heard us exchange greetings. He was sitting at a typewriter stand pounding out a letter and leaned way back to see who had come in. When he saw who it was, he got so shook up that he fell backwards with stand and typewriter bouncing off his chest. It looked like a bad fall, and we were concerned that he had injured himself but he declined to seek medical attention. And what about the inspector? He had merely come in to use our telephone.

GOOD TIMES AND LEARNING

The matter of continuing education of agents had interested the Service for some time, and, the year before I came to work, a small group of people had attended a six-week session at the University of Michigan at government expense. This proved to be rather expensive, and the Service introduced its own advanced course in 1959. Five of us from the state were selected to attend one of the first such courses in Nashville. The district contributed one of the three instructors, and he turned out to be the best one of the lot.

Having only recently moved, we reluctantly locked up our comfortable house and, while the family went to stay with Grandmother once again, I flew to Nashville to report for duty. We were housed in the Sam Davis Hotel downtown, two to a room—still customary then—and class was held at the First Baptist Church, which was within walking distance. The course was difficult, and Sunday-school rooms did not turn out to be the most suitable accommodations; in fact, we came close to having to find new quarters after just the first week. In those days most men were smokers, and no restrictions were placed on lighting up in class. What nobody realized, however, was that air-conditioning in the educational building was an integral part of the system which cooled the sanctuary, and on Sunday the congregation walked into a church filled with the blue haze of stale tobacco smoke normally found in a sports arena. Nashville is the home of the Southern Baptist Convention, and the uproar was what anyone would have expected. Either Uncle Sam was a well-paying tenant, or local IRS officials were influential members of the church, or perhaps both, and they decided to let us stay provided we stopped smoking. That, of course, was unacceptable to the troops; they had to plug up the air vents in a small room with lots of windows, and that was where the addicts gathered to puff away during break, or whenever they had completed an assignment.

The school was a good one, mainly because of the personality of the instructors. One, a lawyer, was an agent from Memphis, another was a supervisor from Nashville, and the one we brought along was also a supervisor. The two men from Tennessee had an inexhaustible supply of jokes told at the beginning of each session—some of which I remember to this day. The most hilarious periods were when skits were organized to test our ability in dealing with difficult taxpayers (a role played by the instructors), and only a few of us managed to stand up to the abuse meted out by them. In time, we came to realize how valuable these sessions were.

The assistant division chief at home kept up with us like a mother hen and later berated me for not having dropped him a line occasionally as the others had apparently done. It was amazing how the course affected my work, and they immediately began feeding me more difficult cases. The nice thing was that a promotion soon came along, enabling us to start exploring the world on vacations, something which was to become a passion with us in time.

It seems that one never appreciates one's circumstances, however temporary, until they are ancient history. I enjoyed the times that I filled my briefcase with a dozen or so tax returns and headed for the country early in the morning and returned to the office before quitting time to fill out a daily report. Eastern Carolina is (or was) tobacco country, and the growing season has distinct stages just as cotton has in Mississippi. Subsidized by the government, farmers raised their crops under a system of allotments, and many were making a living from what grew on as few as two acres of land, even though their farms were considerably larger. The lower leaves of a tobacco plant mature first, and the progress of a harvesting season becomes evident from the length of the bare stalks. Leaves are tied at the stem and are draped over a long stick which is hung in a small barn for curing—essentially a drying process for which most farmers used fuel oil. Auctioning took place in big warehouses which competed for business. Auctions started in Georgia, moved up through the Carolinas into Virginia, then to Maryland and Kentucky. Most of the tobacco is bought by the large cigarette makers and goes straight to their redrying facilities after which it is stored for some time. Foreign buyers rely on independent redryers where leaf is shredded, redried, and packed in hogsheads (huge round barrels) for shipment.

Local redrying plants employed hundreds of seasonal workers, most of them women. On Fridays, one plant traditionally prepared a batch of seafood gumbo, enough to feed everyone on the premises and then some. I watched them dump ingredients consisting of rock fish, many bottles of catsup and tabasco sauce plus salt and pepper into a black pot in which people once used to boil laundry and which was placed over a gas burner. The contents simmered all morning and at lunchtime managers, foremen, and visitors were invited to pull up to a makeshift table to partake of the delicacy, which was best consumed with copious amounts of soda pop to cool the tongue. As soon as everyone had their fill, what remained—more than enough—was turned over to the workers who swarmed around it like flies.

Late in the fall, farmers butcher hogs, and many a homestead sports a pig's carcass hanging from a tree limb on a cold morning. It is said that no better barbecue exists anywhere and that the most famous is served in Goldsboro and Wilson, two towns twenty-five miles apart whose respective newspaper editors would crank up a lively debate at least once a year as to who had the best of all. When taken home, leftover barbecue should not be stored in glass jars because of the substance's visual impact after it congeals with one-third meat at the top resting on a layer of pure pig's grease taking up the bottom two-thirds of the container.

In 1961, the Kennedy Administration took over, and things began to take on a different look. The new Commissioner of Internal Revenue stressed that the overwhelming majority of Americans (some ninety-seven percent or more) were obviously honest since they voluntarily filed their returns and paid their tax each year without grumbling and that we therefore only had to worry about the three percent which did not. Perhaps this last group didn't quite know how to file, and we were therefore to put forth every effort to assist the public in order to lend credence to the word "service," which, after all, was part of our name. We soon found out what was wanted because the filing season began in earnest only a short time later. Where the public had been left to its own devices in filing returns—some ninety-seven percent doing a pretty good job—people now began coming to the office in unanticipated droves since they understood that it would be done for them. We, however, understood nothing of the sort and in desperation took evasive action like stuffing the telephone in a file cabinet and sneaking out of the office whenever we had to leave. Our workload didn't diminish, and supervisors began making veiled threats which made us feel like we were between a rock and a hard place. There wasn't much of a problem in large offices where the task could be assigned to low-level personnel, but in outlying posts of duty we had to do all of it ourselves. When service didn't measure up to what was promised, complaints began coming in, duly amplified by the news media, and this soon led to a buildup of new personnel engaged to enforce the edicts coming from the regional office.

Each district office has an administration division whose task it is to look after personnel matters, training, the furnishing of supplies, problems of building maintenance, local leases, and so on, but which otherwise has nothing to do with the examination of returns or the collection of tax. But that did not deter the recently appointed chief of our administration division from meddling in all our activities. In fact, we began to see more and more of him in the field, and even our usual training sessions were preceded by one of his pep talks during which he presented a graphical display of beans and carrots which made absolutely no sense to anyone. When troops began to ask difficult questions, he started bringing the district director along by way of intimidation. Fortunately, being the valuable asset he was, they soon promoted him, and he secured a high position in Washington. However, it appeared that he had been a mere precursor of kindred souls who came floating through on their way to greater things. Once we caught on to the fact that these intruders were only interested in becoming managers, a modus vivendi developed which eliminated most friction between workers and non-workers.

The tax laws began to change, too, initially in the area of depreciation, a jealously guarded specialty of marginal personnel who had managed to survive year after year by vigorously arguing with taxpayers over how long a period the cost of a particular asset could be recovered. Their bible was an IRS publication known as Bulletin F, wherein suggested lives were provided for practically every object known to man. The more sophisticated (or cynical perhaps) taxpayers made it a sport by deliberately charging off items whose costs were recoverable over an excessively long period and then arguing about it during interminable conferences which enabled accountants to increase their fees. In time, lawyers got into the act, and fees really began to soar. Tragically, matters of real consequence went unnoticed at an inestimable cost to the government and, of course, the taxpayers. New laws and regulations were the beginnings of an intense effort to change this nonsense, but no lasting success was ever achieved until the Reagan years, when people were encouraged to more or less do as they pleased.

ANECDOTES

Our stay in Goldsboro lasted almost ten years. In retrospect, Ruth and I both wish that we could have spent my entire career there—indeed, the rest of our life! But as pleasant as it had been, it was a mere interlude, and we never even got the chance to buy a house. On the other hand, things were to change drastically in time, first with the integration of schools and later with the all-out attack on the use of tobacco, which changed an entire way of life. Moreover, a disastrous hurricane flooded huge areas of the eastern part of North Carolina in the last year of the century. At any rate, faced with many unusual situations, I do wish to pass on a few anecdotes in random order.

The Gambler

Chief executive officer of a medium sized business, he was traveling abroad when arrangements were made for me to audit his company's tax returns, and we didn't meet until several months later. It was always my habit to be exactly on time for an appointment, but, as usual, I was kept waiting, this time for almost an hour. Finally, the door to his office swung open with a bang, and three strange-looking characters came out and passed through the reception area without saying a word, and stormed out the front door.

"You can go in now," said the receptionist.

The man did not get up to greet me, complaining that his back was hurting and curtly motioned for me to take a chair facing his desk. He never uttered a word while I presented my findings, a process which took about fifteen minutes.

"Is that it?" the man asked at the conclusion.

"Yes, sir," I replied.

"All right—now you listen to me, you son of a bitch," and he proceeded to give me his opinion of the US Government and all it stood for, finally concluding with, "and now you get your ass out of here while you still can!"

That obviously turned out to be an unagreed case, and I thought I had the answer for such strange behavior when the business folded not long afterwards. However, that was only part of it, because the real reason came out a couple of years later when I came across the receptionist in another setting. She told me how embarrassed she had been and wanted to know if anyone ever told me what had happened to her old boss. A compulsive gambler, he had stopped in New York upon his return from overseas and had lost a great deal of money, much of which had been borrowed on a short-term basis, just long enough to make arrangements to repay the amount once he got home. Unable to make good on his promise, it so happened that the three "gents" who kept me waiting so long that day were representatives from the underworld who had threatened her boss with physical harm if he didn't pay up in so many hours. In view of his bad back, he might even have been given a taste of what to expect, and the poor fellow told me what he didn't have the nerve to tell those men. They certainly looked the part with their dark suits, wide-brim straw hats, and black-and-white wing-tip shoes.

A Magic Recovery

What old money doesn't always seem to realize is that there is plenty of it around nationwide and that those who have it can't possibly all be descendants of that select group who came over on the Mayflower or those who signed the Declaration of Independence, but they often will try to give one the impression that they are anyhow. This one really had airs and became downright insulting once he saw that his superior status didn't make much of an impression. The best legal and accounting advice were at his command, or so he thought, and he came barging into his accountant's office where we were discussing his case one afternoon. Having just come off the tennis courts, he had a towel draped around his neck and didn't smell so good. As he began lecturing his accountant and me, I noticed that his lawyer—a man well advanced in years—had decided that it was time for a siesta and was asleep on the sofa. Suddenly his client wheeled around and imperiously demanded, "Isn't that right, John?" It was amazing how fast John awoke and regained his composure to answer, "Absolutely!" while he never even heard what it had been all about.

A Message (from Heaven?)

George lived down the street from us and was an accountant whom I often dealt with. An unassuming man, he and his wife always sat in the same pew upstairs in church and didn't notice that we had taken a seat directly behind them one Sunday. It so happened that a new face was passing the collection plate around, and I noticed George trying to show his wife something he had written down on his church bulletin. She merely shrugged her shoulders.

As so many people do, George left his program on the seat at the conclusion of the service, and I picked it up to see that he had written, "Who's that?" The next day I got the name and address of the one taking up collection at the church office, wrote it down under the question on the program, and mailed it to George.

Quite some time later we happened to be haggling over something involving one of his clients and George wanted to know how in the world I had picked up such information. I casually pointed out that there were certain ways, just as he had found out the name of so and so in church that day. He blushed and said that he and his wife were still talking about that mysterious message, and he seemed genuinely relieved to finally have the answer.

The Mob

It seems that lots of places in America have a notorious area where real or imagined danger lurks and which are to be avoided. In the South, a place often seems goes by the name of such-and-such a "hollow" whose inhabitants are reputed to be on the lawless side. I blundered into such an area once in pursuit of a hard-to-find man who had taken liberties with the law and who had paid very little tax. He and his wife operated a country store in what seemed to be a real jumping-off place. It didn't take long to reconstruct their earnings on the crude but effective cost-plus percentage mark-up method, at the conclusion of which I handed him the result plus the usual agreement for him and his wife to sign, whereupon he excused himself and left me alone in that spooky place.

After what appeared to be eternity, I decided to wait in my car and, as I stepped out the front door, I caught sight of a group of people who came resolutely marching down a path in the woods. There were men, women, and children, and a couple of persons even had on a military uniform. One of the latter politely but firmly inquired what that piece of paper I had given his daddy was all about. Standing there surrounded by what appeared to be a mob, I bravely tried to answer, but what came out didn't make much sense even to myself. For some reason, it seemed to satisfy all the adults, who were nodding as if they understood everything. When I finished, the young man told his parents to go ahead and sign that piece of paper, after which I got in my car and took off as fast as I could. When I related my experience to those in the office later that day, I learned that I had been in one of those hollows and had been lucky to get out alive since it was known that strangers who went in there often disappeared without a trace, vehicles included. Upon reflection, I decided that the young fellow in a marine's uniform had merely wanted to show his family that he was a man of the world, and his parents proudly accepted his advice.

About a Corpse

While working in a funeral home, they had us (my on-the-job instructor and myself) seated in the reception area where people had been coming and going all morning to pay their respects to an old friend. Shortly after lunch, the close family members came in. They had just arrived by plane from New York. After mingling with the crowd for a few minutes to accept condolences, they moved on to an adjacent room where the open casket stood, and we could tell from the sudden commotion that something was amiss. Funeral home employees came running up to several women who were becoming hysterical. Our first thought was that the corpse had come back to life, until we heard someone say something about a wrong body. The remains had come from the State Hospital for the Insane and had been misidentified. It took a long time before the whooping and hollering subsided that afternoon.

Our Landlord

He had come over from Greece before I was even born and had set up a hot-dog stand in what was little more than a hole in the wall on main street. In time he became the owner of the most popular restaurant in town. He had married the local hotel's housekeeper (a gracious lady), and they raised two daughters who married well.

Bill had become a rich man and had built five houses in a row across from the high school athletic field. He occupied the one in the middle and rented the others to what he considered to be worthy tenants. Two of those had been physicians, who lived there before building their private mansions, and we were fortunate to be able to move into one of these. We evidently showed more pride in our abode than anyone had ever done before, and this pleased our landlord. Even though Greeks are apt to be clannish, we became good friends, and I learned a lot of history from him. He told me how one of the principal officers of the local bank had mercilessly pressured him to buy stock in the institution during the Great Depression and laughed about the fact that he had only recently made a cool hundred thousand dollars when the bank was acquired by a much larger competitor. He told me many times that the owner of a café should always worry less about what comes through the front door, and more about what goes out the back. Food theft by employees is a common problem, and he was always the last one to leave and lock up.

He frequently went back to Greece and became a major benefactor of the town where he spent his childhood by having a new church built entirely at his expense. Later, when his health deteriorated, he took his personal physician along—one who used to be a tenant—and, who, incidentally, was the most prominent in town.

A Sure Enough Clown

This was a full-fledged fraud investigation of a small-town physician who seemed to be having a hard time making ends meet, a fact deemed suspicious in and of itself. We had analyzed his bank accounts, interviewed people, all to no avail. We did discover that he had a large safe-deposit box in a bank, and after much discussion were able to persuade him to let us examine its contents. To this end, I picked him up at his home one morning to drive him into town. The man appeared to be a real maverick and talked a blue streak all the way in. He related how his colleagues had ganged up on him to deprive him of hospital privileges, and he had much criticism for the way medicine was practiced in general.

"Go to any hospital," he wailed, "and see how many wives and children of doctors are patients. You'll find none! And you know why? Because those places will kill you! The bastards have quit scrubbing before performing surgery and are relying on antibiotics to keep infections at bay. Trouble is, more and more germs are building up a resistance to all that fancy stuff."

It was a half hour trip into town, and I eagerly listened, realizing that a renegade—while apt to exaggerate—can be a good source of information. The special agent was waiting at the bank and seemed to be annoyed that we were late. Then the doctor couldn't find his key to the safe-deposit box, and we were beginning to think that he had deliberately misplaced it, perhaps even left it at home, when he suddenly produced it. We noticed that his hands were shaking when he reached for the box (a good sign) and then handed it to me instead of to the special agent, who snatched it out of my hands. He opened the box and found nothing more than a wadded-up, dirty bandage. Bank records showed that no one had opened the box for a long time, and I had a hard time keeping my composure because this clown had his act down pat.

Too Much of Something

The middle-aged, well-to-do couple had lost everything in a house fire, and the loss they claimed on their return was obviously out of reason. Among the items set forth on page after page of detail were forty brassieres costing a respectable amount of money because of their alleged quality. Their attorney had the habit of never cooperating, and we advised the agent to just sit there looking sad, shake his head, and never cease asking how anyone could possibly have forty of the things. It worked, and the parties eventually agreed that the entire loss should be halved which, as it turned out, was only slightly more than their insurance reimbursement; hence, virtually the whole of the amount claimed in the return was wiped out.

Citizen Abuse

When a taxpayer files a claim for a refund of tax which is contested by the government, a US District Court assumes jurisdiction. This means that the Department of Justice handles the case rather than IRS counsel. In this instance, an assistant US attorney was sent out all the way from Seattle because of a personnel shortage. It was the first time the fellow had ever been in Dixieland, and he appeared to be fascinated by it. About the second or third morning, he came into the office in a somewhat pensive mood, which he did not seem able to shake off. I asked if something was the matter.

"Well, not really . . . , but I did see a disturbing thing as I looked out of my hotel window while dressing this morning. A policeman drove by several times in front of the hotel on a three-wheeled motorcycle, which had a cattle prod lying across the back—surely they don't still use those things against colored people, do they?"

It took me a moment to realize what he was talking about. The city had no parking meters, which were deemed to be one-armed bandits by the local citizenry. To enforce the two-hour parking limit, police would mark car tires with a piece of chalk clamped in a long stick which did look like a cattle prod. Our guest seemed genuinely relieved to hear that no black citizens were being abused.

A Public Remorse

There was a traveling salesman who would call on us from time to time although we could only pass on our needs to district headquarters and never favored him with an order for anything. We happened to run into each other in a neighboring town one day as we were about to enter a cafeteria for lunch, and we decided to eat together. As we later chatted over a cup of coffee, the man suddenly began to cry. The place was crowded with people (lots of whom were my past customers), and I was sure they were thinking that there was no telling what that sorry *revenooer* was doing to that poor man. I managed to calm him down, and he told me that he had failed to file income tax returns for several years and was deeply worried about the consequences. I explained to him that he had just then made a voluntary disclosure and that he should go home, get all necessary information together, and bring it to our office where we would help him file his past due returns. There would of course be delinquency penalties but no fraud penalties. Phew, talk about being embarrassed!

The Gold Mine

The small radio station looked like a place in trouble. Initially quite ornery, the person running it eventually came across with a most unlikely story as to the cause of his predicament.

The station's broadcasts of mainly rock music were directed toward a small town about twenty-five miles away, and in recent months advertisers had begun complaining that its signal was becoming weaker by the day, which had caused some people to cancel their patronage. Technicians were called in to check all equipment but could find nothing wrong, until somebody decided to visit the site where the antenna was located. There they found that a heavy copper ground cable pointing in the direction of the main listening area had been tampered with. Located close to the Neuse River, it had become exposed during recent flooding and was discovered by a couple of vagrants who began chopping a piece of it at a time which they offered for sale at a local junk yard. The goldmine soon gave out, and the culprits had moved on, leaving the station's owner holding the bag.

THE MAJOR LEAGUE

It was the week before Christmas in 1964, when one of the men in the office stuck his head in the door of the barbershop to announce that the chief in Greensboro wished to talk to me.

"Did he want to know where I was?"

"Yep," was the answer.

Too bad, but we had long ago decided that since hair grew on company time, there was no reason why it shouldn't be cut on company time. Anyhow, the boss answered the telephone himself when I returned his call.

"How would you like moving to Charlotte?" he asked.

"For a promotion?"

"Sure."

"How long do I have to think it over?"

"Oh, two or three days."

"I'll let you know, sir, and thanks!"

It was an offer to move into the highest grade an examining agent could attain, and I was ready to go but had to talk things over with the family first. We all loved it where we were and agonized over the decision for three days. The children had recently gotten full-sized bicycles and were proudly riding them to school. Ruth had a kindergarten class at the church which nicely supplemented our income; hence, why move? I had only recently turned down a job offered by the owner of the largest local manufacturing firm who had gone into semiretirement and who was impressed by the way I had gotten along with his tempestuous son, who was taking over the reins.

Compensation was to have been three times what the government would pay, but I had already seen too many men putting in sixty-hour weeks and never regretted my decision, even though it ran counter to the American dream. Hence, only one way remained, and that was to accept a promotion.

On our way south for the holidays, we stopped in Charlotte to look around and immediately regretted our decision because the place looked simply awful! But what we saw was mainly the downtown area, which soon was to be transformed by the Federal Government's Model Cities program. Charlotte was one of ten cities selected nationwide.

January 1965 turned out to be a beautiful winter month with lots of snowfall, and the children had the time of their lives, which made the prospect of leaving all the more heart wrenching. I reported for duty the second week and was handed a real bummer of a case; it had been shunted from one agent to another because of its multitude of problems. The man who had originally started the examination had retired on disability and died of cancer not long afterwards. The taxpayer's chief financial officer was happy enough to see me and had an expensive desk and leather chair brought into his spacious office. For the next two weeks, we worked in perfect harmony while facing each other. The first thing each morning I was forced to look on as a group of subordinates received instructions for the day in a brief and efficient manner. The man actually had a miniature hourglass on his desk and an employee was expected to communicate any problem within the time the sand ran out. My requests for information, on the other hand, were treated with far less urgency and were either misunderstood or simply ignored. After two weeks of playing games, I wasn't any wiser, while my host was becoming testy and finally inquired how much longer I intended to stay. I told him that it was going to be as long as it took to perform an audit and that I really hadn't even started yet.

"Well," he hissed, "perhaps I'd better have a little chat with your supervisor because you're wasting your time and ours as well."

I told him that I thought such to be a splendid idea indeed.

There were two audit groups in Charlotte, each with about a dozen men, a secretary, and a supervisor. Cases were rotated between groups, and the return assigned to me had recently been reviewed by an agent who was now one of those supervisors but fortunately not mine. The man was a certified public accountant—a rarity among agents in those days—and I soon found out that he was in the habit of second-guessing his men while maintaining open lines of communication with all the accounting firms. A good many of his men were resigned to having to play gofer and the group was generally a lackluster lot. Those who resisted the trend were members of the group I was in, headed by a relatively new supervisor. I understood that the telephone conversation between him and my client was brief and to the point, and when I came in the next morning, my gorgeous mahogany desk had disappeared, and I was escorted to a storage room in the back of the building where they had squeezed in a rickety table and a chair which had four legs but only three casters.

"No problem," I told the embarrassed assistant, "this is more like what I'm used to."

Finding suitable housing was once again my primary concern. We wanted to buy in a settled neighborhood rather than in one of those suburban developments on the outskirts of town, but what was available was either too expensive or in a state of disrepair. The owner of the real estate firm happened to be pinch-hitting for our salesman one day and took us out to see a multiple listing house which appealed to us at once. It was located on the periphery of the most respectable section of town, and school was within walking distance. We were told that the area's original developers had big plans for the neighborhood, and the evidence was visible, until one went a few blocks further. It happened to be a buyer's market, the price was good, as was the general condition of the property. We met some of the neighbors; they seemed congenial enough, and we bought. Ever the idealist, there were a few things I naively overlooked, and these were to bother us to varying degrees during our stay in excess of twenty years. Little did I suspect that I would constantly be reminded of the predictions offered by the auditor and ex-revenue agent at the air base in Mississippi.

The Piedmont section was synonymous with textiles, and Charlotte was the center of the industry. Thousands of men and women worked in the mills, where they were generally mistreated when compared with those who labored in other industries. For example, most plants shut down the week of the Fourth of July each year for major maintenance, and workers were furloughed without pay. Mill owners had successfully kept out labor unions, and it was distressing to hear people gratuitously offer anti-union slogans during an ordinary conversation. Brutalized at work, people apparently sought solace in religion, and there are an astonishing number of churches in the area. It is a place where it is not unusual for one stranger to ask of another whether he or she is "saved." Street preachers—common in the hill and mountain towns—strutted up and down sidewalks and could be heard for several blocks in all directions. They were banned in Charlotte, where they officially considered them to be a traffic hazard but more probably because they were a public nuisance.

It was in this climate that Jim and Tammy Baker established their radio ministry through the PTL club which initially operated out of a house on Park Road in Charlotte. PTL stood for People that Love, which, among the more cynical minded, came to mean Pass the Loot. In time, the operation moved to a 2,700-acre tract of land across the South Carolina state line, where an ambitious building program was undertaken which became known as Heritage Village. It was carried out on a grand scale and was actually done rather tastefully. Admission to the grounds was free, and all one had to do was pass an officious-looking guard house staffed by young people who waved visitors on with a cheerful greeting of "God loves you!" The decorations at Christmas were spectacular with countless tiny lights strung up in the trees. There was little doubt, however, that the Bakers were an embarrassment to Charlotte, which preferred to be identified with Billy Graham's brand of evangelism.

Now, all this is not to say that Charlotte had no redeeming features at all. On the contrary, after all its downtown was razed and rebuilt, it became a handsome city, thanks in large part also due to the influx of northerners, who first came as personnel of companies establishing branches, followed by individual entrepreneurs and, increasingly, by well-to-do retirees. These elements are apt to be strident and, in some ways, overwhelmed the existing power structure of mill owners and slum lords, improving the public taste in the process. However, they generally had one thing in common with their hosts and that was a conservative political outlook. That was bad news for a civil servant, particularly one engaged in tax law enforcement who was regarded as nothing more than a pariah. Such then was to be my lot for twenty years, the sad part being that my family was accorded equal honors.

It took me six months to ferret out sufficient information before presenting my first large client with notice of a hefty deficiency in tax, which caused an uproar not only within the company but apparently sent shock waves through the ranks of local consultants as well. Nobody had ever spent as much time on a case, and even my supervisor had become nervous enough to begin asking when I planned to finish up. My standard answer was, "When you want me to, but I still have a lot to look at." Apparently, I was enjoying the confidence of the chief at district headquarters and that was that.

Standard operating procedure was for agents to meet with a taxpayer and his representatives and present findings orally upon conclusion of an audit. This worked fine so long there weren't too many issues or when issues weren't too complicated. Commerce was rapidly expanding, however, and so were the problems engendered thereby, which necessitated a more orderly presentation of factual material, accompanied by well-reasoned arguments which, in my humble opinion, could only be done in written form. I had accordingly begun presenting written proposals in some instances even before arriving on the local scene and had run across criticism from both within and without the organization, but none matched the reaction I got here.

"What the hell is this?" demanded the comptroller when he leafed through three modest volumes I handed him after having cooled my heels for a couple of hours in the waiting room beside his office, the final insult during my stay. I explained that those were changes we proposed to make to the company's tax returns. The changes resulted in certain deficiencies in tax, and I suggested that perhaps he would like an opportunity to study the material first before discussing them.

"You're supposed to discuss changes before issuing a report—this is an official report and constitutes an illegal procedure in that it doesn't afford us the normal rights of appeal." He then picked up the phone to summon the tax manager of one of the accounting firms collectively known as the "big eight" in America (and lately, the world) and turned around to continue working on something on the credenza behind him. While we were thus waiting, a secretary stuck her head in the door to announce that the people upstairs wanted a copy of whatever I had brought in sent up at once.

"Dammit, how the hell do they know about this thing—you didn't tell them anything, did you?"

Her reply was that someone had probably seen me waiting for a long time and must have concluded that I was bringing something of importance. Realizing that the man's problems were mounting and whereas the arrival of the person summoned had brought an immediate shouting match, I told them to look things over and call us when they were ready to talk business and walked out. The case ultimately wound up in Tax Court.

Not only taxpayers' representatives had a hostile attitude toward written proposals, but the most vehement reaction came, in fact, from some of my colleagues who were not at all anxious to leave tracks as to how much was subsequently conceded. However, not a sound was coming from the chief who, as I heard through the grapevine, was keenly interested in the developing controversy.

THE CHALLENGE THAT SEALED A CAREER

A strange twist of events had previously caused the tax department of one of America's largest corporations to be located in Charlotte. Its tax returns were in the process of being examined by two older agents—one from each group—who looked and acted as if they were US senators. They were accordingly treated with appropriate deference by both the public as well as their fellow employees. The one from our group was afflicted with rheumatoid arthritis, had spent seventeen years in bed until the drug cortisone was introduced, and walked with a stoop. Being the black sheep of a local prominent family, he had been a professional boxer of some renown, and was the boxing coach at the University of North Carolina when the dreaded disease laid him low. He was a truly delightful person, and we became friends before he died several years later. The other man had transferred into the district some years earlier, and we had briefly served in the same group in the eastern part of the state, where he had held conferences on some of my cases. He was a courtly gentleman, and we had always gotten along very well, but promotion of a much younger man to his own grade level had apparently offended him, and he had stopped speaking to me. I was sent out to assist these two senior agents who were in the process of writing a report for a year on which the statute of limitations was about to expire.

Upon entering the grand reception hall of the building, housing the headquarters of just one corporate division, it occurred to me that this was going to be big stuff for sure. I asked the receptionist to please notify our personnel at their extension that they had a visitor and she invited me to take a seat. I had barely managed to get comfortable in one of the overstuffed leather chairs when I noticed an elderly gentleman briskly approaching me. He introduced himself as being an assistant to the tax manager and asked what he could help me with. I told him that I had come to join the other two agents on site.

"Young man," he said, "we don't need any more of your people; the ones here are doing just fine and, besides, we are running out of room."

"Bbbbut, sir . . . ," I stammered and couldn't think of anything better then to chuckle before continuing, "I have been ordered to report here for duty, so would you please take me to the gentlemen in question?"

"No!" he said. "Now will you please leave?"

After we looked each other in the eye for a second or two, I shrugged my shoulders, turned around, and left. Everyone in the office had gone out to lunch, and I had to wait for my boss to return.

"Back so soon; what happened?" he asked when he saw me sitting in his office reading the paper. After I got through telling him, he shook his head, grinned, and just sat there for a moment before picking up the phone to call the agents on site. He told whomever answered that I was leaving the office, to go and sit in the reception hall and wait for me and, when I got there, to introduce me to the tax manager. "The tax manager, d'you hear?" and if they pulled any more crap, he was coming out himself.

Creighton was waiting for me when I entered the building the second time that day, and he took me to see the tax manager (who looked impish, but who was otherwise quite cordial), and then took me to where he was working. He was alone and his partner, Jack, was on vacation. We never saw him again for, while on leave, he decided to retire and returned to his home state without saying goodbye to anyone.

It was hard not to be intimidated by the size of everything, especially the large dollar figures which overflowed into the margins of the tax return—a return comprising two volumes, each six inches thick. Once on the premises, our hosts became friendly, and I was quickly accepted by the group which lunched together in the cafeteria. I learned that the tax manager would soon retire and that his department was in the process of being reorganized. A boisterous New Yorker, we were to run into each other for many years at the popular Kiwanis Travel Show, where he would hail me for all to hear with, "Well, how are you; I thought you were dead!"

It was evident that the two agents had been at loggerheads, quarreling over perfectly silly things. They had identified the usual "big" issues, which they talked about in the office for everyone to hear. These were of an inconsequential nature, the kind that produced tax one year which would be returned the next year and which were referred to as "flip-flop adjustments" in the trade. One agent had been writing an explanation of just a few items while the other (the one who abruptly retired) had been busy preparing the transmittal letter consisting of page after page of material lifted verbatim from the most recent annual report to stockholders. And what about any tax deficiencies? As always, one million dollars, more or less, which routinely earned them a much-publicized pat on the back from middle management. Taxpayers' employees just couldn't be more complimentary about the pair, and one soon had to conclude that Uncle Sam had been took, indeed, took real bad for a long time. Unfortunately for them, things were about to change.

My partner had always used a simple filing system: none! He lugged everything around in a bulging leather briefcase which folded open flat. The latter would occasionally fall off his desk, causing him to spend several hours to bring order out of chaos. He was writing his report at the rate of a sentence a day and was holding conferences with people whose indulgence knew no bounds. My supervisor and I decided that he was really quite an asset because he was diverting their attention long enough for us to consult all kinds of experts while building a case regarding later years. Government sources were amazing, and we discovered that there were international agents, valuation engineers, even economists, ready to help whenever asked. By the time we concluded the examination of another return (about a year later), we surprised the taxpayer with issues they never even considered the IRS was capable of raising. Our proposed adjustments hit them like a thunderbolt, and for the first conference they had lined up a bevy of consultants with truly impressive credentials. As we listened to them hold forth most of the first day and part of the second, our confidence in what we had presented began to evaporate, and we were particularly worried about the apparent lack of concern on the part of a valuation engineer from the National Office. He seemed to be asleep most of the time. In fact, when it was his turn to present his case, it seemed as if he was going to falter altogether, but he did finally look up to ask if they were through. Yes, they were. Good. He began to speak, haltingly at first, to give a summary of arguments offered the last couple of days before launching into his own comments. Within half an hour, the smugness on the part of taxpayer's personnel had disappeared, and by the time our man had finished his masterful presentation, entirely without notes, they appeared devastated. The saddest part of it all was that practically no one had seemed to be aware of the fact that the US Government had numbers of such people on the payroll just sitting there waiting to help.

New personnel began appearing in the tax department, and we heard that the entire activity would soon be transferred to New York, where it was to become a division of the legal department. On one of our visits up there, we accidentally learned that they were maintaining a color chart, which covered a wall on one side of the library and on which the entire corporate structure was depicted. Whenever a change occurred (practically every day), it was recorded with a Polaroid snapshot of which we were denied a copy. Fortunately, the law required that each foreign change be reported on a special form attached to the tax return, and this enabled us to painstakingly reconstruct overseas possessions from one year to the next. The time came for another return to be filed of which we were also denied a copy because, they argued, for us to look at it would amount to a premature and therefore unauthorized examination. We knew that they were in the habit of hand-delivering the company's tax return at the IRS computer center in Georgia on March 15 each year. We alerted personnel there to make a copy of it the minute it was received. On March 16, I caught the first plane to Atlanta, drove out to Chamblee, and was back in Charlotte in plenty of time to walk casually into the tax manager's office with a copy of the huge documents under each arm, gently place them on his desk, and then start asking questions about some items. When they realized what I had, the reaction was positively electrifying, and that was the part of the game that was enjoyable. Far more often they got us riled up about something, and once we actually caught them in the act of slapping their knees in merriment when we returned to the conference room unannounced to retrieve something we had left behind. To the casual observer, we would have appeared to be bitter antagonists, but we were merely representing our respective employers and actually had excellent relationships. It was professionalism at its best.

LIFE IN THE LATE NINETEEN-SIXTIES

The late 1960s were difficult years for families with teen-age youngsters. Outright rebellion afflicted countless households, and fear was universal among parents as children began disappearing. In Charlotte, there existed a halfway house into destitution reportedly run by the offspring of a well-known national political figure. No matter how much it infuriated the local citizenry, there appeared to be no legal remedy available to close the hated place down, let alone run the operator with his live-in girlfriend out of town, and the specter of potential disaster came closer and closer as one's neighbors and colleagues became affected. A son or daughter would fail to come home and, after some time had passed, a phone call would be received from a stranger to announce that they were in good hands and perfectly safe. Safe indeed! In the Greenwich Village section of New York City, there were swarms of the wretches running around barefooted, filthy dirty, dressed in hippie garb, and sleeping on the street. Piedmont Park in Atlanta was another hangout for thousands of them, and the neighborhood became a disgrace.

With two teenagers at home, we desperately sought ways to keep them busy and never let them out of sight. The church was totally useless due to my status as a tax pariah, but there were other ways. Although they were to keep us struggling financially for many years to come, we began having extravagant vacations and, in the process, explored not only much of the United States, but large parts of Canada and Mexico as well. At home we discovered and joined a gem and mineral club, which met regularly in the local Nature Museum. North Carolina is a rockhounds' paradise, and the club arranged monthly field trips to various mining locations, where we could dig to our heart's content. The first such outing took us to an abandoned garnet mine in a remote part of the mountains. Upon reflection, I realized the danger of the venture, which found several dozen men, women, and children digging in unsupported mine shafts radiating in all directions at various levels. Ignorance is bliss, however, and we never had a more enjoyable adventure. Sooner or later, all rockhounds come upon valuable material, and most acquire at least the basic tools with which to make cabochons, which are unfaceted stones with a polished, convex top suitable for mounting in inexpensive ready-made rings, brooches, and bracelets called "findings." A few talented people eventually progress to the more difficult art of faceting stones, and some even cast their own findings in silver and gold. True masterpieces are often created—sometimes by the most unlikely people—which are usually displayed at shows. Two notable members of the club were a man and his wife, both of whom were once high-school science teachers and who had quit their jobs to open up a hobby shop. The husband gave us some of the most informative lectures I have ever had the privilege of attending. In time, however, the club gradually came to be dominated by persons with a flea market mentality who were more interested in putting on an annual show to generate income for which nobody ever bothered to give an accounting, and the quality of the membership began to decline. The shows became bigger and bigger, even though little more than pure junk was brought in.

For anyone interested in gems and minerals, the place to visit is Spruce Pine in the North Carolina mountains. At the intersection of the Blue Ridge Parkway and State Highway 226 stands a mineral museum operated by the National Park Service while, about five miles east of Spruce Pine on State Highway 19E, one runs into the Gem Shop owned by Mr. McKinley, who is an excellent jewelry craftsman. He has his shop in his residence, where one is always welcome, even as a browser. Desperately ill at one time, he somehow recovered to keep adding to the world's treasures.

THE COMPUTER AGE

At some time in 1968, the job of large case manager was handed to the man who had been our best instructor in Nashville some years earlier. An intelligent Irishman with an immense ego, he regularly got away with more foolishness (commonly referred to as Irish roguery) than anyone was apt to in the Service. He was able to grasp the complexities of whatever we were working on, but his greatest asset was that he listened and then left us alone.

He moved the two of us who were the nucleus of one of the first audit teams in the district into an empty office, had a blackboard brought in from somewhere so that we, together with visiting experts, could do our brainstorming without disturbing anyone else. He handled public relations deftly and all I had to do was mention a problem somewhere, after which he would arrange for the two of us to go out and find out what the cause was.

Amounts of money involved were generally substantial and were purportedly due to honest differences of opinion as to how applicable tax laws should be interpreted. Tax managers of large companies were all members of an organization called the Tax Executives Institute, which aggressively lobbied for tax benefits and then did the interpreting. They eventually wound up controlling the process of tax administration insofar as big business was concerned, while the IRS seemed to be increasingly preoccupied with adapting the organization to the use of computer technology. I was repeatedly selected, either singly or as one of two people, to represent the district at computer seminars, for which I lacked both aptitude and interest. Some, of course, were informative, like an early one conducted at the Georgia Institute of Technology, where we were privileged to spend a week in an amphitheater resembling a war-room while a distinguished professor provided us with an overview of the subject. Everything having to do with computers was initially called Automatic Data Processing, or ADP for short, and that first introduction was followed not long afterwards by a course in programming at the regional computer center. This time two professors instructed a select group in theory the first week, and the second week we worked a night shift so we could run our programs on the giant main computer after it had cooled down from the day's operations. The whole affair was an enigma to me, and I succeeded in getting a very simple program to run only after about the twelfth attempt. At the conclusion of the course, we were called in by the assistant regional commissioner for a roundtable discussion of what we had learned. I sat next to the man, and it was my misfortune to be the sole dissenter as to the computer's utility in tax examinations. Until the end of my career, I remained convinced that it was an agent's job to get the big picture and determine whether a taxpayer had treated income and expenses according to law and not to get bogged down in detail. Apart from myself, all those people who attended the course eventually moved on to management positions dealing with computer applications. They were all smart fellows, and I continued to be in touch with a few as time went by, but we somehow lacked a common outlook. It seemed that they gradually spun themselves into a cocoon which became an end in itself rather than a means to an end.

So-called computer specialists began to be recruited from the ranks but were ineffective because of a lack of proper training, while data-processing machines were continually being replaced by more sophisticated equipment, i.e., *real* computers. A handful of people who had worked on the outside were able to extract information for us, but they weren't too effective as agents; they were, as the professor at Georgia Tech had stressed, a special breed of human beings.

In due course, another pilot project was introduced, this time dealing with statistical sampling. Three groups of about thirty agents attended separate sessions in Dallas, Columbus, and Manhattan, and the instructor was an elderly professor from the City University of New York. He was the author of several books on the subject and showed us how one could extract information with ninety-seven percent accuracy by selecting one hundred items from a virtually infinite mass of detail. The course was split into three parts scheduled at one-month intervals, each session lasting three days. We were very much enthused with the prospect of putting our new knowledge to work—that is, until "graduation day," for which two officials out of Washington came all the way to Dallas.

"Congratulations to all of you for passing the course," the man who mounted the lectern said. "However," he continued, "we now want you to forget everything you learned because we are developing our own method of statistical sampling and this course was strictly meant to be an introduction to the subject."

We were stunned, to say the least, and were left wondering what exactly they did have in store for us. Those instructed in Dallas came from places generally south of a line running from San Francisco to Richmond and were the first exposed to the course. We later heard that something akin to a riot occurred in New York when the men were told the same thing at the end of the course there. A former colleague who had moved up rapidly in management explained that such reactions were commonplace up north, as had been his experience when he became an assistant chief of audit in Chicago and decided to make a goodwill tour of all posts of duty to introduce himself. In one place, he commented about the nice physical facilities (decidedly scarce in the Federal Government) and upon coming to work the next morning found a grievance on his desk filed by the employees in that office. They accused him of intimating that changes in working space were going to be made without the union having been notified first.

As soon as it became known that the IRS was experimenting with statistical sampling, greatly alarmed taxpayers began impeding the flow of information in new ways, but they need not have worried because the program which eventually came out of Washington was merely a variation of the traditional practice of checking expense detail. Instead of a scientifically proven sample of a hundred items extracted from an enormous amount of detail, we were to stratify individual expense accounts into five segments, and one hundred items were then randomly selected out of each stratum for examination. Aside from violating the basic tenets of statistical sampling, we were forced into burying ourselves with unimaginable quantities of detail. Not long afterwards, computer specialists arrived on the scene. They had been freshly trained at government expense at various universities, and they were able to address large computers to extract whatever information we thought was needed, but they were under orders that statistical sampling was to be carried out in accordance with the methods developed in Washington.

Commanding far greater resources, corporate taxpayers immediately began frustrating the implementation of the new program. One thing they objected to—and rightly so—was having to track down detail connected with the sampling techniques, and, in one instance, a company had *all* purchase invoices brought in and placed them in row upon row of file cabinets (about one hundred and fifty of them) in the basement of its office building. We were invited to help ourselves, and it was soon realized that the three audit aides we brought in weren't up to the task and the project was abandoned.

NEW YORK

The slogan "I love NY," which adorned the bumpers of many automobiles, had not been introduced when I first returned to New York on official business, but my fondness for what many consider to be the world's capital was rekindled at once. Upon awakening the first morning in the old Hotel New Yorker on the corner of 8th Avenue and 34th Street, I was treated to a spectacle as exciting as the one I saw twenty years earlier through the open door of my cabin aboard ship. It had snowed during the night and the Empire State Building a block and a half away was framed in all its majesty in my hotel window against a dark, wintry sky.

Contrary to popular belief, I have found New Yorkers to be the most genuinely friendly and tolerant people in America provided, of course, one considers that the city's reputation has probably been tainted by the influx of so many different people who have come to the place seeking their fortune. One of my coworkers came home terribly upset once and related how, while attending a training session on Long Island, he had stopped someone on the street in midtown Manhattan to ask directions and how the man had backed off to shout "fuck you" and walked away. I merely asked if it had occurred to him that those might have been some of the few words he knew in English. On later occasions, the same fellow and I explored several parts of Manhattan, foolishly walked across Central Park after dark, and once got lost in the area where the great ocean liners used to dock. We never found the one which was supposed to have an open house, but along the way back to the hotel we passed a parked car with what looked like a dead man sprawled on the hood while a small crowd of onlookers gave us dirty looks. In a minute or two, an ambulance came screaming down the street to attend to the matter.

The Manhattan street scene offered entertainment at all hours of the day and night. When alone, I never strayed far from Midtown, whereas with two or more, we often went exploring, and never encountered any fearful situation. When a path respectfully opened up for us in Greenwich Village, where thousands of unkempt runaways clogged the sidewalks, we concluded that they mistook us for plainclothesmen. Returning to our hotel one evening, my partner ran across the street to beat a red light while I hesitated. As I watched him, I noticed three youths sitting on an iron fence make a backwards somersault into the subway entrance beside the hotel, while a girl with them panicked and almost got run over by a cab as she ran away. When I caught up with him, we discussed the disturbance and decided that those kids thought we might have been after them.

Occasionally, when there were formal conferences for which the case manager would be in town, we would be invited out to lunch at one of the venerable feeding troughs of Manhattan. This was no treat for me because I much preferred to eat a sandwich somewhere, followed by a stroll through the streets, but my boss called the shots, and it was, after all, the equivalent of a Roman feast for our hosts to eat at their employer's expense. The bill for a party of six amounted to about $300 on one occasion.

Following one of those "scandals" which periodically plagued the IRS, we were reminded in no uncertain terms that accepting freebies was strictly prohibited, and it infuriated those who invited us out when they were informed that we would foot our own bills. This was just another instance where attempts at enforcing honesty became counterproductive because going out to lunch together became a rarity when tax department personnel also had to pay for their own meals. They were no longer considered to be entertaining anyone, and what little cooperation we received immediately following such treasured outings ceased at inestimable cost to the government, but tell that to the taxpaying public. It was one of their own kind which brought about a scandal by inviting a case manager on a Florida fishing trip and then maliciously bringing such to the public's attention. It turned out that in that instance a record had been maintained of minutiae such as how many cups of coffee were served to IRS personnel during the audit. The case manager was called out of retirement to stand trial and was convicted of accepting bribes. He lost his pension on top of going to prison, and all others on the team were reprimanded.

FAMILY REUNION

North Carolinians are beach people and seafood lovers. Those living in the eastern part of the state either go to Atlantic Beach in Morehead City, or to Carolina Beach near Wilmington. Those living in the Piedmont and Mountain sections generally prefer Myrtle Beach in South Carolina.

There is a big difference between North and South Carolina beaches; Atlantic Beach is rather pristine—probably because of the state park at one end of the island—and is family oriented. The fifty-mile-long strand at Myrtle Beach attracts people from everywhere and was beginning to look more like Miami Beach, but that was where we had started staying once we moved to Charlotte. Wherever money flows freely, crime is not far behind, and we witnessed an unusual event early one Sunday morning at the motel we frequented. As I sat on the front porch reading the paper, a helicopter skirted the beach and swung inland to set down on an empty lot across the street. Two young men climbed out and walked across to the motel to join a group gathered by the swimming pool. Introductions were made by first name only which, as someone in the party announced, was their custom. The ones who had been sitting around the pool were guests at the motel, and two of these owned a couple of dilapidated VW vans normally driven by hippies.

One doesn't see helicopters every day, and I decided to examine the sleek model parked so close by. Papers on the front seat indicated that the craft had been rented in a town not too distant from where we were. As I walked around the machine to admire it from all sides, I caught a glimpse of the party at the swimming pool. They were silently eying me and thereafter followed every move we made until we checked out to go home. This was about the year 1967 or 1968 and, after discussing the incident at work the next day, I decided to make some inquiries about the motel's ownership, only to come across some unsettling information. It was a comfortable old place with a swimming pool overlooking the ocean, but we never stayed there again.

Our children were at a precocious age, and we were becoming ever more vigilant concerning their safety. We never took a liking to Myrtle Beach, partly because of that, but also because of the long distance one had to travel over bad roads to get there. While on the way home after an extended weekend at the place during the summer of 1970, the girls harassed us continuously about going back the next weekend, and I wasn't particularly happy after just having dropped five or six hundred dollars. There was still a long summer ahead, and as soon as we arrived home, I started out for a travel agent to see how much it would cost for the family to visit Holland for a couple of weeks. I was pleasantly surprised and arranged to do so on the spot.

First came the necessary inoculations, and to the children's protests as to what they needed them for, I replied that I had gotten them all my life and that it was time that they got theirs. But when we went to get our picture taken for passport purposes, the cat was out of the bag and the excitement became unbearable.

Only Pan American was flying the giant Boeing 747s, which had only recently been placed in service. The Dutch airline was still flying stretch DC 8s, and we were picked up by an attendant in a station wagon to go less than a quarter mile from one terminal to another at Kennedy Airport (imagine such service today!). Seated next to me on the plane was a couple who had emigrated to New Zealand the same year I came to America. They were also going back for the first time, and we talked most of the night, comparing our experiences.

Twenty years is a long time, and I found that Holland had been transformed into a state of prosperity which, happily, included my sister and her family. I did learn that there had been some serious doubt about that at one time. The steamship company in the Indies—which her husband had represented as agent in one of the major port cities—had folded when the Dutch were finally forced to leave the new Republic of Indonesia. They, with thousands of others, came to Holland, and severance pay had long been depleted. As the family was taking its usual desultory stroll one afternoon, practically without knowing where the next meal was coming from, they ran into the city's mayor. The man had worked under Piet's father before the war and was surprised to learn about the dire straits they were in. Mayors in Holland are appointed by the Crown, and he was able to get Piet started in a new career (rather late in life, to be sure), which eventually resulted in a more than adequate standard of living.

Any knowledge I had about Holland I had picked up during relatively brief postwar visits, so everything was practically as new to me as it was to Ruth and the girls. We had a hard time locating my sister and her family among the crowd of welcoming passengers at the airport, which is still the practice whenever a plane arrives from faraway places, but there she was with the traditional bouquet of flowers in her arms. They had come to pick us up in two separate cars and I was aghast when we quickly accelerated to 120 kilometers (75 miles per hour) in a vehicle scarcely as big as the hood of the one we parked at the airport at home. With the engine howling, we had difficulty carrying on a conversation with those in the back seat who seemed to be sitting on bleachers, and I did notice that Ruth was kind of green around the nose. The trip home was mercifully short.

Americans were still the rich cousins in those days, and we settled in what looked to be a fairly new motel at a convenient location. It had an excellent restaurant, but the room furnishings consisted of four ugly iron bedsteads of varying dimensions. The oversized bathroom had a commode, a bidet, the utility of which I was unable to explain, and a shower. We rented a large car (at least by European standards) and went sightseeing, to the utter delight of my sister who accompanied us everywhere we went and learned as much about the country as we did in the process. But first we had to get used to the traffic, which was already becoming difficult to negotiate and which, in time, was to turn into a nightmare. Roads are festooned with all manner of traffic signals, and one needs to maintain a sharp lookout as to who has the right of way, which is indicated at virtually every intersection. If you miss seeing one, watch out! However, speed is the biggest worry. Seventy-five miles per hour is the official limit, but it is wise to triple check before entering a passing mode lest one gets clobbered by a Mercedes or BMW traveling almost twice as fast. Occasionally we were treated to a spectacle where a car was tailgating another at an excessive speed, wildly flashing its headlights, and then passing on the emergency strip. Things were to become much worse during subsequent visits when I became so rattled that we headed straight for the garage to turn in the car and continued getting around via public transportation. There is no doubt in my mind that the aggressive behavior we have to cope with on the roads at home was picked up by people visiting Europe. Visitors from over there find our traffic running much calmer and smoother.

Amsterdam was still a charming city, although it was exhibiting signs of coming trouble. Hippies of undetermined origin were roosting on a monument in front of the royal palace on the Dam; they had gained notoriety and were obviously enjoying it. Anyone attempting to take a picture of the scene got the sun reflected in his face by means of a small mirror. Some months later, royal marines took it upon themselves to forcefully evict them and earned the gratitude of the citizens.

Not long before our visit, my sister and her family had moved into a new eight-story apartment building across the street from an equally new shopping center. The unit they occupied on the second floor had a spacious living and dining room facing a busy street, two bedrooms on one side of a hallway leading to the entrance on the back of the building, and a kitchen, toilet, and shower on the other side. A small balcony off the dining room had space for about four persons to enjoy the outside on summer days. All units were alike, and the place had a particularly festive look when the large orange awnings over all living room windows across the front were lowered. The building was owned by an insurance company, and the very reasonable rents were controlled by the state. She and her husband were to live there in comfort and without a worry in the world until they died within four months of each other about twenty-five years later.

We covered a lot of ground during that first visit and were fortunate to see the country at a most attractive period since the war. Much was new and fresh with the old blending in nicely, but everything would change drastically in just a couple of decades. It was the first time I got to hear a detailed account of life in Japanese prison camp from which most victims never fully recovered.

By the time we boarded the plane for the flight home, we were thoroughly exhausted, but more adventure awaited us when we transferred from Kennedy airport to Newark by helicopter, which made an intermediate stop at LaGuardia. On lifting off at Kennedy I spotted one of our suitcases sitting on the tarmac. It contained all the souvenirs we had collected—some of them valuable—and I worried that we would never see it again. It was delivered at home the next morning while we were having breakfast.

THE GOLDEN YEARS

The 1970s were exciting, and civil servants with their low but steady income—thirty percent less than what was paid for comparable work—seemed to prosper despite rapid inflation. We even got a taste of luxury when we were able to stay at none other than the Waldorf-Astoria while in New York, courtesy of an oil company travel club. The Big Apple was facing bankruptcy, and the commercial crowd had to make do with more modest lodgings, if they traveled at all. Richard Nixon was president and, except for the time that Ronald Reagan occupied the White House, government workers simply seemed to fare better under a Republican administration.

Early in the decade came the Arab oil embargo, and we all had the happy experience of standing in long lines for ten gallons of gas. Rationing was left up to the individual retailers with unfair results (good ole boys seemingly getting all they wanted), and that more than likely contributed to the eventual demise of the corner service stations which once provided thousands of jobs for unskilled workers, not to mention a fairly reliable living for the proprietors. Just as everyone suspected, there never was any real energy shortage, and output at home was curtailed to jack up the price. Texans partially shut off the supply of natural gas to the Northeast in the middle of a harsh winter and sported slogans on their cars such as "Let them freeze." This came to haunt them in time.

In Holland they told us that there were never any shortages in Europe, although prices had increased sharply and the dollar had lost value when we returned for another visit in 1974. This time we rented a diminutive Dutch car called the DAF, which was very popular among older people, most of whom had never driven a car before. It was powered by a spirited 1100 cc engine, and it had a variable transmission which needed no shifting. The car was actually driven by two rubber bands moving up and down a steel cone which provided a constantly changing gear ratio depending on the speed of the engine. Aside from a distracting whine, it performed superbly under all conditions.

We spent the first few days with my niece, Annette, who lived in a huge new housing development built in a pasture, complete with a train station, schools, and even a shopping center. The layout of the streets was so convoluted that we never did find her condominium on the first try. It seemed such a pleasant place and I particularly enjoyed taking my grand nephew for a walk on the splendidly landscaped grounds. The place unfortunately deteriorated in less than five years due to the elements which bedevil society in all parts of the world.

We had come to embark on the traditional circuit for most first-time visitors to Europe, except that we did so on our own, which has both its advantages as well as its disadvantages. The main advantage is that it costs about half as much and that it gives one a sense of real adventure. The less pleasant aspects are finding places to eat with a reasonably priced menu, finding parking space near hotels in the center of town and, of course, encountering a lack of comforts one takes for granted in America. Most prewar housing in Europe lacked adequate bathing facilities, and the average citizen once made do with one bath a week in a public bathhouse. It is said that some places in Paris still lack indoor plumbing, but that is hard to believe. In older hotels, guests went down the hall to use a common bath or toilet, and these places were naturally unacceptable to the American tourist who was once king of the trade. Europeans have long since developed an aversion to lack of private bathrooms as well, and modestly priced hotels now have at least a private toilet and a shower, but many are strange contraptions which require acrobatics on the part of a user. Then, too, just about everyone has some sort of a defect such as a slow drain or leaking faucets, while most furnish a stream of water resembling what comes out of a spray bottle.

As rockhounds we made it a point to visit Idar-Oberstein which is nestled in the German mountains about forty-five miles east of Luxembourg, as the crow flies. The city is famous for its jewelry industry, which is carried on in handsome old homes backed up to the Nahe River flowing through town. Showcases in the front part of the houses display endless varieties of masterpieces crafted out of gold, silver, and semiprecious gemstones. Raw materials come from every continent and were stored in open wooden boxes on the riverbanks which, someone later told us, is no longer the case because the river has been covered up. Finished products are distributed worldwide.

Our hotel was a jewel befitting the surroundings but contained the usual booby-traps for unsuspecting American travelers. Proceeding down the hall, one had to turn on a light which burned long enough to get to either one's room or at least to the next switch. Missing one of these caused us not to notice a step down in the hall, and Ruth fell flat on her face. A meeting was going on in a room just beyond, and a number of men came bolting out of the door to investigate the disturbance. They were as upset as I was, although the damage to her face and spectacles appeared to be minimal. The hotel's proprietress was summoned and, while we waited for her, several of the men were urging us to sue. The lady insisted on taking us to the hospital in a cab and despairingly carried on a conversation with its driver as to the dreaded consequences, but she need not have worried; a Turkish doctor discovered nothing more than a hairline fracture of the nose which Ruth had sustained playing basketball in college. Newly built on the side of a mountain, the facility was spacious and well equipped. There was a full complement of nurses on duty, even though there seemed to be no patients.

Next day we drove on to the Rhine Valley, thence south through the Black Forest toward Switzerland. It was summertime, the weather was perfect, and as we reveled in the scenery, we wondered what on earth caused people to ever want to leave and seek their fortunes in far less agreeable places. It was my first visit to continental Europe, too, and my mind wandered back to the stories my father used to tell about Germany, a place he loved dearly. During the First World War, before he went out to the Indies, he regularly visited Berlin, and he recounted with much emotion the ordeal of a people at war. I doubt that he ever realized, however, what they wound up doing to his kind the next time around.

In Austria, we spent several days in the Tirol region where, in the late afternoon, we would sit on a bench overlooking a valley to wait for the sound of countless cuckoo clocks in people's homes strike the hour at more or less the same time. For this reason alone, the summer has got to be preferable to wintertime to make a visit. We crossed into Switzerland at the bottom of a remote valley where the border was guarded by two surly militiamen armed with automatic weapons while a German police dog took in the scene. Even though they snatched our passports, they did not examine them, but they gave us a disdainful look without returning our greetings. Spectacular as the country is, its inhabitants are less endearing (they don't even bother to turn away while they pee on the road when a car approaches) and, in time, we learned to avoid the place altogether except for coming through it while on a train. One high pass was closed due to bad weather, and we were forced to take another where the road was clear but where snow was banked up on both sides twice as high as the car was tall. Just after starting our descent, we came upon a hapless elderly motorist who had driven his fancy new Peugeot into the side of the mountain. We drove his wife to an emergency telephone and back, and they declined our offer to stay with them until help arrived.

Zürich was frightfully expensive, and it was my turn to run into one of those European booby-traps when the sliding glass door of a hotel entrance hit me on the side of the head. The doorman looked at me as if I was crazy, while the price they quoted at the desk to stay there was absurd. Not much further away, we lucked into a nice place close to the lake. Run by a Dutchman, it attracted his countrymen and one, who came all the way from Sweden, inquired with eager anticipation about the impending arrival of a group of "chicks" while he was eating breakfast two tables away the next morning. As the manager stopped by our table, he bade us good morning in Dutch, whereupon the man from Sweden turned red from embarrassment. I put him at ease when I explained to him that Ruth was American and didn't understand his remark about the girls. He was a computer engineer and worked for a firm in Stockholm. His employer only paid for his airfare home once every three months, hence he didn't get to see his family very often.

It was in Zürich that we first got into the habit of boarding a streetcar to ride it to the end of the line and back. You get to see much of a city that way, but it has its hazards. One is that conductors have been done away with in many places, and passengers must buy their tickets from a machine. Dire warnings are usually posted that to be caught without a ticket earns one a stiff fine, and we always heed those warnings except when the directions on the automatic dispensers are just too complicated. Fortunately, inspectors rarely come aboard to check. In most cities one can buy a pass for a certain number of days at a tourist information center for little or nothing. Any sightseeing trip by tram should not be taken late in the evening, lest one winds up spending the night in a barn at a terminal.

In France, I rear-ended a lady who had just learned to drive and who was taking her children to school early one morning in a brand-new car. We had spent the night in Vesoul, not far from the Swiss border, and were behind her as she was starting to pull into traffic on the main highway not far from the motel. As I looked over my shoulder to see if all was clear, I failed to notice that she had hesitated and stopped. It was more of a shove than a collision, which occurred next, but there we were, facing a hysterical French woman on her own turf. In fluent broken French, I managed to persuade her that we should go to a police station where, upon arrival, what seemed to be an entire platoon of gendarmes circled the car to survey the damage. Shortly, a civilian drove up who must have been the prefect, and the entire party moved indoors amidst much chatter and gesticulation. The situation was becoming alarming when, suddenly, the gendarmes were ordered out of the room. The prefect helped us fill out an accident report, after which he suggested that we stop by the lady's insurance agent. It all ended well, and I was able to straighten the Daff's bumper out with my bare hands.

We stopped for lunch at a wayside restaurant where we had the opportunity to observe the French working man consume enormous amounts of food. Cars and trucks were parked all over the place, and while some of the clientele looked downright poor, they sure ate and drank well. How in the world they managed to do any work the rest of the afternoon was beyond understanding. While making her rounds, the proprietress came by our table for a chat and shook her head when she learned that we were headed for Paris. Perhaps we should have heeded her advice to find accommodations somewhere on the outskirts and take the train in the rest of the way. Avoiding the beltway, which was only partially finished, we had no trouble finding our way into the city's center. The problem was getting out. With a map in her lap, Ruth called out the landmarks as we passed them, invariably wedged in the middle of a stream of traffic until we reached the Place de la Concorde, where we got a chance to fan out. We learned too late that, to avoid being cut off, one must resolutely aim for the exit of one's choice, regardless of the swarm of motorists all around and, as novices, we were forced into unknown territory where we spent the afternoon traveling in different directions, occasionally squeezing into a parking place to see if we could find accommodations for the night. There was absolutely nothing available. Finally, at about 6:00 in the evening, we spotted a sign for De Gaulle Airport, which we never did see, but we did notice that we were gradually leaving the city and correctly concluded that we were heading north. We were running out of gas and tanked up at a station which closed for the night the minute we paid the bill. Way down the road, at about 9:00, we came upon a restaurant which was in the process of closing its doors but where they were kind enough to serve us a leftover bowl of soup. Well, if push came to shove, we could always head back to Holland where, at the speed we were progressing, we figured we should arrive in time for breakfast. The road was narrow, and trucks refused to dim their lights. While they were not as big as in the States, one nevertheless had reason to fear them. Around midnight, I began to glimpse traffic seemingly running parallel to our road and when we took the next intersection to investigate, we came upon the main *autoroute* to Brussels. What a find! Heading north, we shortly came upon one of the first Novotels, all lighted up on the other side of the divided highway. There was a parking lot on our side, and a phone call brought a van, which took us through a tunnel to the front door of the hotel. It was 1:00 in the morning when we turned off the lights.

It was our intention to return to Paris the next morning until they told us that the tunnel the courtesy van took us through was not for private vehicles and that the next overpass where one could turn around was about twenty miles up the road. Besides, did we have reservations in Paris, monsieur? No? Well then, we would not advise you to go back before you do! Since our budget didn't allow us to stay at even a modest hotel—assuming that we could have found the place—we decided that it would be best to conclude our journey, but when we came upon a turnoff to Calais, we figured that a trip along the coast would be worthwhile. Road signs advertised hovercraft service to England, so we decided to at least go and have a look and, well, why not just go across? Cars and trucks were standing in line, and a ticket wasn't all that expensive.

It was a hazy day, and the hovercraft didn't become visible until it rounded a tall dune. To see it come out of the water and come lumbering up the beach toward a smooth area in front of us was a weird sensation. When the main engine was cut, the rubber skirt around its periphery deflated with a loud hiss and, almost at once, a ramp was let down over which an astounding number of vehicles exited. It soon was our turn to drive aboard and, after parking the car, we had to go upstairs to take a seat in a cabin resembling the interior of a wide-bodied jet. The trip across the channel lasted about forty-five minutes, and we saw nothing but spray due to the heavy seas, which made it seem as if we were riding a bucking horse. However, it was nothing like the pitching of a ship which is liable to make one seasick. We landed at Ramsgate, cleared customs, and headed for London.

It takes five days to become accustomed to driving on the left side of the road and even then it is easy to become confused upon entering a divided highway or street. Consider the fact that people drive on the left side in Australia, South Africa, Ireland, Egypt, Japan, India, Pakistan, Indonesia, Malaysia, plus quite a few other places in the world, and one concludes that about a third of the world does so. The English countryside is magnificent, particularly in the midlands where there are those enormous hills (denuded mountains, really) which we were to see on later occasions.

We spent the first night in a bed-and-breakfast in Canterbury where, upon visiting the cathedral, we stupidly ignored a privacy sign beside a gravel path and were much embarrassed when we encountered two clerics engaged in earnest conversation while taking a stroll. They must have been used to brash tourists because they nodded and gave us a pleasant smile, after which we beat a hasty retreat. Was it the archbishop? Who knows! One still had to put coins in a heater to draw warm water to take a bath as well as to turn on the hearth to ward off the chill in the room. I remembered having to burn wood chips in a water heater in Australia before taking a bath. People were so polite everywhere we went, and we hated to leave the place the next morning.

Getting around London in a car with left-hand drive proved to be a challenge, and we wasted no time parking it for the duration of our visit. Our hotel was not far from Victoria Station, and it took only a short bus ride to reach the popular tourist attractions such as Trafalgar Square, Buckingham Palace, and the Houses of Parliament, but we still did a lot of walking. Ruth had promised her parents to look up her brother's name in a war memorial book kept in St. Paul's Cathedral. A short service was in progress, and we had to wait until a cleric became available to show us where to go. As we finally managed to approach one, we heard him exchange some sharp words with a man who was carrying a suitcase which he had previously parked in an aisle before taking a seat. He later explained to us that he had to keep an eye on the individual during the service to see that he didn't depart without his baggage because, if he had, they would have had to evacuate the church and call the bomb squad, courtesy of the Irish Republican Army. He showed us what we had come for, and I duly recorded the event by taking a picture to show Ruth's mother.

On leaving London on Sunday morning for Harwich to catch the night ferry to Hook of Holland, we had a difficult time finding our way out of the city. In a quiet neighborhood, a gentleman tending his flower garden patiently explained how to reach the loop road around the city, on which we next drove mile after mile without getting to the sign the man told us would direct us toward Harwich. At one point, we pulled up behind a car parked beside the road which was occupied by a Sikh and his family who were as lost as we were, and we wound up leading him, a London resident. The sign finally showed up around lunchtime, and we had a pleasant drive the rest of the way. There was plenty of time to survey the countryside around Harwich, and the beach was crowded with people. The tide was out and many of them were looking for sharks' teeth, of all things.

Having made no reservations for the 10:00 p.m. ferry, we spent some anxious moments first standing in a line of cars early in the evening and again when the train from London disgorged hundreds of people, which rendered securing a cabin improbable. Our name was finally called by the purser, and we wound up in a stuffy enclosure devoid of any facilities other than one bunk stacked up on top of another, but it was private and we managed to get some sleep. When we took the same ferry two years later, we were pleasantly surprised that our travel agent had reserved one of four luxury cabins (of which there were two on each side of the ship), and we traveled in splendor. It forever eliminated any desire to book a trip to nowhere on one of those love boats filled with dancing waiters and beautiful people singing, "If you could see me now."

Arrival in New York from abroad is always an adventure, as we were to find out again upon return this time and on future occasions. On approaching Kennedy Airport, the 747 suddenly encountered severe turbulence, which caused a number of people in the rear of the craft to become airsick, sending cabin personnel scurrying. After circling the airport for the better part of an hour because of a thunderstorm, the captain announced that he was running low on fuel and that he was heading for Montreal. Before landing there about an hour later, everyone was advised to stay on board because Canadian customs officials would not permit anyone to leave a small waiting area, not even to use the restrooms but that plenty of telephones would be available to call relatives, if anyone so wished. About one hundred people—including myself—scrambled for a place in line for what turned out to be one telephone. A fight almost erupted several times as the inevitable phone junkies could not resist making useless conversation, and the phone was finally yanked out of one man's hand by someone who became sufficiently frustrated. The incident caused much cursing but fortunately little else. I finally got a chance to call Antoinette and Lynda, who were just ready to leave for the airport at home to pick us up.

As we waited for the refueling to be completed, several of us got a chance to learn about the less romantic aspects of an aviator's life when we witnessed the captain and the purser struggling with a problem of logistics. A crowd of 350 hungry people needed to be fed, and the only food available on short notice were floppy sandwiches wrapped in cellophane. The captain was an elderly man, and one couldn't help but feel sorry for him because he must have been on duty in excess of twelve hours, yet he never for one moment seemed to compromise the safety of his charges, some of whom were getting to be rather hard to handle. One was a lady with three children—the smallest a mere infant—who had departed Moscow at 6:00 local time that morning on her way to San Francisco. Like most of us, she had long since missed her connecting flight when we finally landed in New York at about 10:00 in the evening. The ordeal of clearing immigration and customs was more than she could cope with, and she suddenly went into hysterics. About half a dozen flight attendants appeared out of seemingly nowhere to sweep up the children as well as all the lady's baggage. The last we saw of them was when they were being loaded into a station wagon. Those who needed them were issued courtesy passes for cabs as well as a place to spend the night. Ours turned out to be a substandard hotel not far from LaGuardia Airport, where we caught an early plane home the next morning.

The terminal at Kennedy used by foreign airlines was expanded a great deal as the years went by, but they never seemed to be able to bring order to the arrival area on the lower level where huge crowds had to funnel through immigration and customs. As we stood around the conveyor belt in the baggage area waiting to retrieve our luggage on one occasion, someone casually walked off with a nearby passenger's shopping bag, filled with expensive goods bought at a so-called "duty-free shop" at the airport in Amsterdam. The owner had placed it on the floor beside him as he stood talking to a fellow passenger and never noticed what happened. The place must have been invaded by a group of itinerant thieves because soon an announcement came over the public address system cautioning everyone to guard their belongings. In later years, some of the customs officers began carrying guns as the public became more and more unruly. While we have never had to open our luggage for inspection, others didn't come off so lightly. We once stood in line behind a couple who had to unpack everything. They appeared to be tour guides, and the man was sneeringly addressed as "doctor" by the inspector as another one packing a gun stood by to watch. They were particularly nasty to the lady and opened two or three tubes of makeup from the bottom, presumably looking for drugs. They finally demanded that she turn her purse upside down and dump everything on the counter. We were shocked at such rude behavior, but shortly afterwards I began working with a man whose father was a customs officer in New York and I learned from him that I need not have been. What these people have to contend with is often unbelievable. Moreover, when, some years later, they joined our union, it became evident that they had been—and were being—treated in an abominable fashion.

There were rare occasions when humorous incidents occurred. Once, when the arrival concourse was so badly congested that even airport personnel had become jittery, we were standing in the inevitable long line waiting to pass customs when an apparition came into the hall and proceeded toward the exit without bothering to fall into line. She was a huge woman, dressed entirely in black with a short skirt above the knees and black stringy hair. She was pushing a baggage cart loaded with soft-side suitcases piled so high that she was having trouble keeping them all on there. If she wasn't actually drunk, she was putting on quite an act, and the people watched appreciatively as she tottered along and the whole load of baggage on her cart suddenly came crashing down. The crowd roared with laughter, but customs officers became enraged and yelled for porters to come and clean up the mess. Two of them loaded everything onto a much bigger cart and escorted the lady out the front door to where the cabs stood waiting. Well, laughter abruptly ceased as people wondered what kind of a show they had just witnessed. Wasn't she supposed to go through customs? What the hell was going on here? No explanation was provided, but I guess that just happened to be New York!

ABOUT TRAVEL AND LEISURE

We were to make three more trips overseas during the seventies, and my job continued to be engaging. Much of my work was in Asheville and Winston

Salem, and I would leave early Monday morning, spend the night, return late Tuesday, stay in town Wednesday to catch up with administrative detail, then repeat the process Thursday and Friday. Rumbles emanated from intermediate management, but the top brass at headquarters had no comment and appeared satisfied with the results.

Large companies carry on activities all over the country, and one thing I would always insist on was to become acquainted with some of these. As a result, we wound up visiting all kinds of manufacturing plants, oil refineries, coal mines, salt mines—just to name a few—and discovered that these companies' personnel were as eager to learn about what their employers were doing as we were. Some of the time my immediate boss (the case manager) would come along, while at others I would be accompanied by a specialist such as an engineer or international agent. If any problem subsequently arose, we wouldn't have any explaining to do but could quickly resolve them.

To visit a coal mine, a company's tax manager and I traveled to Harlan, Kentucky where serious violence once occurred between mine owners and workers. To get there, we flew into Tri-Cities Airport in the eastern part of Tennessee and continued by car alongside a seemingly endless creek, which was decorated for the most part with what appeared to be toilet paper hanging from the trees. The latter mystery was cleared up when they later explained that the creek had recently flooded causing toilet paper to become entangled in the tree branches. How come the toilet paper? Because the majority of dwellings lacked plumbing—stupid!

Coal was extracted by means of drift mines which are horizontal burrowings into the sides of mountains. They took us on a tour of one such facility which, because of the large company which owned it, had the latest state-of-the-art equipment and strictly observed all safety rules. We were required to don overalls and boots, were issued hard hats, miners' lamps and survival gear, and had to hand over any smoking paraphernalia such as matches and cigarette lighters. Accompanied by a home office executive, we gathered at the mine entrance to crawl aboard a train consisting of three-foot-tall cars with open sides, and promptly departed to enter another world. It took about half an hour to reach the mine facing, which is the area where they were actually digging for coal. They informed us that we were two and one-half miles inside the mountain and thoughtfully omitted the kind of remark a park ranger makes in Mammoth Cave to the effect that if something were to happen, we couldn't possibly be buried anywhere deeper and cheaper. We had switched on our miners' lamps (which burn eight hours) the moment we entered the mine and noticed that the walls and ceiling were a dirty white color. This is because they were coated with lime to keep down coal dust, which is a fire hazard. To keep the ceiling from collapsing, about a one-foot-wide, heavy steel plate is installed overhead every six feet or so, kept in place by long steel bolts screwed into the rock overhead. This takes the place of the old wooden roof supports. As soon as a quantity of coal has been dug out, a machine is rolled in place. It drills holes overhead to accommodate the bolts which hold up the ceiling support. Until the roof supports are in place, this is an extremely dangerous area into which I innocently wandered until someone unceremoniously grabbed me by the collar to yank me back into the safe zone. In an area just around the corner, a machine which did the actual digging had pulled up to a mine facing and was about to start up; before it did, sirens warned everyone to get out of the way. Operated by a man who sat right behind the giant claws up front, this enormous device—also about three feet high—created a dense cloud of coal dust which, after it settled, made us all look like miners. As the machine dug, the coal fell on a conveyor belt which carried it all the way beyond the mine entrance, where it was dumped on a pile.

We were able to walk upright wherever we went once we stepped out of the train, but coal is found in veins which are often of a thickness that makes it no longer practical to mine because of the size of the machinery. In times past, they went after it with picks and shovels and dragged it out in baskets to the point where it could be loaded in carts which were hauled out to the mine entrance by mules. These mules had been born and raised inside the mine and were blind because they had never seen daylight. The president of the mining company had been in the business all his life and fascinated us with stories for several hours after dinner at the VFW club that night, until the question of unions came up. What did I think of unions? Well, as far as I was concerned, society couldn't do without them. That started an acrimonious debate that quickly ended the meeting, which caused the man from the home office to get all shook up, but he later confided that his father had been a stalwart member of a union and he had to agree with me. He took great pains to keep me away from mining officials after that.

From the looks of the area, one couldn't help but conclude that miners lived in great poverty. We learned that, whenever they got a chance, families would move north to one of the large cities in order to improve their lot. More often than not, however, their luck would run out. They would return in a wreck of a car—their most prized possession—which soon gave up the ghost and would either be left sitting close to the shack in which they lived or rolled into a nearby hollow or creek, which made the whole region look like one vast junkyard. But that was just the readily apparent misery, and I was to hear worse tales later from one of our own agents at home whose father owned a gas distribution business in the area we were visiting. A by-product of mining is methane gas, suitable for household use, and the young man used to help his father install gas appliances during the summer months when school was out. He told of one house where half-naked children played amidst food remnants on the floor and where they came across the ghastliest thing ever when they had to open a closet. Here was the family toilet, consisting of a straight-back chair propped up on bricks over a cardboard box three quarters full with human waste, the stench of which was overpowering. It was midwinter, and the box would be emptied in a nearby creek as soon as the weather turned warmer.

It was the mid-seventies, and coal was in great demand because of the oil crisis. If the miners lived in poverty, this did not mean that the mine owners suffered likewise. When subsequently auditing a firm which sold airplanes, they told us about the time one aircraft costing slightly less than a million dollars was delivered in the area to a mine owner who arrived on the scene in a late-model Rolls Royce, which was barely recognizable as such because it was coated by a thick layer of coal dust. He paid in cash as they were sitting inside the car, which had a bag of coal parked on the rear seat. Could the man fly? Nope! Where, then, was his pilot? Well, he was dickering with a couple of fellows, and as soon as he was able to hire them, would they mind coming back to show them how to fly the thing?

A great contrast with the coal mine was a salt mine we once visited. Here we had to descend one thousand feet to enter what looked like a brightly lit factory with all sorts of machinery moving about as if they were above the ground. We were invited to take a seat in what looked like one of those German army command cars during the war and were driven for miles in an underground maze of tunnels wide enough to let two vehicles pass one another. At one point they told us that we were riding under some large city.

Salt is dirty brown or nearly black, just the opposite of what one would expect, and most of it is used to be spread on icy roads during the winter. The humidity in the mine is very low, and they have no problem with anything corroding. All machinery, no matter how large or how complicated, has to be taken apart so it can fit in an elevator and is reassembled one thousand or more feet below. Sadly enough, some people lost their lives in an accident not long after we were there, one of them an engineer who had shown us around.

Going one thousand feet down a hole in the ground takes some getting used to but, once there, one forgets about any danger. In some places, salt is flushed out of the ground with hot water, but we didn't get to visit such an operation.

Not long afterwards, after having passed Mobile in Alabama on the way back home to Charlotte, we found that eastbound traffic on the causeway was rerouted on the westbound lane due to a tropical depression which had made landfall during the night and which had partially flooded the highway. That storm moved up into Pennsylvania and flooded the valley between Scranton and Wilkes-Barre, causing enormous damage. The fellow I was working with showed me around the area later and recounted how the Susquehanna River came out of its banks uprooting graveyards and wrecking homes, but the weirdest thing that happened was when the roof of a mine collapsed, causing permanent flooding of valuable anthracite mines. They tried to stop it by dumping railroad cars loaded with dirt into the hole with little or no effect because they simply disappeared. I wasn't at all impressed with the area, which is one of the oldest in America. Leafing through the telephone book in my room one night made me feel as if I was in Czechoslovakia.

SPECIAL ASSIGNMENT

Having once worked for a steamship company, I was delighted to be assigned to assist in the examination of a return of a large concern which had recently bought such a company. It just so happened that I had come to the United States in 1950 on a vessel which was owned by it, although the nature of the enterprise had long since changed. Thrown in with the package was a recent acquisition of an oil company operating in the Middle East. This time I wound up working with two different engineers and two international examiners in addition to three regular agents.

The shipping company had caught the attention of the then chief of examination, and a number of office auditors were mired in an unbelievable quantity of petty detail contained in boxes stacked up in a large room on the taxpayer's premises. They were looking for evidence of petty fraud while far more significant matters were being ignored.

The taxpayer had two people on its staff whose sole function it was to thwart the examination, and this was something new we had to contend with. It necessitated spending almost three weeks on site in Elizabeth, NJ, followed by a week's visit to Puerto Rico. Nobody in the office allegedly had the authority to show us around, least of all to take us on board one of the company's ships so we took the liberty to simply walk aboard a couple of them during a lunch break one day. Pathetic is the only word which would describe conditions aboard them. They were scarcely habitable rust buckets with minimal amenities for crew members, none of whom were anywhere in sight. These were container ships, and our engineer wanted to see the loading and unloading of one with those huge mobile cranes. A customs officer arranged for us to do so, and he picked us up in his station wagon because it was freezing cold and much of the harbor was covered with ice. On the way to the dock area, he repeatedly warned us to stay right at his side so as not to afford a crane operator the chance of "accidentally" dropping one of those containers on us. We thought he was joking, but he was perfectly serious; even in those days before rabble-rousing talk show hosts, those were the sort of things public servants already had to face.

Container ships were relatively new. Through the ages, cargo had been loaded and unloaded on board ships by stevedores, or longshoremen, as they are called in America. Nowadays, everything is loaded into semitrailers pulled by trucks alongside a ship where the entire body (called the container) is lifted off the wheels and hoisted aboard by means of giant cranes. Starting deep down in a ship's hold, the individual containers are placed on racks and, when the holds are full, the rest is piled four or five high on racks above deck. At their destination, they are unloaded and placed on individual trucks, which distribute them to receivers. Huge amounts of special equipment are needed but the system is fast, so fast in fact, that apples grown in New Zealand are on American tables in less than three weeks. Container ships now circle the globe on tight schedules.

Four of these ships had been sold in Puerto Rico, something which had to be verified, and two of us took a three-hour plane ride out of Atlanta to check on matters. I had not looked forward to this trip because of the restrictions placed on an agent's activities when away from the United States, even though these were not altogether applicable in a commonwealth state. We were received with the utmost courtesy wherever we went and were careful to respond in kind. Our quarters were a stone's throw from the fashionable Hotel San Juan, located on the beach, and each night we entertained ourselves by sitting in its lobby, which sported the biggest chandelier in the world (so they said) while watching the arrival of crowds from whichever cruise ship happened to be in port. They came to rid themselves of money, of which they appeared to have plenty. Those were the days when mostly the elderly retirees seemed to be the only ones who could afford cruises, and they were a sight to behold—doddering old ladies on spiked heels, escorted by well-cooked gentlemen wearing pink coats, flowered shirts, and yellow or green white shoes. One night the excitement in the casino appeared to be so great that we just *had* to take a peek as to what was going on, but we were simply dressed in pants and shirt. That was no problem because security officers at the door loaned us their red coats so that we could meet the dress requirements.

Our hotel was quite nice, too. It happened to house a tennis club, and I enjoyed watching them play from my window on the third floor. Strangely enough, only the individual guest rooms upstairs were air-conditioned, whereas the public rooms downstairs were not, but there was always a nice breeze blowing off the ocean. I really had expected to feast on tropical fruit for breakfast, as one does in Mexico, but none was available; they apparently grow very little of anything in Puerto Rico, and the people are dependent on food brought in from the mainland. It is nice, however, not having to worry about sanitary conditions, which are more or less the same as those at home.

Cars apparently were very expensive, and most people depended on used cars brought in from the States. We didn't bother to rent one and got around by cab instead. We did make an official tour inspecting facilities for a whole day and traveled to Ponce on the south coast, thence to Mayagüez on the west coast, before retracing our steps to San Juan. A low mountain range runs from east to west in approximately the middle of the island, which is green and verdant in the north due to abundant rainfall, and arid on the south side. Being of average size, I was the smallest in the party and wound up in the middle of the back seat of the car. About halfway back to San Juan in the afternoon, I decided I had been nice long enough and asked someone to exchange seats with me, but I had waited too long and wound up with a bruised coccyx (tail bone) which, the doctor later told me, commonly takes about a year to heal. Fortunately, mine didn't take that long, but I was uncomfortable for quite some time. Did anyone ever wonder why the Japanese have been reluctant to buy American cars? Well, for one thing, after the war they, for some reason, quit exporting them with steering wheels on the right side while lots of countries continue to drive on the left side of the road. The other complaint foreign buyers have is that the back seat is not fit to sit on, and they wouldn't be seen sitting next to the chauffeur in the front where the seats are comfortable.

It was pleasant to ride around Puerto Rico if for no other reason than to enjoy its vacation atmosphere. Splendid hotels exist up and down the beach in San Juan, and the old town around the famous fort is a shopper's paradise. Unfortunately, raw sewage is discharged directly into the ocean—at least, it still was at that time—and swimming was risky. The one thing that stood out was the artful use of wrought iron on most dwellings and commercial buildings, with honorable mention going to one entire house, including a car in the garage, which was enclosed in an iron cage commonly found in a zoo.

Shortly after returning home, a special emissary from Washington came to bring us the news that unpleasant things could happen to us when moving about New York during the audit of the oil company and he had been instructed to give us some advice on how to proceed in such a case. I was the only one of the team in town that day and was fascinated by the man. He had been an international examiner for a long time and apparently had done his job so well that he was rewarded with two lengthy overseas assignments, the first one in London, followed by one in Paris. As for the danger, we never noticed anything out of the ordinary, although there were lots of rumors floating around. We never ceased to wonder, however, about a long hallway in the oil company office, which was festooned with numerous photographs of Kuwaiti sheiks. Now, what could possibly induce an American company to pay homage in this manner to foreigners, I thought, until I learned that oil production was completely controlled by western interests at the sufferance of a bunch of questionable characters, few in number, but so rich and lazy that they probably had someone flush the commode for them, to put it politely.

Our assigned quarters were high up in the Associated Press Building in Rockefeller Center, overlooking the famous skating rink, and we took full advantage of this unexpected privilege. Weather permitting, one could take a peek in the back of the building at members of Radio City Music Hall's Rockettes taking a sunbath. I did go back and look one day, but without binoculars, things weren't worth watching. Besides, we were engrossed in something really interesting, and our casual request to interview the company's president was acted upon favorably. This could only happen in New York because, anywhere else, one got to talk only to underlings, who needed several weeks to gather appropriate misinformation relative to even the most routine questions. This misinformation was then presented with much fanfare in a meeting attended by a bevy of the taxpayer's personnel, each presenting his (and, later her) special knowledge about a matter. This time we got full and frank information of astonishing magnitude, which we communicated to our petroleum engineer, who passed it on through proper channels and which—we later learned—was summarily rejected on grounds that we didn't know what we were talking about. Perhaps that happened to be the danger they had warned us about!

CHANGING TIMES

Jimmy Carter had been in the White House a year and a half when we returned from our trip and, like most people, we seemed to be doing reasonably well. Yet, there was a nagging feeling of "malaise," to use that unfortunate term the President resorted to and which later came to haunt him. The derision which had been rampant in Atlanta during his presidential campaign was becoming prevalent everywhere, and we were feeling the effects of it in carrying out our duties. Longtime managers were retiring, to be replaced by far less able men (and women), and an undesirable atmosphere was developing—one of mutual distrust and hostility.

District headquarters had come under the leadership of a person who had started his career in the IRS as an office auditor, and he was generally not considered to be the most astute of personnel. He was reported to have originally studied for the ministry but had changed his mind and went to work for the government. He was quickly identified as management material and came to us to replace a stern and respected professional who brooked no nonsense, whatever the source. It liberated a flock of men of far lesser caliber, who began to assert themselves and who quickly managed to create a country-club atmosphere spiced with brotherly love for all—or almost all. The new director insisted on being called by his first name, and people were soon judged by their golf scores rather than their ability.

The system of review and disposition of cases with unagreed deficiencies in income tax was faltering because of the ever-growing multitude of "tax specialists" on the outside. They enticed delinquents to use their services, which consisted mainly of delay and obstruction. Of the enormous number of unagreed cases, once reported as 80,000 in the district (rather doubtful, I thought), only a dozen or so ever came before the US Tax Court. During my entire career only one of my cases ever went before this body and was deemed so complex that the Court took two years to render a decision. The truth was that we had the taxpayer over the barrel, yet they still got away with half. According to our counsel, the judge had sought advice from appellate personnel in Washington rather than seek clarification from him and became confused as a result.

There was a definite lack of respect on the part of personnel up the line for operational personnel, i.e., people in the field who raised issues. The bottleneck was the appellate staff, consisting of revenue agents who had once served in the field and who were presumed to be of superior ability. Some were, indeed, but as time went by, that standard was seriously affected by persons who were picked simply because they had managed to pass the CPA exam but who otherwise were deficient in many ways. Complex cases were arbitrarily dismissed, particularly if there was the slightest hint of intellectual endeavor present. There eventually developed a mutual contempt between field agents and appellate staff, which cost the government millions. Nothing was more unsettling than to receive a telephone call from a conferee months after a case had been submitted—seeking clarification about an issue, only to find that the man had not even bothered to read the agent's report and was relying solely on what was stated in a taxpayer's protest. Some even went so far as, without hesitation, adopting innuendo offered by taxpayers' representatives about examining personnel.

Although Ruth and I were only in our fifties, we found ourselves thinking more and more about retirement, for which I would be eligible in another six years. Perhaps we had been unduly influenced by our brother-in-law in Holland who had been counting the number of Christmas trees before he could throw in the towel, something he wasted no time in doing the minute he became eligible, which probably added about fifteen years to his life.

GOLDEN YEARS INTERRUPTED

We felt we had reached a crossroads in our life. I was fifty-three years old, and it occurred to me that my mother died at that age. Even though I was healthy, my enthusiasm at work was steadily declining.

During the Carter administration, authority in the IRS had become increasingly concentrated in regional centers, ours being in Atlanta. Emphasis was placed on identifying executive talent, and there was a constant turnover in management, which was becoming much younger. Members of the old guard were leaving the moment they qualified for retirement, to be replaced by personnel from other parts of the country—apparently according to the principle of divide and rule—and these people seemed to be solely interested in managing for management's sake. For a time, our work appeared to terrify them, and they avoided becoming even remotely involved in anything smelling of controversy. However, sycophants clustered around them like leeches, and as these were rewarded with intermediate management positions, they came to rule with an iron hand.

Taxpayers' personnel were becoming outright contemptuous, and we soon were the laughingstocks of the accounting and legal professions. Eventually, what was once a proud and capable civil service came to be demonized by the political establishment, something simply deemed unthinkable at one time. In short, I thought it was time to start thinking of retirement, the only question being, where to? We considered many options but concluded that the die had been cast long ago when the girls went to Mississippi to attend junior college. In the end—shortsighted as it was—we could visualize only one place as being the feasible one, and that was to settle where Ruth had been born and raised. I had really come to like the hill country and remember the countless walks in the woods, as well as standing behind the parental house overlooking a pasture, wishing I could stay forever.

In the spring of 1979, a large part of the Jackson metropolitan area was inundated by the Pearl River, which caused a subsequent migration of many people to the countryside. One of the first to do so was Ruth's oldest brother, who acquired three acres of land on which he personally constructed a house. The person who sold him the land informed Ruth and one of her younger brothers that she would gladly sell them a lot as well. Broke as ever, the latter nevertheless jumped at the offer and bought five acres right next to his brother. After much soul searching, we decided to make a more modest acquisition of two acres and, in time, bought six more, which turned out to have been a wise move because it provided us with a natural barrier when we built our house. Once landowners, we did little else than come down several times a year and attempt to clear an area on which to stake out a house site, but Mother Nature frustrated our efforts by growing things faster than we could cut them down.

A long-standing rule in the IRS was that an agent was not allowed to examine the tax returns filed by any person or corporation more than twice in succession and, as a result, I was assigned the audit of a bank, an extremely boring task. It did have a challenge of sorts in that taxpayer's executives took every step to thwart the audit, and we were at odds right from the start. They assigned us a space on about the twenty-fourth floor of a tower which had recently been constructed but which had many vacancies because law firms and insurance agencies were constantly attracted by fancier quarters, which were added to the city's skyline as time went by. While we had a splendid view, we had to go all the way down to a plaza to go to an adjacent building when we needed to see personnel in the tax department, which was located on about the sixteenth floor. Prior years' records were stored in a building across the city's busiest street, and we gave up jaywalking after one of us almost got run over by a bus; hence, we wound up spending much time on street corners waiting for traffic lights to change.

A bank man's business is the buying and selling of money. There would really be little to audit because the comptroller of the currency does a thorough job every year, but tax department personnel steadfastly refused to make the results available for our inspection, and we were forced to get bogged down in piles and piles of detail. Despite unimaginable boredom, we did have our occasional moments of laughter. Bank officials are apt to be stuffy, and, during many hours riding elevators, we overheard much bragging by youngish bank officials. One day, we decided to spin a fantastic tale ourselves. Gold was in much demand as people sought to protect themselves against inflation, and a deliberately muted conversation between two of us on a packed elevator as it made its way from floor to floor went somewhat as follows:

"Well, how was your trip to Johannesburg?"

"Oh, all right I guess . . . , but we had a few hectic moments on takeoff as the 747 freighter seemed reluctant to leave the ground. Those gold bars were heavy, and they were spread all over the deck from front to rear. Fact is, we had to walk over them any time we needed to use a toilet way in the back."

"You've got to be kidding!"

"No sir . . . I'm serious!"

An odd silence occurred on the elevator, and we seemed to be regarded with some awe during the rest of our stay.

The bank wasn't the only place where we were treated with contempt. It was the same everywhere, and why not? After all, President Reagan fired the entire staff of air traffic controllers for daring to go on strike and allegedly urged that tax collectors should be treated like junkyard dogs. I can recall only a single instance when a chief executive officer of a large company agreed to be interviewed by us, which is not to say that they didn't always know exactly what we were doing. One was openly hostile and tried to jab me with a long steel bit sticking out of a heavy industrial drill as we both were trying to negotiate the front door of his office building. Worse still, he rudely pushed my wife out of the way as we were going down an escalator at a shopping center one evening—actually physically touching her—because he was in a hurry.

It was about this time that I was selected to go to Washington to join a small group of people called in from the field to prepare training material. I have never liked the place, notwithstanding the fact that it is the nation's capital, where there are many things to see. It was around Thanksgiving, and we worked in Crystal City, across the Potomac River. The subway went as far as the National Airport—one stop beyond where we worked—and I had to ride in a courtesy van to my hotel in Fairfax, which served the most delicious lamb chops I have ever eaten. Quite often, the van would be loaded down with the same crew of an Air Florida plane that crashed into one of the bridges across the Potomac just a short time after we finished our assignment. Even though no pleasantries were ever exchanged—air crews being very standoffish, just like doctors—it gave me a strange feeling when the disaster was announced.

An agent from Albany, New York, and I were requested to prepare text material sufficient for two days of classroom training about foreign income tax credits. They weren't at all happy to hear that I didn't know enough about anything to keep a class busy more than half a day—indeed, if that long—and that I would be glad to make room for a substitute, but that fell on deaf ears. The task took its toll, and one evening I must have fallen asleep during a performance of the National Symphony Orchestra at the Kennedy Center. I was embarrassed to death when I found people staring at me because I had probably been snoring. Needless to say, I beat a hasty retreat out of the hall and, furthermore, was never invited again to prepare training material for the National Office.

It wasn't long afterwards that I was in Washington, this time to accompany an international examiner to see someone in the Treasury Department. Ruth and I drove up on this occasion and she went on a tour of the city while we worked. As they passed the Treasury Building, the bus driver emphasized that very few people ever gained access to the place, which of course was nonsense. All they wanted to see on entering was our pocket commission and they didn't even ask us to open our briefcases. Even though the gentleman we talked to was well up the line of authority, his working quarters were nothing less than pathetic. He sat at a huge, beat-up old desk at the end of a hallway and had a tiny personal pocket fan to circulate the air. We sat there most of the morning without a break, and our international agent thought he had convinced the man without keeping in mind that at that level he was operating in the rarefied air of politics—international politics at that! We were through at noon, and I met Ruth for lunch at the Smithsonian with the intent of afterwards viewing exhibits we had not seen before. By mid-afternoon, I was feeling ill and could barely make it back to the hotel to lie down. However, a short repose revived me, and I had to admit afterwards that the tense situation at work, together with the hustle and bustle of the immense city, had momentarily gotten the best of me. It was the last time I was in Washington, a place I never liked.

Not long afterwards, I made my last work-related trip to New York under less than desirable circumstances as well. Preparatory to an upcoming trial, our district counsel wished to take a deposition from a key witness who was allegedly in ill health. The man was an engineer and had rendered a highly questionable opinion as to the value of property sold, and our own engineer had taken exception. After spending most of a day discussing the matter in our district office, we took a late plane out of Greensboro during a violent rainstorm and arrived in New York after dark. Our attorney was ready to go right back to work without bothering to have anything to eat. In a situation like that, an unwritten rule was that we tailor our affairs to suit him, but I didn't accept that, and I suggested that we have dinner first in my favorite little restaurant in what was known as German Town. He adamantly refused, and I told him that I would see him later, which threatened to blow up the party, but they came around to my point of view and later admitted that I had been right after all. Returning to the hotel at around 9:00, we set up shop in a corner of the lobby and worked until 4:00 in the morning, getting no more than an hour's sleep before moving on to an office building in the lower part of Manhattan.

A young woman dressed in rags (a common sight on the streets of New York) joined us in the elevator and we instinctively moved over to give her all the room she needed so as not to be accidentally contaminated by some dreadful disease. Imagine our distress, however, as the same person joined us shortly afterwards in the hearing room, handsomely dressed and looking quite attractive. She turned out to be a court reporter who laughingly told us that she always moved about the lower end of Manhattan disguised in rags to avoid being accosted by undesirable elements. Once more—such is New York!

Earlier in my career, I studied law by correspondence, just as I did accounting. They even conferred a degree, which I thought preposterous and never flaunted it. It should be noted, though, that my superiors took careful note of my enterprise and promptly rewarded me with a promotion the minute I completed each course which, altogether, took the better part of ten years. Anyhow, if people persisted in wanting to know more about it, I would call myself a half-assed lawyer, which always seemed to give them great satisfaction. This particular day, in New York, I had the privilege of witnessing a real professional at work who spent the entire day interrogating his quarry and finally, at 5:00 in the afternoon, devastated him by announcing: "So, you did not tell the truth then, did you sir?" to which the man meekly indicated his agreement.

We hastily packed up our papers because we had a plane to catch, only to discover that it had been snowing outside. About six inches lay on the ground and, oddly enough, there seemed to be little traffic. We had no trouble hailing a cab, and I was looking forward to a restful evening when our attorney directed the driver to take us to LaGuardia Airport. Remembering one instance where I spent hours waiting for a connection and arrived home well after midnight, I was tempted to let them drop me off at the hotel where we stayed the previous night but was told that we had much work to do at our office the next morning.

The terminal building at the airport seemed totally deserted, until we entered the front door and found a huge crowd of angry people milling around. As expected, our flight was delayed indefinitely, and we joined the throng at one of the bars.

"Don't fret," said our attorney, a Chicagoan, "we're gonna get out of here tonight." To him, this was merely a little diversion and, sure enough, within an hour, they announced that our flight was getting ready for departure. Our other companion was headed for Atlanta, and we left him sitting forlornly at the bar. These were still the Eastern Air Lines days, the airline everyone professed to hate, just like they "hated" New York, simply to be fashionable, and we got back to Greensboro perhaps an hour late. By the time I got back to the motel, I was so tired that I left my room key sticking in the door, and anyone could have walked in on me during the night. But that wasn't near as bad as what the attorney did. He was distracted by his children when his wife picked him up and left his briefcase on the plane, something he discovered on the way home. Fortunately, the plane wasn't going any farther than Greensboro.

END OF CAREER

Just after Easter 1985, the realtor put up a FOR SALE sign in the front yard, and our house was sold three days later. We ordered our contractor in Mississippi to immediately start building a new one which he had promised to complete in three months, and he wound up doing exactly that. We did our own moving, making two initial trips in a fifteen-foot Ryder snub-nosed panel truck with the engine partially inside the cab. For the final trip, we used a conventional twenty-four-foot truck, which also towed our second car behind on a dolly. We had spent twenty years in Charlotte, and leaving wasn't exactly easy.

Even though retirement parties were no longer in vogue—most people being given a sendoff with a luncheon in a cafeteria—my friends and colleagues insisted on having a traditional one for me in a local country club. It was once the custom that this sort of affair was attended by the chief of the audit division or, at the very least, by his immediate assistant, but that was no longer the case. One of two branch chiefs came down one day and I was treated to breakfast by him and my supervisor.

The usual service awards were handed out during the retirement party, after which there came a pleasant surprise when a former agent stood up to make a presentation of a handsome plaque awarded by the Carolinas Chapter of the Tax Executives Institute which was inscribed as follows:

In Recognition
Of Your Many Years
Of Outstanding Service In
Tax Administration

This was not merely a perfunctory award but had real meaning because the organization, consisting of lawyers and certified public accountants, was our greatest adversary. On some occasions, I had all but come to blows with some of its members and routinely accused them of being nothing more than a bunch of criminals. Fortunately, all had been kind enough to consider the source. In fact, a week before our final farewells around the city, Ruth and I were treated to a delicious dinner at a Chinese restaurant by three couples of whom the husbands had possibly been my most devious opponents over the years, but, as noted earlier, we carried on as professionals and managed to remain the best of friends.

Chapter 7

Home Sweet Home, 1985–2008

RETIREMENT

Initiation

It took the better part of a year to acquire a new lifestyle and there were many eye openers. I had first thought of maintaining partial ties with the accounting profession and contacted an employment agency in Jackson, Mississippi, to leave my name for anyone who might be interested in my experience but found out that such was not the way things were done: one was a job applicant who was expected to sign a contract, just like anyone else who walked in off the street. Well, I was merely thinking in terms of part-time work during tax filing season or maybe getting called in occasionally to help someone get straightened out with the IRS. So much for that, and I never gave the idea of working, either part- or full-time, another thought.

During the thirty years we lived in North Carolina, we had hosted many members of Ruth's family, some of whom were annual visitors. It had lately occurred to us that, whenever we came back to Mississippi during the last few years before we moved, we were being used as caregivers to her father because the maid who normally looked after him was promptly dismissed for as long as we were there. His appointments with doctors—even his visits to the barber shop—were always scheduled during our stay. While we had no problems with any of this, we were beginning to detect evidence that the family might have expected us to make taking care of the old man our responsibility, something we had never intended.

During a conversation with a fellow who sold me a lawn mower before we left, the subject of retirement came up. When I asked him about costs of certain equipment to tackle the job of clearing land, he inquired about where I was going.

"Man," he said, when I told him we were heading to rural Mississippi. "The missus and me just recently got rid of everything we had in the country and moved into town, and I am an old country boy! You ought not to even be thinking about what you're about to do. One thing for sure is that everybody and his brother you'll be dealing with will be taking advantage of you."

How right he was! We were presented with demands for payment for work never done, and each time we expressed even minor criticism about the quality of what was done, it seemed that it became that much harder to get someone to perform any kind of service at all. While at a local lumber yard one day, a grubby little character walked up to the counter to loudly tell his fellow "bidnisman" to watch out for so-and-so, who had just failed to keep an appointment with him and who owed him money. From this incident, I had to conclude that some unofficial, better business association existed in the area which enforced demands of members regardless of merit.

Church visitors were not far behind phony creditors. I had earlier resolved to join the little church where we had been married thirty-five years earlier but, when the time came, I just could not bring myself to it. As a matter of fact, I had no religion—at least, not in the traditional sense of the word. Early in life, I recall my mother taking me to Sunday school on Sunday afternoons but never to church, and when she died, a well-known preacher she had befriended (probably during her previous marriage) was called on to perform the graveside service. The only time I remember entering a house of worship during my youth was when my sister got married and, not long thereafter, a synagogue, when my father made a futile attempt to expose me to something he scarcely believed in himself.

The four-year exposure to Anglican church rituals in Australia taught me to appreciate (and admire) elaborate pomp and circumstance, but I steadfastly refused to accept any of the religious dogma they tried to force on me to the point of almost being expelled from school. They finally gave up—not I!

The somewhat inauspicious start of life in the Bible Belt, though not an entire failure, was more or less the beginning of our gradual alienation from local society, which didn't suit me—or perhaps it was the other way around. The question, then, begged consideration as to why things were as they were, and for this I relied on the experiences and insights of my wife Ruth who was born and raised here.

In the first place: her forebears had been prosperous but, like so many people, had suffered dreadfully during the Depression. She never forgot—nor forgave—the fact that her parents and their ten children, ranging in age from two to twenty years, were evicted from land and home which her father had both inherited and bought from his relatives. A neighbor who owned adjacent property was active in local politics and happened to be serving on a committee which was consulted on how much farmers should be able to borrow to raise their crops. Notoriously covetous, this man saw to it that his neighbor got not a penny more than fifty dollars with which to purchase fertilizer. Already two years in arrears paying property taxes, her father was unable to raise much of a crop, and all his property wound up being sold in a sheriff's sale. The "good neighbor" who was in the timber business wound up being the purchaser and began cutting trees on the property even before eviction proceedings had commenced. The question remains, of course, why the rightful owner (i.e., Ruth's father) didn't avail himself of this remedy. The answer was that no market existed for timber except for someone who was in the timber business. To this day, my wife can scarcely contain her fury when she relates how her mother, pregnant with the last of her fourteen children, started crying when she, accompanied by her whole family, first saw the dwelling they were forced to move into. All this occurred not long after the Japanese attack on Pearl Harbor. The oldest son, who had recently finished training in the air force, was killed not long afterwards during the Allied raid on the Ploesti oil fields in Romania.

Hatreds continue to simmer below the surface in the county which, once sparsely populated, now is one of the most prosperous in the State. The gaining of political office still causes the fiercest contests of all, and outright fraud has yet to be completely stamped out. Since we have lived here, the State of Mississippi had to move in to dismiss an entire board of supervisors as well as the chancery clerk (top dog in the county). Out of the next batch that filled the office, one member wasted no time in demanding a bribe for which he served time in prison. Until a county manager was hired, the chancery clerk ran the whole place and doled out favors and destroyed reputations at will. His duties included acting as registrar of deeds for which he collected a fee. Out of the proceeds, he paid his office staff and other incidental expenses and stuck the rest of the money in his pocket. In North Carolina, as well as in any other state where I had to refer to country records, it was my understanding that the registrar of deeds was paid a salary which was in line with the remuneration of persons with comparable jobs. The metropolitan area of Mississippi's capital city spills over into two adjacent counties which benefited enormously from white flight. This resulted in the chancery clerk of our county enjoying a net annual income of over $200,000. Redneck politicians used to flock to county jobs like vultures to a carcass and were able to jack up their compensation as a result of the disproportionate income of the top dog.

Prior to the time we actually had our house built, the heavily wooded lot had to be cleared, and we asked Ruth's brother, living in a trailer next door, to oversee this activity and collect the proceeds from the sale of timber for us. A surveyor had tentatively established boundaries and attached ribbons to an oil bush (a common piece of vegetation around these parts) of which Ruth had taken particular notice. After we had moved, we noticed that the ribbons had disappeared and that what we had understood to be the boundary had been shifted twenty-five feet to the north of the east-west line. The house consequently looked misplaced on the lot, and when we made inquiries about where the usual permanent steel stakes were located, we were given the runaround. Ruth was anxious to start landscaping, and I spent hours trying to locate the stakes without success.

Not long after the place was beginning to get a settled look, a sister in Texas and her new husband expressed an interest in building next to us and asked if we would sell them any spare acreage for the purpose. We were happy to accommodate them, and, after the passing of earnest money, we began marking a tentative boundary and identified desirable trees and fauna to be protected. Strangely enough, the husband didn't seem the least bit interested in making any definite commitments such as engaging a surveyor, and I went into town and found a reputable firm who would be glad to do the task. I was told that finding my property lines was relatively simple once I found the point of beginning, which would likely go back to the first lot on which the oldest brother had built his house five or six years earlier. I went home and found that stake without any trouble and began following the lines described in deeds registered at the courthouse. I immediately found the cause for the strange configuration of our lot and asked the brother about it, who became outright hostile. It was New Year's Day, and he and his wife were watching the Rose Bowl Parade on television and didn't like to be disturbed, so I confronted the younger brother living immediately next to us. He confessed to having participated in an irregularity. He did so again in the presence of my wife Ruth, as well our daughter and her husband, explaining the reason for the situation. His brother had built a workshop either too close to the line, or on top of it, and they had been in a quandary as to what to do about it. As with everything else: the stupid city boy would never know the difference, so why not just move the line? Such matters like disproportionate configurations of the lots, as well as subsequent corrections to deed registrations (which required involving the assistance of their good friend, the registrar of deeds) seemed to have never bothered them, and I soon found out that challenging an elder in the family meant taking on the whole tribe.

Settling Down

It seemed to us that we had merely moved to another place and found a new job which we took on with much enthusiasm despite many difficulties. Behind the house lay an enormous pile of debris, which had been pushed up by the bulldozers and, with winter approaching, I thought that all I would have to do was to take my chainsaw and lop off pieces of protruding logs for firewood to feed our fireplace insert we had bought as soon as the weather cooled. These contraptions were the rage in those days and, consistent with local custom, they managed to unload an outmoded piece of equipment on us for the price of one far more efficient. The wood I assiduously harvested under hazardous conditions on the junk pile was usually wet and not suitable for firewood in the first place. Our insert soon became clogged with creosote, and the amount we so proudly saved on electricity had to be paid out on an all-day cleaning job by a chimney sweep just a couple of years later. Chimneys regularly caught fire because of a lack of cleaning, and burned-out remains of houses used to dot the countryside. It wasn't until we spotted snakes sunning themselves on top of logs the next summer that we had a bulldozer dig an enormous hole further back from the house and bury the entire pile without a trace, at least for the time being, because fifteen years later, we continue to dump assorted debris in the constantly sinking hole.

It was surprising how fast one learns to cope with all sorts of mechanical breakdowns without calling on experts to come and fix them. Living thirty miles out of Jackson, the cost of service calls is nothing to sneeze at. There are qualified technicians living close by, but they all work for firms in town. Local yokels, who claim that they can fix things, can really mess things up in a hurry.

The person inspecting our home for the loan company during the building stage had believed it seemed to be a quality-built structure, and so it probably was, except for some serious defects. In the first place, the roof had to be replaced the sixth year after we took possession. Building materials had been supplied by one of Jackson's most respected companies, but the shingles were experimental, and we were duped, along with dozens of others, when shingles began to crack. Of course, they readily agreed to pay for replacement, less depreciation, without including cost of labor. Price to replace was $3,000, but the amount of reimbursement amounted to slightly more than $500. The bad roof had earlier caused the overhang, consisting of soffits and fascia, to deteriorate, which we had covered with aluminum siding at a cost in excess of $4,000.

The roof power ventilator soon started making an awful noise, and I thought I'd better take a look at it. This meant having to extend the attic flooring to reach it, and in the process of doing so, I found that its installation had been an obvious hazard. They had simply fished a hot wire out of the insulation and attached it to a thermostat which controlled the fan. The wire—tautly stretched and part of an unidentified circuit—was hanging on a single nail. I rewired the whole thing and put a switch where the air conditioner unit was located so that the ventilator could periodically be oiled without switching off the circuit. The fan motor had to be replaced for lack of maintenance and, in time, the whole unit had to be replaced by a wind-driven turbine. The house has a minimum number of circuits, which makes any expansion of the electrical system impossible without spending a lot of money.

Finally . . . who built the house? Well, let's just consider one thing. While our builder somehow enjoyed a good reputation, ours was the last one he built before being expelled from the county the old Southern way by the sheriff notifying him to leave before sundown if he wished to avoid arrest, for it became known that he had regularly been molesting his twelve-year-old daughter. This kind of justice is of course only available for the good ole boys.

While flood insurance was sponsored by the federal government, it seemed to be a virtual unknown in these parts. This was unusual, since seventy percent of the State of Mississippi is deemed to be a floodplain. To find out whether we were in a flood zone required the services of a surveyor, and our insurance agent, although he represented several top companies, resisted putting the wheels in motion to get this work done. Anything new seemed to paralyze even people with a good deal of influence, and I finally talked to a man working for a Farm Bureau agency who knew what to do and who got the man who did the original survey to certify that we weren't in a flood zone. While we weren't farmers, we were extended the courtesy of being covered by insurance, although they did so reluctantly because, the agent explained, they had had so many cases where people deliberately burned down their property when they got tired of living in the country. We promptly received a bill from the surveyor (whom we had previously paid a substantial amount) for additional work he never did and should have done in the first place. When I refused to pay, the man curtly informed me that he would see me in court. A sheriff's deputy scared Ruth half to death not long afterwards to serve a summons for me to appear in court.

We met in what is called "Justice Court" where what used to be a justice of the peace holds forth seated behind an imposing bench while wearing a black gown. When I walked in, plaintiff and the judge were engaged in a lengthy tête-à-tête which continued until the bailiff walked in and called the court to order. The four of us were the only ones present during the trial. The plaintiff was invited to verbalize his complaint, after which I was given an opportunity to respond. Judgment was swift and abrupt, the plaintiff being awarded half of what he claimed and me having to pay court costs. What I didn't know until quite some time later was that Ruth called the judge at his home and blessed him out for what she thought was an unfair decision. The man was in her second-grade classroom when she started teaching and apparently never finished high school. I have been particularly careful to avoid having to return to his court, and this has put me in many an awkward situation over the years. For example, most Mississippians have contempt for all "laws'n riggulations," and this is most noticeable on the highways, where they consistently ignore the speed limits. There seem to be no more than half a dozen members of the highway patrol in the whole state, except on special occasions, when dozens can be seen directing traffic and visiting one another. The trouble is that speeding tickets are expensive, and I observe all speed limits, which means that I'm constantly being followed by a string of cars and huge trucks trying to get around me, and this is nerve-wracking.

If there was one thing positive out of moving to the country, it is that we have so far been able to maintain a state of physical well-being through hard work and exercise. We never even considered retiring in the strict sense of the word and have maintained a regimen such as always being appropriately dressed, eating nourishing meals on time, keeping our surroundings in an orderly state and—most important of all—never idly viewing television, having it on only to watch the evening news and tuning into a very select number of programs, usually on PBS. Both of us wound up with an aversion to the inane blather and atrocious noise on the airways which passes for entertainment. One thing which we found astonishing when we returned to Europe was that American country music had become pervasive in everyday life. When my niece and her family came to visit us, they couldn't get enough of the stuff.

Thanks to my sister's habit initiated long ago, and continued by her children after her death, I regularly received a heavy packet of Holland's foremost magazine, which carries detailed news articles from around the world. It nicely supplements the increasingly sparse reading materials in Mississippi.

About five years after retiring, the urge to investigate the world around us began to reassert itself. Neighborhood trips had mostly been to visit the Mississippi Delta where our story started decades ago. As in all places, things had changed but not necessarily for the better. Greenville had grown and, unfortunately, once comfortable residential areas had turned into slums. The once attractive downtown area had lost the battle of survival against a shopping center, notwithstanding the installation of a serpentine street bordered by neglected vegetation and small rest areas, presumably meant for shoppers. The once proud air base, where thousands of young men had learned to fly an airplane, was merely a skeleton and had become the new Greenville airport, where a small commuter plane picked up passengers in the morning and deposited others in the evening. A plant had been built which manufactured small aircraft, but activities ceased before we made a later visit to the place. Famous Doe's Restaurant in the old section of town was still serving hot tamales and huge steaks, but the floor of the place is eaten up by termites and has holes in it over which pieces of linoleum have been stretched. The owners must be quite well off because they keep introducing their delicacies in various places around the country, the most recent one in Washington, DC. What really made them famous were their two-inch-thick steaks which are cooked to order in a huge furnace like one sees in a steel mill. The marina at the popular downtown levee has long since been filled with gambling boats, which brought in fancy new motels practically next door to some of the worst slums anywhere.

Pressing on with our renewed curiosity, we made a two-day trip to the northernmost metropolis of Tupelo (birthplace of Elvis Presley), where we discovered that the countryside looks very much like that of the Carolinas. To get there we used the Natchez Trace, that marvelous creation by a once caring and responsible government. A luxurious motorhome took up prime space in the motel where we were lucky to find a room, because Ole Miss was playing Alabama in Oxford some fifty miles to the west, and lodging was tight in the entire area. The vehicle was obviously owned by a rich (and therefore popular?) alumnus to whom throngs came to pay their respects. For lack of a better place to take our exercise after dinner, we used the parking lot and couldn't help but admire the handsome vehicle each time we passed it, until

Ruth suddenly gasped and said that the owner was walking around inside naked as a jaybird. All window shades were up and, sure enough, there the hairy old goat was, with a beer mug in his hand, looking at something. These types of people must not only be excessively wealthy but excessively taken in with themselves as well. What utter bores, the British would say, or better still, what utter pigs!

New Orleans was our next choice for a visit. Come to think of it, I find it strange that after having lived in America for half a century, I haven't been back more than half a dozen times. It was a lovely place in the late forties, but less so in the fifties and later. The mini–World's Fair in the mid-eighties had rejuvenated the lower end of famous Canal Street, and the Audubon Zoo is impressive. We stayed at the Pontchartrain Hotel on Saint Charles Avenue and found the furnishings magnificent. It has one of the top restaurants in town, and a menu displayed on a tripod told us that it was well out of our range. We found the Superdome truly awesome but were left to wonder what had happened to the naughty French quarter of years ago. It had a contrived atmosphere, and many of the eating places had become dubious joints operated by hippies.

We took several long walks through what is known as the Garden District, where many of the handsome homes appeared to be suffering from benign neglect. Here and there on St. Charles Avenue, there were establishments that had a cozy Parisian look, particularly after dark. Streetcar service had recently been revived, albeit with ancient equipment. We used it a couple of times but were soon back in our car which was parked in a garage behind the hotel. Upon departure, we found everything topsy-turvy that wasn't tied down inside or in the trunk, indicating that the car might have been subjected to rough treatment. We soon discovered that valet parking must have required bigger tips than I offered the doorman for bringing the vehicle to the front of the hotel each time we went somewhere because, when we got home, the transmission needed repairing which, fortunately, was covered by extended warranty.

We came across one secret paradise early after moving to Mississippi, and that was Gulf Shores, fifty miles southeast of Mobile Alabama. While the children were growing up, we became addicted to the beaches of both North and South Carolina, where we spent countless weekends and holidays. While they are not as grandiose as those on the west coast, they are exceedingly comfortable, and the seafood is beyond compare. However, as time went by, Myrtle Beach became overcrowded, while access to the place posed more and more of a problem mainly due to inadequate road systems. Unless one knew certain unadvertised routes through farming areas, a trip home on Sunday afternoon could take six to seven hours due to huge traffic jams in South Carolina. These were alleviated in time through the four-laning of certain road segments but, as usual, North Carolina did nothing unless the federal government did it for them. After the children were grown, we all drove down for a visit, only to find that there wasn't an empty room to be had anywhere and we had to drive back all the way to Charlotte.

We were amazed when we first saw the Gulf Coast in Alabama and Florida after bypassing the area for thirty years. We never forgot the white sand and expected to find the same empty space but now found handsome high-rises and a variety of places to stay. Condominiums seemed to be mostly owned on a time-share basis, and we selected one development where we still stay after many years. The beach area is gradually becoming semi-privatized in that it is accessible by the public only at certain widely interspersed areas: the usual capitalism at its best. We have detected a commensurate development of exclusiveness on the part of property management, which is continually jacking up prices and making further intrusions into one's wallet by charging such things as handling fees and demanding unreasonable deposit way in advance. So much then for paradise, but we did have as good a time with the grandchildren as we did with their parents while they were growing up.

NEW ADVENTURES

After staying close to home for twelve years, we yearned to go back to Europe again. My only sister had recently suffered a mild heart attack, and I thought we should see each other even if it was for no other purpose than to say goodbye forever. She got excited when she heard we were coming and refurnished the guest room in her flat. Her children, on the other hand, were not at all impressed and let it be known that they would just as soon see us stay away for fear that we would unnecessarily upset their mother. Her taciturn husband didn't seem to be enthused, either, but everybody seemed glad we came, in the end. We wisely kept our visits with family short by spending just two nights before going on a fifteen-day trip to France and Italy and, again, a couple of nights before catching the plane home.

My brother-in-law, Piet, was virtually blind and had been for some time. He amused himself mainly by caring for a parakeet named Flip, which had become an important member of the household. The family car had been disposed of years ago, which is no great loss in Holland, where public transport is about as well-developed as anywhere else in the world. A mainline train station was less than half a mile from the apartment and, since we slept with our window open, we heard express trains rush past in each direction any time we happened to be awake during the night.

Like any other place, Holland had changed—for the worst, so it seemed. Things were no longer as efficient as before, and graffiti could be seen everywhere. Local commuter trains, which were once kept so clean, had been vandalized, and attractive pictures as well as route maps had been decorated with big blobs of coagulated spittle. People rode with their feet on the seats and generally looked slouchy. On a couple of occasions, two conductors (it had long since become dangerous for just one to work alone) caught someone traveling without a ticket or had to chase a passenger out of a first-class compartment. As we stood on a platform waiting for a train, another one arriving two tracks away was welcomed by a squad of policemen who stormed aboard. Directly an ambulance pulled up and a heavily bandaged man was escorted to it and taken away.

In the shopping center facing Mil's delightful apartment building, they had recently introduced a McDonald's hamburger stand. It was immensely popular, and people carefully placed trash in big wire baskets near the sidewalk. They soon decided, however, that this was what they thought to be un-American, and a year later, the place was appropriately inundated with litter, to the chagrin of residents across the street, but I'm getting ahead of myself.

We wound up our trip with a nice visit with the family. We brought in Indonesian food one night and, tired of riding the train, took a taxi all the way to the airport. Delta Air Lines' cattle car, in which I occupied a seat with a back which refused to recline, took us on a seemingly endless, nine-hour flight direct to Atlanta. I didn't bother to report the seat problem to the hostesses—assuming that other passengers had done so on countless earlier flights—but, instead, wrote a note which I handed to a security officer upon leaving the plane. For a moment, I thought he was going to detain me, but he promised to deliver it to the proper "authorities."

ROCKING ALONG

It was the latter part of 1991, and we had reached life's late sixties. Thanks to the relentless onslaught of North Carolina's super bullfrog, US Senator Jesse Helms, Public Television was in rapid decline (likely destined to go into total oblivion), and we were forced to watch more and more reruns. One of these, called *As Time Goes By*, has a scene near the end where an elderly character, when asked how he was getting along, replied, "Oh, just rocking along." As our time went by, we came to adopt that motto.

We were still working hard as ever trying to clear land adjacent to where we had built our house, but progress was agonizingly slow. Mother Nature was fickle, and it seemed as if we were climbing a sand dune, taking three steps up and sliding back two, sometimes three or four. What we were trying to accomplish, everyone else was having done by bulldozers, but we were unwilling to incur the expense, even assuming that we would have been able to hire a reliable party to do it. I became proficient in doing many things I never thought I would be doing, and in the process learned to respect more than ever before persons who worked with their hands. We maintained a rigorous routine which was interrupted only when one of us wasn't feeling well, which was seldom. Meals were consumed precisely on time, which must have been puzzling to many, judging by the telephone calls we received during the dinner hour at night. We were always appropriately attired, which earned Ruth many snide comments from her contemporaries. Even though many homes with a front porch around here are decorated with rocking chairs, nobody uses them, except us. Weather permitting, the porch serves as an extension of our living quarters, and we are constantly waving at people in response to their greetings. It just seems preferable to having them shoot at us.

We came here with one dog which was run over and killed before we were able to put up a fence. She was smart and used to pick up the newspaper as well as collect the mail as soon as it was dropped though the mail slot in the front door. We promptly replaced her with a black Labrador retriever who turned out to be half smart and half dumb and who accompanied us for twelve years. Fencing in the yard, which is done by very few people in these parts, cost one thousand dollars and was the smartest thing we ever did. People notice when you treat an animal well and will bring in all kinds of creatures in distress. Even though we chase away strays which are big enough to take care of themselves or call the animal control officer to come and collect puppies and kittens dropped off by people under the cover of darkness, we still wound up with two more dogs as well as two cats. One was a tomcat with the imaginative name of Tom, who for the first year he was with us, had a time establishing his territory amidst an area full of the meanest critters in the world. He would disappear for days and then come home horribly disfigured and bleeding until we took him to be castrated. Big and strong, he became interested in rats and occasionally brought in two at a time which he neatly deposited side by side on a mat in front of the kitchen door in the carport. He liked to go walking with me at the end of the workday, when I took the dogs out into the woods for their daily outing, and would spend most of the time marking his territory.

Clearing the woods caused greatly valued wildlife to slowly disappear. We used to have a flock of wild turkeys which came several times a day to feed on acorns, until someone stopped in the road one day and took a shot at them with a pistol. We were told that it would take two years for them to return, but they never did. Since then, we have seen a pitiful looking straggler occasionally, but that is all.

Several families of owls used to reside in the woods next door, and they would wake up at exactly 4:00 every afternoon to start their day. They moved further back into the woods, but occasionally one would come to pay us a visit while in pursuit of prey. They were never as tame as they were in Charlotte, where a family was nesting in a big old elm tree next door one year. They had half a dozen young ones which entertained us with their antics, even taking a bath in the birdbath set up in our yard. I remember the day when one of them lit on the gutter while I was sitting on the patio and started to sway from side to side, all the time hissing. This had never happened before, and the only explanation I could think of for such behavior was that the bird was saying goodbye on behalf of the family because we never saw any of them again.

Birds are a lot of fun and we maintain several feeders in the yard, which attract swarms by the hundreds when severe weather is on the way. Then, too, during spring and fall when they migrate, we need a book to identify the many different species. During the summer, the hummingbirds take over, which keeps us busy filling three feeders scattered around the house while they carry on their warfare to keep all competitors from eating. They must be the world's best flyers, and they seem capable of speeds approaching that of a tracer bullet.

We used to have a noticeable reptile population, mainly represented by terrapins, which the dictionary defines for us as "any of various edible [?] North American turtles," but most of these have disappeared. For a while, there were lots of king snakes around, which are powerful constrictors harmless to human beings, provided you leave them alone, or just talk to them. Only once did I have to kill a highly poisonous cottonmouth, which put up a good fight. In the beginning of spring one year, our black Labrador was bitten on the nose by an unidentified snake, and her head swelled to twice its size within ten minutes. Since she weighed eighty-five pounds, we had to fetch a wheelbarrow with which to bring her out of the woods, and when she began to choke on saliva which started to coagulate into a consistency of rubber, we decided to bring her in to a veterinarian. It was a close call, but she fully recovered.

In time, we managed to make both the house site as well as the adjacent woods look decent, but the upkeep has gradually become an undeniable burden, Ruth is an avid gardener and when everything blooms in the spring, the place looks very appealing for two or three weeks.

We live in a comfortable dwelling which is condescendingly referred to as "just a little old ranch-type house" by our son-in-law who is in the building business and builds high quality homes. It is stuffed full of furniture and mementos to which we constantly added more during our traveling days. We had to endure a radical change in our lifestyle when we moved here, the results of which have only recently begun taking their toll. Moving from a vibrant metropolitan area with its myriad diversions to a cultural backwater had gradually built up a degree of restlessness, if not outright regret. Perhaps it would have been better if I had stoically accepted the changes which were taking place or found something else to do for another ten years before retiring. I have become concerned that I have entered the early stages of the Alzheimer's disease because the ability to express myself is rapidly deteriorating. That could be due to the fact that English is not my native language; when groping for words and phrases during ordinary conversation, the Dutch version often comes to mind first, and sometimes it is the only one. I have read that this is common, but that doesn't take away the fact that being at a loss for words is quite embarrassing. A less acceptable reason for this affliction is that it is caused by the isolation associated with old age. I have withdrawn into a world of books and periodicals, and cannot even tolerate the sound of television, particularly the jabber of sportscasters and talk-show hosts, without becoming depressed. It would be nice if, in addition to the inane junk crowding the airwaves, we could receive live television programs from all over the world.

And then there is the telephone, once considered a blessing, which has become an instrument of terror in the hands of many lunatics. A member of Ruth's extended family once had to be admitted to a psychiatric institution as a result of harassing telephone calls following annulment of her marriage. For a long time now, we have become the target for harassment, which abated for a while when the guilty party accidentally disclosed itself, not knowing that we had acquired a caller's identification device. Since then, cellular phones have become popular, and one must watch out not to get clobbered while moving about in traffic.

I have tried to complain about telephone communications to the public service commission; my complaint earned me what amounted to a scolding by some young man who said he was an attorney. We have been forced to abandon normal contact with our few remaining relatives in Holland with whom we used to carry on some lively conversations. So much then for life in the computer age, but let me return to other matters, not much easier, but far more pleasant.

Afterword

The next chapter in Erik's memoir detailed his last trip to Europe. He was concerned that this may have been his last, due to his Alzheimer's diagnosis. He seemed resigned to the fact that it would be the last time he'd see his sister.

> *Arrangements had been made for us to be entertained by my nieces and their families during the entire weekend preparatory to the whole family attending a formal dinner in a restaurant that Sunday night. We rode and rode, stopping frequently for refreshments, and we couldn't believe how much food our hosts could consume and still partake heartily of that elaborate dinner in the evening. It was entirely paid for by my sister and her husband, and it must have cost a small fortune. We had noticed a change in their usual mood—one of resignation and it was the first time the husband poured out his heart about his lot in life. Being my senior by some twelve years, he had always been sort of patronizing, but not this time. He had been legally blind for some time as a result of the insidious disease of diabetes, and, as a young man, his very promising career was shattered by the war. He was the only son of a prominent family and wound up destitute (as I have already mentioned elsewhere) and all of this, plus lots more, came out the last afternoon and evening before we left. When we did so the next morning, both he and my sister escorted us to the entrance of the apartment house and then took up a position on an open third-floor passageway at the rear of the building to wave goodbye until we rounded the corner three blocks away on our way to the railroad station. We both realized that this was more of a final farewell than just an ordinary goodbye.*
>
> *Instead of taking a cab all the way to the airport as we had a year earlier, we took the train, which stops underneath the air terminal, a nice and easy ride, made even nicer by escalators, which gently deposit passengers and their luggage on the main concourse. The nine-hour flight to Atlanta somehow seemed much longer than usual.*

Then, after writing about his trip to Canada in 1992 and a trip to the West Coast in 1993, he wrote of his regret in not visiting Europe one last time.

While the trip to the west coast in the Fall of 1993 turned out to be a super one in most respects, we failed to realize that my sister might have been disappointed that we didn't come to see her again in Holland. Part of the reason that we did not had been the apparent lack of enthusiasm we sensed during the previous two visits on the part of her daughters, who again and again brought up the matter of concern about their parents growing old, and that they would much rather see them enter a retirement home for which, after all, provision had been made many years ago. Well, they needn't have worried because in 1994, their mother suddenly died.

Their father had been in the hospital for several weeks with leg trouble resulting from diabetes. The doctors finally decided to operate rather than amputate, and during the long period of subsequent rehabilitation, my sister took a taxicab every day to go and visit him. That must have been a considerable strain for a seventy-three-year-old woman with health problems herself, and one night, when the youngest daughter and her family visited the hospital, she caught a ride home with them and was escorted to her apartment by a teenage grandson while the parents waited in the car. Directly, the son came hurrying back to tell them that something was wrong with Oma, and the daughter went to check on her. She immediately phoned for an ambulance, which was on the scene in moments, and her mother was taken to the same hospital where they had just come from. They followed the ambulance on the way over and could see them frantically working on the patient while traveling faster and faster. Once at the hospital, they took her to the emergency room, where she died of congestive heart failure.

In time, the father was discharged from the hospital and brought home to fend for himself. The very first night at home, he stubbed his toe on the way to the bathroom and fell. Although virtually blind, he was able to drag himself to the telephone in the living room to call for help, but when the rescue squad got to him, he had bled to death.

These two people married in 1939 and had a promising future ahead of them which was shattered less than three years later when both were imprisoned in separate Japanese prison camps for the duration of the Second World War. They came out as physical wrecks, which adversely affected them for the rest of their lives. After being repatriated to Holland for a year's leave after the war, they returned to the Indies where, in time, Piet was promoted to become the agent of the steamship company he worked for in the port of Medan in the northern part of Sumatra. This was a major assignment with infinite career possibilities. However, a turbulent period of resistance and war ensued, which culminated in the expulsion of all Dutch citizens from Indonesia. The last of these people departed during the month of December, 1957, in a fleet of passenger ships hurriedly assembled. Mil and her two children had earlier left for Holland by plane, which had to make an emergency landing somewhere in the Middle East when an engine caught on fire. Most of the hundreds of thousands evacuated, managed to do quite well as time went by.

Such is life, or as the French say, c'est la vie!

The following year after his sister's death, her eldest daughter and her family came to visit our family in Mississippi. He writes of this visit fondly, then in subsequent chapters he writes about nothing other than his final travels throughout the 1990s: Alaska, Puerto Rico, the Florida Keys, and finally Canada's Alberta province.

In 2001, he suffered a heart attack and underwent major heart surgery. His time in the ICU was like a speed course of this memoir: he'd mumble names and places of his life, often at the bewilderment of his doctors and nurses. From this trauma in 2001, and from an entire week without electricity after Hurricane Katrina in 2005, his Alzheimer's progressed exponentially. After a stroke in January 2008, he spent time in the hospital, in rehabilitation, then back in the hospital until his death on June 16, 2008, just a few days after his eighty-second birthday. Erik is buried in the Johns Cemetery, the Mississippi community where "Ruth had been born and raised" and where he enjoyed "countless walks in the woods . . . overlooking a pasture, wishing [he] could stay forever."

About the Author

Erik Smalhout was born in Batavia, Netherlands East Indies. After attending boarding school in Perth, Australia, he served in the Netherlands Air Force during World War II as a librarian in the intelligence service. After the war he traveled the world as a purser with the Royal Rotterdam Lloyd Steamship Corporation before migrating in 1950 to the most southern place on earth: the Mississippi Delta. It was in Mississippi that Erik met and married Ruth Gill, an elementary school teacher and a native of Johns, Mississippi. Erik served his adopted country as an Internal Revenue Service agent in Goldsboro and Charlotte, North Carolina, and retired after thirty-one years of service before relocating to Johns, Mississippi. Erik passed away in June 2008 at the age of eighty-two.

About the Editor

Erika Berry began her career in public education as a middle-grades math teacher in Charlotte, North Carolina. She has since worked in education policy with various state agencies and nonprofits throughout Mississippi, Tennessee, and North Carolina.